GETTING TO
BIG
THE SMALL WAY

GETTING TO
BIG
THE SMALL WAY

Frank Prestipino

New York   Chicago   San Francisco   Lisbon   London
Madrid   Mexico City   Milan   New Delhi   San Juan
Seoul   Singapore   Sydney   Toronto

The *McGraw·Hill* Companies

1 2 3 4 5 6 7 8 9 0   DOC/DOC   0 9 8 7

ISBN-13: 978-0-07-148440-4
ISBN-10:   0-07-148440-X

McGraw-Hill books are available at special quantity discounts to use as premiums and sales promotions, or for use in corporate training programs. For more information, please write to the Director of Special Sales, Professional Publishing, McGraw-Hill, Two Penn Plaza, New York, NY 10121-2298. Or contact your local bookstore.

This book is printed on acid-free paper.

To Enza, Alle, Aaron, Fred, Vanessa,
and my parents, Santo and Maria

CONTENTS

ACKNOWLEDGMENTS

There have been a lot of people who have been involved in the making of this book. It started nearly eight years ago when I was driving back from Port Macquarie, a small coastal town on the east coast of Australia, and was on a cell phone with someone from Singapore whom I hardly knew. This person's name was Don Smallwood, and he was offering me a position where I would live in Singapore and work under his leadership. I accepted. Soon thereafter, we became close friends. The fact that the first part of his surname is "small" is only one of the coincidences involved, with the other being that he is truly worthy of being canonized as the patron saint of believing that doing things right by taking one step at a time is the surest way to achieving success.

Thanks and gratitude go to David Gilman for believing it was necessary to write a book that pointed out another path to success, despite the controversy that would arise from working against current-day dogma.

McGraw-Hill can be proud of Jeanne Glasser. Her guidance and sensitivity throughout the journey of writing were precise, meaningful, and always motivational. I am also grateful for the extraordinary talent of Janice Race and her team, whose small changes made the big difference with the manuscript.

At each economic challenge, there were special people with fortitude and persistence who stood out from the rest. They are the ones who presented me with opportunities and allowed me to be free to accomplish things in different ways. In effect, they allowed me to address issues not by radical means, but rather by finding the simple, basic alternatives to seemingly big issues.

One such person was Darryl McDonough. Anyone working for a company in the early 1980s will recall that the computer department was referred to as "EDP" (electronic data processing). Back then, the class act in this area of business was the Coca-Cola operation based in Adelaide, South Australia. It was in a small, unassuming, single-level square building that a handful of programmers had the privilege of being under the leadership of Darryl, who was the EDP manager at the time. His gift of being able to find that one small thing that solved the bigger problems sparked my ongoing search for those small things that had the potential for the biggest outcomes.

I have worked with companies ranging from the very small to the very large, and some in between, for several years, and these companies have come and gone, surged and merged. Irrespective of their final fate, they all had one thing in common, and that was that they became big. No one could have asked for a better environment for studying company strategy when the curriculum consisted of a stock market crash in 1987, the end of a millennium, the Internet, and the acceleration of globalization.

Thanks go to the many people around the world who believed that for a business to become big, it first needs to get the small things done right. These people provided me with many unique opportunities and learning experiences. My thanks extend to Safra Catz, who opened a new world of learning, and to Charles E. Phillips, Jr., for his unending support during the challenges and successes. Thanks to Judy Sim, one of the most dedicated people I have ever met, who backs up her beliefs with support and who proves each day that incremental advancements are what make bigger and better a reality.

To Derek Williams, an icon of the IT industry in Asia, who will continue to be a mentor. Many thanks to Mark Jarvis for his creative freedom and talent for appreciating that "simplicity can be the difference," and to Jeremy Burton for his instinctive ability to spot what works. To Jacqueline Woods, an inspiration with the rare skill of being able to hone in on those small (even tiny) things that can really make the big difference. To the unrelenting, dedicated team who threw out their job descriptions and worked at whatever it took to make things happen and who lived each day having to find the small differences, namely, Sean Callahan, Patrick King, Matt Tierney, Timothy Douglas, Joe Thomas, Jagdish Mirani, Sean Rollins, Anthony Peake, Alfonso Di'Ianni, Ryan Rathman, Chris Hummel, Lisa Arthur, and Fred Studer. Gratitude and thanks go to Ellen Minter, Peter Graaf, Jeff Stiles, and Andrew Vadyak for their unending support and encouragement even when the odds were low.

Thanks also to Keith Ferrazzi, bestselling author of *Never Eat Alone*, who became a friend and supporter as I wrote this book, and to Greg Botto for sharing his entrepreneurial insights. At work as in life, learning comes from different places if you are willing to listen, and it often comes from where you least expect it. The Mandorlo family is such a source for me, as its members prove every day that life's bigger meaning comes from small moments.

Special thanks to my wife, Enza, who put her heart and soul into this project with countless hours of support.

Finally, to my brother Fred, who is living proof that no matter at what level you start in life or in business, success prevails with taking small steps, one at a time. Without his inspiration, this book would never have been written.

INTRODUCTION

This book is about finding small changes that can be implemented easily and that will bring bigger than expected results to any part of your business. It is not about staying small. On the contrary, it is about accelerating your business toward what you want it to be and where you want it to go. Whether your goal is being bigger or being better or both, taking well-guided incremental steps is a more effective way to get there. This unique approach can get you to your goal faster, at lower risk, and without breaking the company's bank, culture, core values, or resources. This is about a process of *discovery* where those small improvements that will make the biggest impact can be found and made on an ongoing basis.

By carefully making minor adjustments in specific areas, you can achieve any planned objective or solve any problem within the existing operations, policies, and procedures. In the wide variety of projects that I worked on, ranging from large-scale company-wide initiatives to short-term tactical programs, I was able to see firsthand how small but precise changes applied en route, which did not require added budget spending or lengthy management approvals, made significant improvements, and in most cases did so immediately. This phenomenon fascinated me for years, and while my peers put it down to the 80/20 rule (which states that 80 percent of the benefit is derived from 20 percent of the effort), it seemed to me that in a lot of the cases, the benefit came from much less than that.

Another thing that struck me was that while some companies that were successful appeared on the surface to have made radical transformations to achieve this, when these companies were studied more deeply, it was clear that their achievements started with relatively small alterations to their core business and snowballed from there. My investigations led me to the indisputable conclusion that there is a repeatable set of activities that can significantly increase the chances of achieving big results with the smallest of effort. These findings do not mean that thinking big is not necessary for great success; they challenge the idea that it is necessary to make big changes to achieve big ambitions, suggesting instead the alternative of finding small things that can get you to your goal equally well. This process does not eliminate any of the fundamentals necessary to carry out the normal course of business, so it is not an easy way to get out of doing work, but it may eliminate a lot of unnecessary work that amounts to very little.

This book combines my experiences with examples of other companies that achieved similar results in this way. It can either be read in its entirety or used as a reference. Throughout the book, there are frameworks that you can use to implement these ideas within your company or as your personal reference manual. You will be reintroduced to skills that you already have mastered, with the intention of discovering, with a high degree of accuracy, those areas where the smallest of changes may have vastly better success rates than traditional methods. The structure of the book allows you to take ideas from any of the individual chapters or to combine all of the material from Chapter 8, which can be the basis for execution of a project. Equally, the individual chapters can be treated as smaller projects that you can implement at your own pace and at appropriate times, taking seasonal effects into account and avoiding busy periods.

The chapters are arranged to take you through those areas of the business where the biggest impact, in the form of generating more revenues and attracting a bigger market share, can be made. In Chapter 1, we discuss how small changes can have a big impact and look at examples of situations in which this has happened. These examples are contrasted with companies that have taken the plunge into big initiatives, only to be surpassed by those that did things through incremental advances. In Chapter 2, a relationship is drawn between what seem to be contradictory statements: all the people in the company need to understand the clear goal of becoming bigger or better while doing their part by making consistent and meaningful incremental advances toward that end. Company objectives need to be clearly communicated in such a way that every employee is able to appreciate how he or she is involved in the company's success. Random small improvements are certainly helpful; however, they will not necessarily produce the desired results. The beauty is that these goals may actually be arrived at faster through focused small improvements than with traditional big bang methods.

Chapter 3 explores new opportunities that are within the scope of your business today. A solid growth strategy is to move into adjacent markets by exploiting the products, skills, and resources that are already available in your company. Often we find that by making minor changes followed by repackaging, rebranding, and relaunching, seizing opportunities for growth in other markets becomes a natural process. Companies that have taken their first small step into new markets have found their businesses transformed as they pursue new ventures that they had not thought of before they took the first step.

Chapter 4 is about discovering what your business is really about. Often our perception of the value we offer as a business and the things that our customers actually value can be widely different. This chapter looks at a process and methodology that help to bring these perceptions together. We can then develop the right message and the positioning we need in order to represent ourselves as providing something that the customer values. This is one of the least worked areas for a lot of companies that wonder why they are not getting their messages across. The main issues in messaging involve consistency and relevance. The concept of the Message Tree ensures that once the messages have been developed and agreed upon, all other communications with your marketplace will be consistent with those messages.

Chapter 5 covers the structure of the company and ways to make the company easier to do business with by improving individual units of work that are part of the bigger picture. What are some of the internal processes that can be improved by making small improvements on an ongoing basis that will unblock and open the doors to growth? If the business is to become big, then all parts of the business need to be able to scale. Systems that will allow those big opportunities to be processed need to be in place. Often businesses cannot become big because their internal systems simply cannot handle the load or the different variations that big business brings.

Chapter 6 explores ways to find your real competitors and what to do about them. How do you become unique and differentiated, and how can you do this without making radical changes within the company? Useful tools and techniques that can be easily adopted and will give immediate results are presented here. Chapter 7 makes the connection between the overall goals of the company and practical changes in marketing, sales, and channel partners that will ensure that the business is ready to move to the next level.

Chapter 8 brings together a lot of the material in the previous chapters by presenting a plan that sets forth specific steps that can be delegated across the organization to empower all employees to make changes within the scope of their responsibilities. Chapter 9 sets out to prioritize and explain how the rollout of this new culture needs to be done. Introducing the idea that everyone is now involved in the welfare of the company, and that each person has a key part to play in its success, requires an approach that ensures that the right attitudes and motivational drivers are in place.

Chapter 10 looks at ways to manage and measure the success of the incremental advances. It uses concepts similar to those of the well-known Balanced Scorecard, with a focus on identifying small as well as big areas of improvement and on how the sharing of those metrics has a positive effect. Information is a key ingredient for success, and it should be available to every employee. This allows better decisions to be made, and when it comes to deciding what small changes will have the biggest impact, it is only with the right information that the right decisions can be made and the right actions taken.

Whether you are the CEO, the vice president of R&D, sales, or marketing, or the company's receptionist, you can apply the concepts in this book. The idea that the only way you can advance your position in the company is by coming up with some entirely new, radical way to do things is not accurate. In fact, in many situations, the fastest way to advance your career could be by making several small incremental improvements. The key is to know where to find the small changes that will make the biggest enhancement and then put them into effect—today.

There is no additional training required to find the small changes that will have a big impact. However, there does need to be a controlled environment with known and communicated guidelines. When this is implemented, it will be perceived as a newly found freedom, and everyone will feel good about finding and carrying out improvements that have always been within their reach, but that they previously may have felt reluctant to act on. Big budgets are not required either. Depending on how you wish to implement the changes, you are free to simply look for improvements for which no additional budget is required. In some cases, you may want to allocate extra resources if an area is seen as having high enough potential to warrant it.

The level of risk and investment relative to the impact of any of the changes will remain firmly within management's control at all levels, irrespective of company size.

The idea of becoming big through small steps is gaining a lot of attention. Where a deliberate strategy of incremental advances has been adopted, the staff members felt less threatened when they heard about big end goals, even when the changes were identified as necessary for the survival of the company. In this hyperfast world, we want things done now, and we want them done right the first time. In many cases, the most expedient way to do this is to resort to previously tried and tested models that are assumed to be current-day "best practices." This reflex action creates instability, especially when several of these strategies are deployed throughout the year. What's just as important, though, is that these models are becoming more dangerous because they (1) involve the replacement of current systems and (2) do not have built-in flexibility to adapt to unforeseen future challenges. Taking the time to formally assess whether a smaller tactic might be a better decision is constantly validated when we hear of companies that have taken the big change route and come out poorly.

Given today's availability of technological resources, the use of technology to accelerate execution is perfectly sensible. For years management gurus have been proclaiming that radical transformation using technology is the only way to keep businesses competitive. Increasingly, though, evidence showing the rising costs of radical change and declining tolerance for the associated risks is mounting. This evidence supports this new approach of taking things in small steps while keeping the big picture in sight. The argument that return on investment is faster and greater with fast execution has a discrepancy when you take the increased *risk of investment* into account. Given the pressures of meeting shareholder and customer demand and the rate of economic change surrounding them, it is easy to become hypnotized by the dogma that thinking big means having to do big. Compared to the established textbook management theories that make up the conventional wisdom of today, any notion of thinking small to achieve the same result appears controversial and even *radical*. The fact is, people have innate natural tendencies to want to make small improvements in their lives, and with prudently administered permission, they can translate this inclination to their jobs.

Volumes have been written expounding on how markets can be revolutionized and new buyer behaviors discovered, and most of these point to the necessity of adopting "think big" ventures, especially with the new economic levers at our strategic disposal, such as the Internet, globalization, and outsourcing, all of which are within reach and in vogue. However, as it turns out, only a few companies need revolutionary changes in order to succeed. Remember the dot-com era, where the revolutionaries got a reminder that they should remember the nuts and bolts of operations.

Every company faces a tension between its vision and how to get there. When outcomes are *not* achieved to their fullest, some may place the blame on poor execution or bad strategy setting, while others will fault leadership or timing. Looking at these variables, separately or in combination, is a valid postmortem activity; however, what such an analysis overlooks is the likelihood that the systematic adoption of incremental but powerful changes will outshine grandiose schemes and produce bigger and better results.

The fact is, there are an inordinate number of interferences with big long-term plans. The fast-paced rollout of these well-intended visions confronts obstacles in the form of inelegant complexities involving people, processes, products, policies, politics, and public relations.

Every business, whether it is small, medium, or large, faces inescapable internal or external pressures until there comes a point where the leadership recognizes that the business must move to a new level of growth, competitiveness, innovation, globalization, or reorganization. At this point, the situation is usually urgent, and the business is in need of a "strategy." This recognition is proclaimed in management meetings that send rumors echoing throughout the organization. The assumption among employees is that some sort of change is inevitable. Then management communicates the new agendas with gloss and excitement, intended to motivate employees and get their enthusiastic buy-in.

In most cases, this procedure has the opposite effect. Big change, especially when it comes from the top, creates fear, anxiety, or stress in most people. This is actually not an issue about having a bad attitude. As it turns out, this is the way the brain naturally functions. Attempting to understand a big change, even a positive one, creates reactions in specific areas of the brain between the cortex and the amygdala—the same areas used for the flight-or-fight response—that initiate fear.

Stacks of well-written white papers, supported by management gurus, have concluded that if a company has reached a point of crisis, then the best course of action is probably a radical transformation of a part or parts of the business. Further assessments will point to areas related to business processes, marketability, or customer retention and growth, and ultimately the recommendations boil down to something like, "Throw out the old and bring in the new," or, "In order to rectify this problem, we need to make big changes."

Examples can be seen in computer software implementations over the last 20 years. Business solutions such as enterprise resource planning (ERP) systems have often been replaced with newer versions from either the same or a different software vendor. Statistically, only 30 percent of these large-scale ERP replacements live up to the business's expectations. Today more than ever there is a plethora of business resources at our disposal, including modeling tools, interactive Balanced Scorecards, business intelligence dashboards, financial simulators, and intricate project planning software. The question, then, is, Why don't things work out as planned more often?

Parts of this book expose the reasoning patterns that go on and show you how you can take a new approach to similar projects and avoid some of the pitfalls that others have endured. Business processes are always open to improvements. Historically, they were originally designed and implemented by the founders of the company, and they have been refined over time with the aim of providing a set of instructions that will allow employees to perform transactions of various types correctly, efficiently, accurately, and legally. Thinking small avoids unnecessary overhauls of core processes, policies, and procedures; instead, the search for big impact takes place within them, in the form of small improvements that have the potential to cascade across other related departments.

Over the last five years, with the increasing pressure of compliance and financial disclosures being so high on companies' agendas, there has been a tightening of the rules by management, with more approval levels being put in place. This is having an adverse effect on employees' ability to think creatively on the job.

In working in large global technology corporations like Oracle and other software vendors for over 25 years in a variety of roles, including engineering, sales, customer service, and marketing, differentiating products and services from competitors' and being the best at solving customers' business issues has been a constant challenge. The interesting point here is that over the years, those companies that made the biggest advances in their technological offerings did not automatically take a leadership position over their rivals. Historically, there has been no correlation between selling more software than the competition and the feature/function footprint being offered. In this book, we look at nuances in go-to-market strategies that do not necessarily require large investments in research and development but that can still give a company an advantage over the competition.

This book shares some of the marketing and business development lessons that I learned on the job, but the context and application of these lessons can be useful in any company. I worked in both the strategic and tactical sides of the marketing function, so this book will touch on these areas.

If we go back to the scenario of executing a strategy for growth, in a lot of situations this entails the replacement of a legacy computer system, the revision of outdated business processes, the need for more innovation in product development, streamlined production plans, or redesigned marketing strategies. The potential damage that can be done by these wholesale changes is the replacement of a lot that is good along with what is bad. The discovery process outlined here will (1) ensure that you take the time to investigate whether minor adjustments can solve the problem, and (2) make sure you look in the right places.

The reality is that new projects have to be executed while the rest of the company is running at a normal pace. Since new projects almost always have tight deadlines and shrink-wrapped budgets, they are expected to move at a much faster pace than the rhythm of normal business. Surround this with external changes in the economy, competitors, and customers' demands, and it is no wonder that with such an inhospitable environment, a radical change is unlikely to be a complete success.

More important, one of the strategies that this book will open you to is a process for arriving at a business recommendation that ensures that any and all of the small possibilities that are capable of achieving the same or a better result and that would make the big project unnecessary have been exhausted.

Companies that have made small changes that subsequently were successful have done so either by necessity or by accident; the changes were mostly unplanned. Embracing the concept of searching for small differences greatly increases the probability that every day someone will add an improvement that increases the efficiency or effectiveness of the business's performance and that also improves the customer experience. This book will provide a structured discovery process to uncover and assess changes based on their potential impact.

Just as when you look for anything in your life, you need to know what it is you want and then establish a likely place to look for it. The systematic methodology and workshop-style process called SMALL Tactics will take you step by step, isolating areas where small incremental changes can give the biggest benefit. This is done while maintaining alignment with the overall company objectives, and it is equally applicable for newly introduced projects or initiatives. The methodology is useful throughout the organization at any level, irrespective of employee rank, responsibility, or job function.

The plan sets in motion a perpetual improvement function. Once it is implemented, everyone engages, and over time an innate sensory acuity for finding small, realistic, and tangible improvements develops; finding these becomes easier as the number of occurrences increases. The benefits are ongoing, with everyone in the company contributing to something "bigger" or "better." Each day you will also see how it can be made safe to empower staff to identify small changes and give them the authority, within specified parameters, to make those changes by themselves. Companies that fully embrace this process may well experience a cultural shift, where employees' alignment with company values and goals moves them a step closer to each other.

Some of the basic differences that the SMALL Tactics will provide are the following:

- There is a communicated process that all employees follow to spot small changes, and all employees understand what *small* means in the context of their areas of responsibility.
- Each change is realistic and is executable within a short period of time, and it shows an immediate result to the individual who performed it, the team that supported it, the business unit that benefited from it, and the management that acknowledged it.
- Once a small change has been made and the results are seen, people are motivated to carry out more small changes, always in sizes such that they can be completed easily and without needing big budgets.
- Since these are small changes, the fear factor among employees is dramatically reduced, increasing buy-in from all levels and leading to unconditioned cooperation.
- Changes are manageable and feedback is immediate, so if anything goes wrong, its impact is minimized and easier to rectify or reverse.
- The aggregate of small incremental improvements may supply more overall benefits in a shorter space of time than a single radical change.
- Big changes will seem ordinary as employees become confident and see the results of the small improvements.

The application of small thinking is appropriate for any industry, and examples from firms ranging from large industry leaders to niche companies are given throughout the book. We will look at what these companies did that became a huge success, offering new learning that you can use proactively in your business. There is also room for innovation and creativity to personalize the planning and implementation and tailor it to individual company needs; in fact, this is encouraged and can be an essential ingredient in building differentiation and competitiveness.

The discovery process starts with basic questions that look at what changes have taken place within the company with respect to what is happening within your industry, your customers, and your partners. For example, questions that probe the business relationship with your market and your industry are these:

- What are your customers asking for that they did not ask for three years ago?
- What are your competitors doing differently from last year?
- What has taken place in the last 12 months to increase revenues?
- If you had to pick one, would you choose market growth or customer retention?

By answering questions of this type in a structured, hierarchical way, a company can develop a roadmap that identifies and prioritizes areas where small changes should take place to produce the biggest impact.

We all know that the all-important customer experience is a reflection of what happens inside a company; therefore, the first round of discovery isolates whether the improvement needed is internal or external. For example, do customer service–related areas need to improve the way each interaction with customers occurs, or is there an outbound issue in the company's marketing material regarding the presentation of the company's message and value?

All parts of the business are considered. However, there are common areas that regularly need attention:

- *Business processes.* Are they fragmented? Is there duplication? Are they slow?
- *Marketing.* Is there a low return on investment? Is segmentation appropriate? What about messaging?
- *Technology systems.* Are there problems with reporting? Is timely information provided? Are the systems slow at everything?
- *Visibility.* What is the level of customer loyalty? What are the current market trends? What is the cash situation?
- *Human resource talent base.* Is it unknown? Are there problems with the hiring process? How good is talent management?

- *Packaged products and services.* What are the current margins? Are products and services competitive? What is the level of customer loyalty?

Communication plays a critical role, especially when it comes to employees. They need to have a full understanding of what *small* means; specifically, they need to know the allowable scope of the changes they can make. This definition will differ across the company based on rank and role. For example, permissible small incremental changes at the shop floor manager level will be different from the flexibility that a production manager may have, which would be different yet again from that of the vice president of marketing or the chief financial officer, and so on. However, when a change that comes from a subordinate is seen as necessary or beneficial across the company, a process is set up that encourages the subordinate to present her ideas to her manager. To make this work effectively it is necessary to have clear guidelines for all areas of responsibility.

Creativity appears logical in hindsight. Once you have gone through this process and started to implement the principles, they will seem obvious and logical. We have all heard and seen continuous improvement programs, idea-generating initiatives, on-the-job intuition workshops, and various other growth and get-well programs for businesses. Unfortunately, nearly all of these programs bypass a basic natural process, which is looking at the path of least resistance for maximum gain. The unique value that you give your customers is what got you where you are today, and potentially something small may be all that is needed to propel you to another level of growth. It is surprising how close so many companies get to their takeoff point, but that then decide to make another leap and replace everything with the new big thing that they expect to somehow move them toward the inevitable success of their vision.

Chapters 3, 4, and 5 will show you just how close you really may be and whether small changes are all that you need. These chapters use a guided learning format with examples to help you understand and take action. Initially, the process will require dedicated time and effort to make sure you are clear about what the core values of the company are and how they relate to the way the company generates revenue. Often the results of determining this are surprising, especially when you take three coordinates: first, determine what changes have occurred in your industry over the last three years; second, look at the advances the competition has made; and third, counterbalance those with your business's advances in the same time frame.

A striking outcome of this exercise is finding out just how stale the company's messages are, signaling that customers may be forming the wrong perception of your company based on the literature and headlines you are sending out. If that is the case, using the Message Tree will take you down the path of message development—where making minor alterations to the overall company's positioning may be all that is necessary.

The exciting thing is that looking at the possibility that a small change may result in a big benefit has many other positive outcomes; at the very least, other related incremental improvements will prevail. While there can be no guarantee that all small findings will revolutionize every business, you can be sure that in the aggregate, small things do add up to something big. How big is really up to you.

CHAPTER 1

THE BIG EFFECT OF SMALL

The gap between what can be imagined and
what can be accomplished has never been smaller.

—Gary Hamel

Thinking small is not about staying small, nor is it about limiting innovative ideas. Every business wants to grow, become more profitable, gain market share, increase customer loyalty, be innovative, be more competitive, be easier to do business with, and have a healthy, happy, motivated workforce. The time frames in which we all want to achieve these objectives are aggressive and urgent. Everyone wants to become bigger or better as fast as possible. But it is important to remember that thinking small does not necessitate slowing down our pursuit of any of these imperatives.

In fact, small incremental advances can actually accelerate the move toward these objectives; by identifying the little details that block strategic plans or that impede the execution of existing processes, larger problems can be dealt with. If you look back at a situation in which your company needed to make a change in order to meet an objective, the decision about the adjustment probably started with the company's leaders and was manifested as a well-worded vision, mission, or strategy statement, made relevant with specific goals in mind.

Thinking small provides a way to retain focus on the bigger picture, which ultimately allows the use of a systematic process for discovering small ways to get to where the company needs to go. Both established companies and start-ups usually begin with an idea. Entrepreneurs and senior management hover at high levels of conceptual thinking, with details rarely being considered during this creative process. What happens next is the development of a strategy, which subsequently is agreed upon and then broken down into tactical plans, priorities, and budgets. After these are approved, owners are assigned, management reviews are scheduled, and the project begins.

This is a typical sequence of events that modern managers have used for decades, so one would think that after all this time, the process would be nearly perfect. Then why do so few projects meet their original objectives?

In most cases, the problem is in the "small stuff"—unanticipated challenges that suddenly surfaced without warning during the execution phase.

In order to understand the concept of getting to big the small way, it is useful to identify common causes of these challenges and the impact that "radical" changes make as compared to what might have happened if smaller incremental adjustments had been used in their place.

Interviews with hundreds of companies, ranging from very large corporations to small start-ups, that had recently undergone a replacement of their computer systems revealed that there were common denominators in their experiences. Specifically, those issues that could have been avoided included these:

- *Feelings that specific business objectives were abstract and vague.* The issue here is that no one was really sure what the business's specific objectives were; they only knew that those objectives appeared to be strategic for the future.
- *Unclear and inconsistent analysis of the initial problem.* This issue involves complaints that there were no specific metrics or key performance indicators, and that the business took little time to investigate the problem in depth.
- *The project was initiated from the top.* This dictated a level of urgency and priority that most of the staff had no warning of.

- *Simple software changes would have fixed the problem.* After going live, the company realized that minor software modifications or tweaking of business processes would have been sufficient, but these actions were not considered because they were seen as interim solutions and not beneficial for the company in the longer term.
- *The biggest gains were in areas with the smallest investment.* Several companies concluded that they seemed to have used a sledgehammer to crack a nut, including implementing modules that they did not need.
- *It took twice the anticipated budget to get half the anticipated benefits.* When everything was added up, the business had overspent.
- *The company was obsessed with selecting the right software package.* In this situation, evaluation teams focused so intently on comparing vendors that they lost sight of the objectives and what the task was supposed to achieve.
- *The company altered its priorities halfway through the project.* In doing so, the implementation of any remaining modules was halted. Instead the company took whatever benefits it could from the modules already installed.

These issues are symptoms of a failure on the part of the business to investigate whether there were any small changes in the current systems that would have achieved the objectives or affected the initial scope of the problem. In other words, these businesses neglected to ask themselves, What incremental small changes could have been made that would have allowed us to arrive at the same, if not a better, end point?

The Success of Big Strategy— Details, Details, Details

In much the same way that the nanotechnology and biotechnology industries deconstruct particles and molecular systems in pursuit of cures for viruses, cancers, and energy deficiencies, businesses should utilize an inside-out approach when dealing with problems that affect, interact with, and coexist with other parts of the corporate ecosystem.

There is no argument with the idea that starting at the macro level in the development of strategy is essential; however, because the future is unknown and planning for uncertainty is difficult, allowing for adjustments during a project's execution plays a significant role in determining that project's success. Business scholars assert that flexibility needs to be built in at the initiation of any strategy as a preventive against failure. By the time an important strategy is aired in a business meeting, it has undergone various degrees of diligent scrutiny, has been supported by data, and has been turned into a well-rehearsed, polished presentation. With credibility and reputations now at stake, most strategies will come across as *definite* and certain to be successful.

Putting a strategy into effect, however, requires a meticulously well-designed tactical plan with appropriate well-articulated milestones, which are necessary if you are to arrive at the desired outcome. This identification of details is often left to line managers, who have to figure them out from the flat, abstract document that is the only remaining record of the official strategy and that is made available only after the roundtable deliberations are over. The saying "the devil is in the details," attributed to Gustave Flaubert, was altered from the original statement, which when literally translated was actually "God is in the details." I agree with the original formulation, as it is alarmingly true that attending to the smallest of details can often save a project.

Improper project implementation is rarely the result of a lack of funding. This is because budgets are set and approved at the project scoping phase and remain one of the few constants. While some may argue that there is never enough money allotted to any given project, the fact is that project owners and managers know from the beginning of the project how much money is allotted to it and can plan the project accordingly. The unforeseen *challenges* are what bring delays, which absorb precious time and money. So when projects run out of money, it is not because they were not given enough to begin with, but rather because of the cost of something unforeseen. Typical documented causes for projects not being completed on time include the following:

- Lack of *alignment* with the rest of the organization
- Wrong *timing* given changing market conditions
- Not enough focus and *commitment* from management at the division level
- Competitive *pressures* resulting from globalization
- The idea that this is a *long-term* strategy, so the fact that it is delayed doesn't matter
- Not enough consideration of *change management*
- Inadequate or nonexistent *communication*

In Figure 1-1, each of these official reasons for project failure is compared with an example of the actual reason for the failure.

From a careful review of the factors involved in the actual cause, it is clear that the impediments could have been resolved with minor corrections, much smaller than the size of the investment.

But thinking small is more than just attention to detail or being more prepared. It is about "mini-innovation" or "microcreativeness" within specific parameters. Small changes materialize as a result of adaptations and the implementation of necessary *preapproved* adjustments. These changes, which often occur in midstream, are the aggregate effect of small efforts and have the potential to maximize the project's potential for success.

Often a new mission statement, strategy, or project coming from the top is interpreted as requiring revolutionary change in a specific companywide objective or across departments. Big change may sometimes be justified and valid, but in light of past performance, an evolutionary tack is proving to be a far more suitable way to effect change in today's economic climate.

The reality is that success lies within the operational capability that we have come to know as *execution*. One of the key principles of thinking and acting small is releasing permission in a controlled way, such as allowing each employee to make changes within his

Reason Given for Failure	Actual Cause of Failure
Alignment with the rest of the organization	Employees were not advised of the impact the project would have on their respective daily routine jobs even though the project was centered around one business unit of the company
Wrong timing resulting from unforeseen market conditions	The plan was conducted in an isolated location of the company away from day-to-day interruptions, with a very rigid plan managed and executed by outside consultants under time constraints
Not enough focus and commitment from management at the divisions	Less than a third of the management team knew anything about the project or were invited to any of the briefings, planning sessions, or even the launch of the project; all the line managers heard about it from their subordinates on the grapevine before learning how they were involved
Globalization—international competition reacted faster than anticipated	Assumptions were made concerning the availability of a small component of the final product, which, it turned out, could not be sourced easily; engineering was not consulted in the planning process
This is a long-term strategy, so delay is irrelevant; it's about the bigger picture	A minor compliance regarding a product-naming convention was held up in the legal department for months
Change management was handled badly	Employees and supervisors heard about the launch of the product in the staff bulletin days after the press release
No communication at the user level	The system went live with only a handful of users adequately trained

Figure 1-1 Official and Actual Reasons for Project Failure

or her job function. If these changes prove to be beneficial across departments and along other company hierarchies, the end result is to make the employee feel empowered. In other words, a simple change in one area of the company may have a beneficial ripple effect across other lines of business. Albert Einstein was noted as saying that the greatest mathematical discovery was compound interest. Small incremental advances follow a similar mathematical path in that their usefulness is compounded when other areas are willing to accept them.

To illustrate, in any business operation, certain interdepartmental processes interact with others at a transaction level, as seen in Figure 1-2.

In each of these basic transactions, there is a flow of work involved in processing and promoting the transactions and moving them on to the next logical destination in the company. For example, a customer's product order is taken by sales, which enters it into the system. Distribution then takes the product out of inventory and delivers it to the customer, who receives the product and pays the invoice to the accounts receivable department. Accounts receivable then processes the payment, and it is summarized in the finance department, which produces the financial reports for management at the end of each month. In each of

Operation	Transaction
Manufacturing/logistics/ distribution	Sales orders, components, parts, inventory stock, spares
Purchasing	Invoices, orders, pricing
Finance	Revenue, expenses, cost centers
Human resources	Employee records, benefit plans, payroll
Sales	Products, services, pricing, discounts, quotas
Marketing	Leads, customer data, market statistics
Management	Budgets, revenue, quota, expenses, profit/loss

Figure 1-2 Process Interactions

these individual parts of the work, there is room for small incremental improvements that can contribute to the efficiency and effectiveness of related departments as the transaction flows through them.

How does thinking small play a part in the framework of a company?

To answer, let's use a simple scenario like going on vacation. You start with what you want to do and your destination (*objective*). Then you determine how much vacation time you have available and how much you are prepared to spend (*budget*). That done, the tactical plan kicks in: finding the best price options for getting to your destination, the mode of transport, hotels, attractions, and so on (*project plan*). As long as everything goes according to plan, your strategic enjoyment will have been accomplished. Simple enough—at least in brochure form.

Your willingness and ability to make relatively small adjustments are completely *within* your control en route to dealing with the myriad of fluctuations that can affect your door-to-door journey, from the time you get to your hotel until you finally get back home.

In a business setting, the number of activities is larger and the process is vastly more complex, with many more internal interactions, external factors, and goals running in parallel; however, the example of the vacation helps to clarify the context in which small thinking enters the process and where it can play an essential role in ensuring that the overall objectives and goals are met. In summary, thinking small is akin to making fine adjustments midstream in a project or in the work being carried out day to day.

While simple and obvious, the concept of small thinking requires a deliberate management emphasis on encouraging employees to intervene in the daily executables by making beneficial changes that are within their capability and rewarding them for doing so.

Existing variants on this theme can be found in Six Sigma, but thinking small is intended to work with processes that are in place today rather than to introduce new ones. It involves implementing an overall philosophy that says that small changes are permitted, so that people start to believe that they can make a big difference.

Regardless of the size of your company, when these seemingly minor adjustments are aligned with company goals and applied daily in harmony and compliance with company policies, the aggregate of these adjustments delivers big overall improvements. As long as the objectives are well communicated and the reasons clearly understood, everyone can continue improving long after any project has been declared complete.

The Small Things That Count

Take, for example, a study of 40,000 women between 46 and 71 years of age. The *Journal of the American Medical Association* concluded that losing as few as five pounds can make a difference in vitality in performing everyday activities, no matter how much the women weighed to begin with. Even the heaviest women in the study reported improved physical functioning and less pain after losing only modest amounts of weight.[1]

To quantify these observations, for every 3,500 calories a person eats that is not expended through metabolism or exercise, that person will gain a pound. By cutting just 500 calories a day, you will have lost a pound in a week, without as much as putting on a pair of track pants or getting a glimpse of a gym. Now if you exercise as well, which is highly recommended, a brisk walk lasting around 20 minutes will shed approximately another 230 calories, meaning that you need to cut out only 270 calories per day to lose a pound in a week.[2]

Finding the Big in Small Things

The students at Bradley University in Illinois were not taking advantage of the on-campus food court. The students' lack of usage of the food court created two problems for the university:

the area was intended to be used as a study space to supplement the students' course work, and the food court was running a promotion whose aim was to encourage students to sign up for the university's "in-dining services program," a feature that would teach students easy ways to make healthy meals. For some unknown reason, this promotion was having the opposite effect; it actually discouraged students from visiting the food court. As a result, a minor change was implemented: the food court was split into two sections, which were branded differently; one served typical fast foods, such as pizzas, burgers, and upscale sandwiches, while the other featured new healthy dishes and recipes each day. This minor change resulted in an increase in participation in the in-dining services program by 40 percent.

Montrachet, a restaurant in New York City, was seeing subpar Monday night attendance. As most of the evening diners were local, it decided to make Mondays a BYOB (Bring Your Own Bottle) night. Customers were delighted at the opportunity to have a French-style meal with their private wine selection, and patronage increased from an average of 40 diners to over 175.

Pinxav (pronounced "pink salve"), a diaper-rash cream, was not selling; mothers were skeptical of the benefits of switching to the cream, despite the manufacturer's money-back guarantee. In response, the manufacturer slightly altered its money-back offer, replacing it with an offer to not only refund dissatisfied customers' money but also to buy the mothers any other brand of cream that they had previously purchased. This dramatically increased sales to the point that it is now standard practice. Greg Steiner, the CEO of Pinxav, commented, "You're often not reinventing the wheel—you're simply polishing it a little."[3]

A relevant observation concerning these small changes is that they were implemented by employees as they were doing their day-to-day work; the changes were not as a result of intense strategic analysis in any given company's organization. As you learn more about how to apply these principles to your business, let's expand on the characteristics of these types of changes:

- The changes were small, but their impact was big.
- The changes occurred in one place first and then rippled through other parts of the company.
- The changes were done quickly—faster than competitors' changes.
- Most of the changes had no budget to begin with.
- The changes did not require a new skill or expertise to be introduced, at least not in the first execution of change.
- The changes all achieved or exceeded their initial results.

Thinking Small at All Levels

Small changes can be beneficial at any level of an organization. They are effective at the strategic level and are relevant to setting direction, product innovation, customer service, distribution, sales, and marketing. Take, for example, Starbucks, one of America's best-known brands, which decided to go from selling coffee beans to serving coffee in a corner coffeeshop. Strategically, the move was not a big leap, nor did it involve volumes of research and comprehensive planning. The outcome, however, consistent with the overall objective of selling more beans, was that Starbucks now sells an average of 18 cups of coffee to customers each month, overcoming the brand loyalty of incumbents like Nestlé, which had been in the same business sector for more than 10 years before the Starbucks move.

What looks now like a revolutionary change of course started as a simple adaptation to demonstrate the quality of the coffee, with Starbucks never having to stray from the original company objectives. To demonstrate the applicability of this process at all levels within Starbucks, at one time its agronomy office organized the supply and quality inspection of coffee using manual records, mainly on spreadsheets. The process required "verifiers" in Africa and South America to create farm inspection reports; send them to Costa Rica, where they would be sent for review and checked for standards in Oakland, California; and then send them to Seattle,

Washington. Then this elongated and tedious process was centralized using online systems that gave everyone along the supply chain access to the reports and information and that provided transparency and accountability to the farmers. This process made the certification and approval process much more efficient, and the online presence and feedback of farmers gave them wider visibility, providing them with the added incentive of deepening their commitment to organic standards.

These easily executable, low-cost changes provided big benefits not only within the company but also within its operations, partners, and suppliers. That one small idea created a *ripple effect* of other changes across the rest of the organization. Success bred success, and other locations responded by improving on the initial offerings with more varieties of coffee. Starbucks now has a culture in which each barista (coffee server) is free to make feasible small changes to improve service and the customer experience.

The skill of thinking about small but significant differences can be easily inculcated at every level of a company and can be managed, monitored, and measured. Ideas for small improvements have an immediate feedback response, and because they usually occur within the tactical operations of a business, they give other employees a feeling of empowerment in their day-to-day jobs, instilling in them a sense of the importance of making worthwhile contributions. The power of small thinking combined with immediate executable actions for better results is that, while a single unit of change, when studied in isolation, may seem relatively minor, in the aggregate and in concert, small thinking can make a big difference, especially when the benefits roll across the company.

Employees today can bring a wealth of experience to their jobs, but they are sometimes hesitant to stray from the instructions, procedures, and policies prescribed by legacy processes, which are often based on "the way things have always been done." With job insecurity on the rise, employees are pulling back from making any suggestions for fear of sounding negative or going against proven methods or abandoning the Employee Handbook. Thinking small is not about disrupting the core processes needed to perform work; it is about improving them, one small improvement at a time.

If you ask a unit manager to think of new ways to do the same job (to "think outside the box"), in most cases he or she will struggle with the concept, feeling that making the biggest impact will require rethinking almost everything. This is where seemingly minor but consistent changes outperform larger ones. In essence, several orchestrated small changes can achieve more than a few large ones. The fact is that with small changes, you have an equal or better probability of success with less disruption, cost, delay, and anxiety, and without losing sight of the bigger enterprisewide objectives.

In his best-selling book *The Tipping Point*, Malcolm Gladwell gives evidence of how little things can, in fact, make a big difference. A conclusion he draws is that, inside a company, the proliferation and intensity of any impact made by small changes are containable because there are fewer external consequences from social or environmental factors, so that the danger of small changes disrupting the "ecosystem" of the business is much more manageable.[4] The key to building a culture of small incremental changes within an organization is remaining consistent with the strategy of the business. As stated earlier, objectives and goals *must* be clearly communicated. Small incremental changes also need to be simple. Simple changes make for quick wins, as they can be implemented faster and with more confidence. As long as guidelines are followed, there is little or no need for bureaucracy to intercept these changes. When employees feel safe in making simple changes, they are able to develop a natural self-confidence and hence can bring more ownership to their jobs.

The conventional wisdom regarding increasing revenue growth, becoming more competitive, capturing larger markets, and cutting cost habitually leads managers to take the "rip and replace" route. How often have we heard exhortations to "think big" as the way to get bigger and better?

An example that disputes the argument that big outcomes need big changes comes from a contemporary work by Professors Chan

Kim and Renée Mauborgne in their book *Blue Ocean Strategy*,[5] in which they consider the notion of value as compared to cost. They debunk the assumption that companies can provide better value only at a greater cost, and also argue against the belief that less value comes at a lower cost, holding instead that you need only to investigate a different view of the business. In fact, more value can be gained by finding differentiation and creating "value innovation," which they claim can lead to new markets. In this way, Kim and Mauborgne also reveal that there is no hard correlation between making big changes and having a sizable impact on the extent to which the company can develop new markets from old ones.

In everyday working life, there are problems both big and small, and they all need to be addressed as soon as this is practical. However, more often, the decidedly small problems are left unresolved. This isn't particularly surprising, given that 95 percent of us procrastinate, chiefly because we lack either confidence or an understanding of the importance of finishing our jobs.[6] But when the issues grow to the point where they reach upper management, steps toward resolution are taken, but with a wider purview that affects more than the otherwise less disruptive approach of rectifying the impediment at the source would. Even in cases where the fix requires a series of small steps in a chain of connected sequences, such a series would still be more effective than most replacement options.

Why Big Strategies Fail

In any size company, it is critically important that there are clearly defined goals. Often strategies are communicated to the administrators of an organization, but much is lost in translation at the worker level. Unless the goals are specified, it is difficult for staff members to intuitively identify how the new vision relates to their day-to-day jobs.

A surfeit of studies by management consulting firms highlights flaws in the way managers communicate company strategies, and reveals why so few workers understand these strategies:

- The strategy is too abstract or vague or is at such a high level that no one beyond the executive management team can understand it.
- The goals and objectives are so new or so different that people hearing them for the first time are surprised by their direction or intent.
- The way the strategy is to be rolled out is unclear or nonexistent.
- There are few, if any, details of the incentives for employees to buy in if the goals are achieved.
- The accountability of the various business units for the strategy or goals is missed.
- There are few controls or mechanisms to manage the strategy's success or to enable employees at operational levels to provide feedback or make contributions to the changes required.

This book will address how to overcome some of these challenges while still inculcating company goals in employees at every level. Employees need to know when to engage. Often employees wait for their managers to tell them to do something that is different.

Knowing when to engage becomes even more critical if the company has decentralized operations or is dispersed across international borders. If we are asking everyone to come to work and think of ways to improve the company that are within his or her scope, then a better understanding of company goals becomes a motivator for improvement, thereby increasing the effectiveness and speed of execution.

In mergers and acquisitions, the need to communicate with the integrating companies is, of course, crucial; however, this is where the notion of empowering small incremental improvement behavior can be optimized. One of the biggest concerns of merging companies, apart from the economics, is integrating the new and old parts so that they work together, hopefully better than they did before.

Blowing Small Out of Proportion

If we look at how problems that arise in everyday business scenarios are dealt with at the management level and observe the flow of typical communications coming into and out of the office of the CEO or other member of management, we find that they cover a wide range of topics and issues, from strategic to very detailed. Broader strategic items aside, the following is a sample across this tactical spectrum of actual day-to-day issues:

- Counteracting or reacting to a new product launch by a competitor
- Deciphering the fine print on union contracts to be negotiated in two days
- Replacing a truck for a time-sensitive, contractually obligated order to a major customer
- Dealing with a lawsuit resulting from an employee's harassing behavior that may land in the media

Management spends a lot of time responding to the drama in order to bring about happy endings. Some would even argue, isn't that why management is there, after all?

By the time they hit management's desk, many of these potentially avoidable issues have had emotional embellishments superimposed. What happens next is that the potentially small problems are "oversolved." You may be familiar with sitting in endless meetings, listening to the ebb and flow of emotionally charged rhetoric, and trying to solve what started off as simple problems. If we look at the previous issues again, this time with the resolutions that came from actual meetings, you can see how a simple operational item can be treated as a strategic matter:

- A competitor launches an unexpected new product under your nose—marketing is not doing its job.
- The union contract issue is being delegated to the wrong people on the shop floor—we need to build a review committee that reports directly to management.

- There are mechanical problems with a truck stuck by the roadside—there is a problem in the maintenance department, or in distribution and logistics, or in both.
- An employee engaged in inappropriate behavior, resulting in legal action—there are issues relating to poor management and leadership.

In management meetings, these issues open tangential doors, allowing bigger and broader resolutions in, because the problem is now *perceived* as needing a *strategic fix*. As mentioned earlier, a common cause of internal problems is a lack of clarity. When issues are presented to management, a number of innate human attributes kick in, causing a distortion of reality. This normal behavior also interferes with problem definition and problem solving. For example, a festering problem or issue will be put through a mental filter that will generalize the context in which the problem occurred, thereby applying a bias that either increases or diminishes the perceived severity of the problem. This then leads to a distortion of the problem's relevance, causing any surrounding relevant facts to be deleted or never mentioned. This is a natural internal thought process for storing our personal experiences with the outside world. But when this natural ability is applied in a business setting under pressure, you can see why problems can easily be blown out of proportion.

A common manifestation of this problem is long e-mail strings generated over a simple matter, with blog-style comments and opinions coming from all corners of the organization. The respondents know that if this issue ever gets raised to upper management, the result will be inevitable: a minor glitch will be inflated into a corporatewide issue. That protracted circular route can be avoided if someone is empowered enough to know that he or she can make the change and take the initiative to fix the problem then and there.

Quite rightly, management is focused on growth. Ironically, this broad thinking and intense focus may actually create tunnel vision that effectively eliminates the ability to recognize the potential of small ideas. Equally, if excellence in customer service, quality, or leadership is on the company agenda, then making sure that the small things are working across the company creates a platform for strong growth.

Big Changes Can Happen for Small Reasons

The fact that minor glitches can be turned into companywide problems is not a reflection on the talent, competence, or experience of either management or staff. Rather, there are two forces at play here, one being the treatment of the issue that has elevated it to an all-encompassing strategic level and the other being how the explanation of the issue is infected by gross natural distortion.

Whatever your job role, I am sure you have seen cases where the obvious fix to a simple problem was a small change. But, more often than not, one of two scenarios is likely to prevail. One is that the problem is ignored and a temporary work-around is found. This scenario arises when employees are uncertain whether anyone has the authority to make the proper change, which also means that, when the problem inevitably occurs again, either another Band-Aid is applied or, because there are no known ways to deal with making adjustments to predefined processes, nothing happens at all. In the second scenario, managers mandate that all issues, large or small, be brought to their attention. In the latter, problems of delegation may be involved. However, if a culture and process that gives employees the freedom to make changes and fixes within their domain of responsibility and skill has been implemented, then a more efficient workforce and management team will prevail.

Thinking small shows its full effect when it is applied within existing operations that touch customers, partners, or suppliers. If the timing of making the small incremental changes is right, your alterations can have a wider-reaching impact on customer service–related business issues. In the majority of cases, customers' complaints occur after their purchase and are directly related to access to information, assistance, or changes. A comprehensive report commissioned in the United States in 1995, during the Clinton administration,[7] identified specific businesses and organizations whose "customers," meaning the public, were most dissatisfied with the level of telephone support they received. The report included federal government agencies, such as Social Security and the Internal Revenue Service, and large corporations, such as American Express, AT&T, Bell Canada, Citibank, GE, and USAA Insurance. Of the top five issues to address, one was to "develop recommendations to improve [your] core processes and empower front-line employees to resolve complaints on first contact."

Timing is all-important, and when front-line employees are uncertain of their scope of authority, they naturally resort to safety zones, bypassing the issue, closing off the issue with "it can't be done," or, worse still, making a promise in good faith to resolve it even though they are not confident that a resolution can really be reached. The practice of giving employees the flexibility to make process adjustments is a dangerously confrontational topic, especially among some managers and supervisors, who are naturally anxious about how to ensure that company policies are adhered to, as well as within departments where the scope of change may have broader companywide or legal implications. The idea that if you give people an inch, they'll take a mile is the crux of the fear; however, if a specific scope or perimeter for each role in the organization is defined, then this issue gradually fades to irrelevancy.

Thinking small not only has a place in providing adaptable changes in the course of executing new projects, but such thinking is also effective in routine day-to-day work. The issue is not just getting deeper into the detail of an isolated problem; companies must fix problems at their roots—(nip them in the bud, if you will) by relying on the people who are the most qualified to fix them—those who are doing the actual work, as opposed to management or supervisors. The key is providing a controlled empowerment.

Taking the Good with the Bad

How often have you heard that if everything is going well, no one cares, but if something goes wrong, everyone knows about it, including management? Managers instinctively focus on solving problems that get in the way of progress. Defaulting to the problem-solving tactics that we are taught in school, we seek out a relevant formula or hypothesis that can give us the answer. Often we need to break apart the issue and examine it more deeply, isolating the problem before coming up with a solution. Thinking small follows this same line of thought: for thinking small to be effective, you first need to look at what is working right, not the other way around. As long as there is a clear understanding of the company's priorities and the direction in which it plans to grow, this approach produces a different response and a more balanced view of procedural problems in the workplace, making it easier to identify the small things to do first that can be leveraged to give the biggest value and benefit.

So far we have touched on oversolving problems that crop up within the company. But issues also arise when companies try to solve problems using the advice of outside influences, such as suppliers and vendors, as they may introduce unnecessarily broad solutions for potential minor issues using their all-encompassing products and services. Operating under competitive conditions, they are eager to demonstrate and sell their extended products and services, thereby positioning themselves as the better alternative to solving problems internally. When they are invited to solve your problems and given only surface details and thirdhand information about company issues, they are likely to explain how their products can eradicate the wider problems that created the fault, and their argument can be convincing. In making this case, outsiders may propose a larger-than-necessary replacement of existing parts, processes, or systems. A study by Deloitte Research illustrates this sentiment from a CIO, who was responding to a survey after looking for a suitable vendor: "Reading through the differences between marketing material and specs is a challenge—

finding out what's different between the old and new versions. Sometimes I'm looking for such a minor feature change that it's often not mentioned."[8]

Let Small In

Companies with good track records of success may try to enter new markets by recycling age-old, previously tried-and-tested go-to-market models, and this can actually hurt them. This is due, says Donald Sull, to a corporate condition called *active inertia*.[9]

Active inertia happens when a company has established patterns of behavior based on previous successes. The company sticks to these models, and even accelerates them, to gain market leadership or a share of new product lines, even when there have been shifts in the market environment that made the models work in the first place. Then there are companies that failed in their ambitious goals but were stuck in their mode of thinking, not willing to make even the smallest tweak to their once-winning formulas. Sull identifies the components causing failure and isolates four areas that are worth mentioning. His analysis reinforces the way in which thinking small would have avoided process breakdown. He categorizes the areas as follows:

- *Strategic frames.* These are based on a set of management assumptions concerning the business, effectively taking a shortsighted look at issues.
- *Processes based on the way things are done.* Basing actions on the way things are done and have always been done enforces routine work while eliminating initiative.
- *Relationships tied to the inner sanctum.* Only a subset of the company's employees, customers, suppliers, distributors, and shareholders are involved, and the company is therefore shackled by predetermined expectations.
- *Values and shared beliefs.* The values and beliefs that define the corporate culture are driven by internal dogma and rant.

Thinking small provides a safe operating environment in which change can be allowed in carefully, thus preventing what I call *corporate sclerosis*. The fact that active inertia exists further justifies considering an incremental approach across all parts of the company, especially when companies feel that they have arrived at operational excellence and conclude that they are suitably flexible and equipped to handle the next step in becoming bigger.

As we unpeel the concepts of thinking small, consider these examples of active inertia. The first involves Atari, the popular video game manufacturer of the late 1980s. Atari was the pioneer of the video game with its infamous Pong. A basic game by today's standards, it captured the world's attention and found a new use for television sets. Despite its unprecedented success in video games, Atari began to decline around 1990 when it began entertaining visions of entering the PC market. This was an obvious next step for Atari, given the company's expertise and investment in software and hardware and its commitment to developing and manufacturing its gaming products. The leap, however, proved too big, and it eventually dragged down the core gaming business. In 1993 the Atari Jaguar, the newest release, failed to compete successfully with new entrants like the Sony Playstation and the Sega Saturn.

About the same time, Wang Laboratories, which was the leader in word processing software and hardware, had a similar experience. Wang, which delivered both software and hardware, designed its products around the needs of a typist. When it wanted to expand and enter the personal computer market faster than its rivals, Wang underestimated the impact on the company of gaining that much larger market share. Although production was stressed to the limit, the company's aim was to build the ultimate personal computer, with everything the competitors had and more. Anxious to get to market, Wang overpromised and underdelivered by a long shot in what is recorded in history as the "vaporware" announcement of 1983, a term that is still widely used in technology circles. Fourteen new products were promised, none of which made their delivery dates. Customers fled to more reliable and versatile brands that were selling "office solutions" and marketed more than just word processing functionality. Ultimately, Wang declared bankruptcy in 1992.

If Wang had taken the path of small incremental releases with enough functionality in their hardware and features, maybe the company would be in business today. Reports at the time surmised that Wang employees "fell victim to the hubris, the insulation from the market, and the sheer bureaucratic inefficiency that goes with such size."[10] Today a growing number of converts believe that momentum can come from a series of small successes. In his book *Bigger Isn't Always Better*, Robert M. Tomasko[11] explains that initial small successes are important and can provide more motivation within a company than bigger wins.

How Big Is Small?

Attempting to define *small* in the context of wins or incremental improvements is like trying to decide what the standard height should be to define *short*: both present technical, ethical, political, and relational issues. However, for our purposes, *small* is not about dimension. It is about the scope of the impact a change has on any one thing or any one person. Therefore, thinking small is not about size or about a lessening of vision or desire. It is about thinking outside the box but within the borders.

The fact of the matter is that small is relative. The concept of thinking small to bring about big changes holds true even when what a company considers small would be big by someone else's standards. In his book *Jack Welch and the GE Way*, Robert Slater quotes Welch as saying, "Making a small call . . . is the easiest job in the world because I've got a big company. 'Small' means investments of a hundred million, fifty million, thirty, seventy million. Making two billion dollar swings or five billion dollar swings . . . where you change the game [is a huge challenge]. You risk the image of the company. You can tip it upside down."[12]

While a lot of companies would not consider multi-million-dollar investments to be small, the point here is that GE's goal remains becoming bigger and stronger, using the rationale that it is far safer for the company to "swing" itself up by way of small increments. A collection of small, quickly executed investments is a powerful and effective way to increase revenues and become more profitable, often with less risk involved.

So, the conception that only big change will elicit a big outcome is outdated.

Life's Small Secrets

In later chapters, we will delve more deeply into the human aspects of thinking small; however, as a further illustration that the concept is a viable option, it turns out that thinking small works as effectively in our personal lives as it does in our professional ones. According to Dr. Robert Maurer, a clinical professor at the University of California–Los Angeles (UCLA) and a practitioner of a "personal application" of Kaizen (a system of continual improvements), asking small questions dispels fear, evokes creativity, and shortens the time it takes to reach personal goals. He goes on to say that by using small thoughts, new skills can be developed and old habits changed. These thoughts lead to small actions that, when rewarded, grow and mount to guaranteed bigger successes.

If we follow this through to our professional lives, thoughts lead to actions when we are engaged in the physical activity of performing our work. The idea that it is reasonable to conclude that employees will feel more comfortable making small incremental improvements reverses any potential trend toward active inertia. Without active inertia looming in the distance, businesses can see increases in agility and flexibility both at the point where employees interface with customers and within the intercompany business processes.

Small Incremental Behavior

Getting bigger the small way and thinking small is based on a change in the way people think about their jobs and how they relate to the overall objectives of both their department and their company. Its application can be seen in a variety of areas and across a number of activities. When and where thinking small is utilized is entirely up to the user, and its implementation can be rolled out in any combination of ways. The places where thinking and behaving small work are:

- At multiple levels within the company structure and hierarchy
- In the design and formulation of a strategic- or tactical-level plan
- At the management or operational level
- For new projects and initiatives or within current projects
- In current business process flows or as an intended replacement for them
- For business partners and strategic alliances with third parties

The first phase of introducing small thinking is to incrementally increase authority at lower levels of the chain of command, thereby creating the invigorating energy that is required if employees are to fully utilize their skills and abilities to effect change with immediate action.

A simple, easy-to-use, easy-to-learn framework and structured process is applied with this approach, allowing every employee in the company to utilize it effectively in his or her day-to-day job. This is what we will be looking at in detail in the coming chapters, but it is useful to introduce at this point the ways in which we will apply these concepts to everyday job functions and roles, as well to any new projects and initiatives that may arise. The application is suitable for problem solving, for running corporatewide projects, or for increasing efficiency at a departmental level.

A framework developed through years of noting not only where small changes made the most impact but also from what part of the company the changes derived is presented here as a structured model that can be easily understood and, more important, rapidly introduced into an organization of any size. The model is called SMALL Tactics, and it contains five basic elements that can be called upon when an area within a company needs improvement. They are isolated here for easier understanding of the concept. Individual activities, in the form of a workshop that is later developed as a plan (see Chapter 8), involve five key considerations. They are revealed here so that other activities and ideas can be generated using the same thought process. SMALL Tactics manifest themselves in real life as one task that can be acted upon when the change is actually performed. There are five aspects of each activity, but they should be performed as one aggregate objective:

- *Selected*. The problem, issue, or fault can be *easily* isolated and identified.
- *Measured*. The impact of change can be *measured* and monitored.
- *Action*. The change is within my given *authority*.
- *Link*. The change is *aligned* with company/department/project objectives.
- *Learn*. There is new and valuable *learning* that others in the company can leverage by *communicating* the change.

The unique aspect of SMALL Tactics is that no special outside skills are needed for its implementation. All the intellectual capital required can be found within your organization today, together with its existing capabilities. Not only can SMALL Tactics be implemented immediately at any level of the company using the exact same principles, but it also can expand the knowledge base of the already-experienced worker at his or her respective work post.

CHAPTER 2

THINK SMALL, AIM BIG

You've got to think about "big things" while you're doing small things,
so that all the small things go in the right direction.

—Alan Toffler

The year 2000 was a turning point on several fronts, especially in the technology industry. The dot-com boom was in full swing, with start-up Internet businesses being developed from business proposals and PowerPoints that could be described as "innovation gone wild." The millennium bug, the so-called Y2K, was prominently on the agenda. It became the catalyst for and probably one of the biggest contributing factors to the outsourcing boom, especially in India, as the Internet, broadband, and immensely powerful server computers swept away many previous network and response issues. "The Internet changes everything" was the global mantra, with a new breed of entrepreneurs believing that business was moving to the online world and that the Internet would eliminate the need for brick-and-mortar stores. History speaks for itself regarding that theory; however, there were movements in the industry that did take place that would prove to be significant.

Y2K itself was an anticlimax. Apart from some slot machines not working and the odd bus-ticketing system failing, only minor damage was reported. However, several companies, scrambling to resolve their century date change issues before the clock struck midnight, found themselves in the new millennium with an over-supply of software that had been "thrown in" by eager salesper-sons supersizing the deals at the last minute. The residual effect was an overflow of fresh software revisions. By early 2001, selling significant software solutions to anyone, and especially to large companies, was a challenge, as most of these companies were still digesting and reengineering their processes for their newly implanted systems. The calm of the postmillennium period cre-ated a vacuum for IT vendors, who, having finished licking their lips after the feeding frenzy of Y2K, now had to find something new to sell.

They soon noticed the market segment that consisted of smaller-sized businesses, commonly referred to as the small and midsize business (SMB) market, which in aggregate had the largest number of potential customers. Conservatively esti-mated at $40 billion, this market includes more than 80 million customers worldwide and is the fastest-growing sector in the technology market. Oracle, SAP, Peoplesoft (at that time), Law-son, Ariba, i2, IBM, HP, Dell, Computer Associates (CA), Sun Microsystems, and a host of others began giving this potentially lucrative segment more marketing attention. The so-called incumbent vendors that had traditionally targeted the SMBs—vendors such as Microsoft Great Plains, QAD, BPCS, JD Edwards (prior to the Peoplesoft takeover), Ross Systems, Sage Group, Epicor, IFS, and SSA—had been marketing and selling to this market with relative success using business and cost models suitable for this type of clientele. They had sustained their growth and competitiveness against their larger rivals for several years based on their good understanding of what SMBs required.

Because of their size, the SMBs had smaller IT budgets, and so naturally these deals had a much smaller per transaction amount than sales to larger corporations. For the incumbent vendors, this was business as usual, and in the main they had had little inter-ference from the global IT vendors. However, things were about to change dramatically.

Aiming Big

How the global IT vendors could get to this huge market in a cost-effective manner was the $40 billion question. The drivers for SMBs replacing their legacy systems included a number of economic factors, among them mergers and acquisitions, globalization, and outsourcing. These factors accelerated the need to replace legacy software, and generally this was a time of solid growth for most vendors. Looking at more functionally rich integrated applications and doing away with as much as possible of their fragmented department-oriented solutions were high on the agenda of chief information officers (CIOs). In addition to the constraints of lower budgets and increasing costs, pressures mounted relating to the decreasing availability of people with the skills needed to deal with the aging systems that these companies had nursed for years. Add to these factors the increasing demand that the systems accommodate new strategies for business expansion, coupled with a demand for more sophisticated consolidated management reporting, preferably real-time and in the form of "business intelligence" or "executive dashboards," and it is no wonder that CIOs were out waving their requests for proposals to find new systems.

Enter global IT vendors, who for several years had been building fully integrated, end-to-end business applications catering to a larger corporate audience. They had just what the SMBs were looking for. For example, Oracle developed a comprehensive business system with multicurrency and multilanguage capabilities, and with localized tax and other financial nuances. This system, which ran on Oracle's database software, was marketed as E-Business Suite and was well suited for fast-growing companies. While it is impossible to define a meaningful delineation between SMBs and larger corporations, the common impression was that many growing SMBs were craving the software that IT vendors like Oracle were selling.

To be sure, there were barriers to entry in this hotly contested market. As Yamamoto Krammer from Gartner reported[1], there was a cost for vendors to enter this market. Krammer predicted that 60 percent of the vendors directing their marketing focus on this segment would fail. Larger players were in fact encountering challenges in credibly moving into and accelerating growth in this downmarket segment using their traditional business models. It should be noted that all the vendors mentioned earlier had always sold and continued to sell to the SMB market. However, with their increased attraction to this market, their attempts to gain share as they had with the larger companies fell alarmingly short of their expectations.

On the one hand, global IT vendors had traditionally directed their sales forces to go after the bigger deals and basically ignore smaller ones on the grounds that the overall deal size would be too small relative to the effort required. Conversely, SMBs had bypassed these same large IT vendors because of the perceived complexity of their products. The SMBs saw these products as being too expensive and having high ongoing running costs. Based on this history, it appeared that two distant and opposing forces were now trying to come together, but they were much like two magnets with the same poles facing: they were repelling each other.

Thinking that they could compete with the incumbent vendors on the same turf because of their perceived better software functionality, global IT vendors were loading their marketing guns and making serious investments. They aspired not only to crack the code for market leadership, but to do it cost-effectively *and* without disproportionately disrupting other parts of their business operations or consuming too many internal resources. Initially the global vendors assumed that the SMBs had simpler business models and therefore needed less complex business software. This miscalculation led to costly reruns of unsuccessful marketing campaigns, until someone dug deep enough into the research that indicated that a larger number of small businesses than had been assumed did in fact have sophisticated business needs. SAP, for example, defined the market based on levels of business process complexity as "simple, sophisticated or advanced."[2]

In reality, for a small or medium-sized business, the cost of the software itself was secondary compared to the cost and impact of ingesting a large-scale system. The overall transaction for a business software application consists of fees—quite a few of them. Some common ones are license fees, support fees, consultant's fees, training fees, hosting fees, subscription fees, service fees, and, if hardware is involved, leasing fees, installation fees, and more maintenance and support fees. What stood out as being of most concern to SMBs was consultant's fees. As the CFO of a $50 million manufacturer told me, "I can negotiate the price on license fees, or on support costs, but the one thing I have no control over is the implementation costs and what the consultants will finally deliver; that is the biggest risk I take here."

It was also by far the biggest exposure for vendors. If you have ever been directly or indirectly involved with a computer system replacement, you will know that implementation is the most critical aspect if the new system is to be a success. It is an important revenue source for vendors and their implementation partners. Implementation costs can typically be anywhere between one to five times the cost of the license fees (or first-year subscription fees if you host the system).

Both hardware and software solution IT vendors faced similar issues. They not only had to make the product's base price affordable, but they also needed to make affordable the related services, such as installation and implementation fees to get the systems up and running. SMBs typically do not have big IT departments. Their heavy reliance on the vendors to bring in the necessary skills and qualified resources risked eroding the vendors' precious margins because of the lower fees they were forced to charge in order to remain competitive.

While this example involves the technology industry, it illustrates a classic market tension and a daily challenge for any business: staying competitively priced and securing profit margins. In any large market, everyone wants to get a big slice. In the SMB market, even a modest business proposal would show large potential returns—in the tens if not hundreds of millions of dollars of extra top-line revenues. For example, IBM, with its partners, was one of the first to launch an attack on this market, with a budget in excess of $100 million aimed at developing marketing programs and customer awareness campaigns.

Others followed suit with broad-based branding and exposure campaigns, but they found that these campaigns generally missed the mark. Given all the marketing variables involved, casting their marketing nets even wider was simply not catching a lot of the right type of fish, and, as is often the case, when the revenues came in, the profitability and return on these marketing costs ended up being lower than forecast. Mass marketing, sometimes referred to as "spray and pray marketing," was not guaranteeing a bigger market share or higher profits, at least not in this case.

In a market of this size, companies' basic instinct is to use the most cost-effective marketing techniques that budgets will allow, often involving previously used templates with generic high-level messages and content. However, in this market, and in other markets in recent times, these strategies rarely provide an acceptable return on investment, as they do not generate enough demand to produce the forecasted sales. Ironically, today, with the biggest world markets ever, mass-marketing strategies are repeatedly showing signs of weakness, mainly because customers want to be marketed and sold to on the basis of their uniqueness and industry-specific needs.

IBM used its distinct advantage of strength in going indirect through its partner relationships and networks. This proved to be an efficient and rapid way to gain *coverage* of the market, but in order to close deals fast enough, further work was needed to gain *leverage*. One of the characteristics of this market is its heavily diversified nature, and a one-size-fits-all approach (which is commonly used in mass-marketing campaigns) was not effective. In today's economy, entering any lucrative market and intending to get big requires a blended strategy that includes both coverage, or providing marketing air cover aimed at the intended target markets, and leverage, which allows the company to execute on sales opportunities by having the right relationships and skills on the ground.

Let's summarize the situation at this point before describing the other market influence that also appeared. Large IT vendors coming out of the Y2K bonanza are attracted to a market segment made up of smaller-sized customers known as SMBs; this segment is the fastest-growing and highest-spending sector of the market. The issue is the perceived complexity and expense of the large vendors' solutions. Marketing departments develop creative offers by repricing, repackaging, and reintroducing their products to this market, competing with the long-standing incumbent vendors who have been successfully selling to this group for some time. Large IT vendors are trying to move downstream, and smaller incumbent vendors are building their muscle and working their way upstream as far as possible to meet their large rivals in the middle, where most of the money is. Large IT vendors have a lot more of the software; incumbent vendors have a lot more of the know-how. Both are aiming big, and both are thinking big, but up to this point both are gaining relatively small amounts compared to the size of the opportunity and the addressable market.

Big Gets Bigger

While all of these vendors were trying to figure out the right marketing strategies and business models to use to market their products effectively, a disruptive technology, brought to us by the Internet, introduced the phenomenon of the online marketplace; it goes under various names, such as B2B (business-to-business) exchanges, trading hubs, and e-markets. Volumes have been written about this "killer application" that would revolutionize the business world. It would basically operate as an online auction; buyers and sellers would represent themselves by bidding for commercial parts, products, materials, and services, and the lowest bidder (not the highest as in domestic-type auctions) would enter into a formal binding contract to complete the transaction. This was the first time that online transactions between businesses were made easily accessible using the Web. This interactive trading post opened doors for SMBs, giving them access to markets all over the world and allowing them to go global *virtually* overnight. Compared with its potential, this application was relatively cheap; there was little in the way of capital outlay for any computer infrastructure, as the application used the Internet, and the technology that made the marketplace available to all parties was usually hosted by a third party. Those third parties took care of the maintenance costs and software requirements and made the system available.

This cost-effective model was particularly attractive to SMBs because the online marketplace represented a fast path to a bigger market. The investment of time required to develop business relationships was smaller than with the traditional way of doing business, and it was smaller yet because of the impersonal nature of the way business was conducted, with relationships starting and ending with the transaction.

These hosting third parties, commonly referred to as application software providers (ASPs), were either start-up independent providers or the same global IT vendors that had been laboring to get into the SMB market cost effectively. These vendors now had the SMB market coming to them. The Internet gave them a clear opening to market their back-office applications and was a natural extension of the technology that was already being used for the subscribed online service. In other words, it would be like signing up with eBay with the intention of selling a personal article and receiving an offer for a software package that you could buy and download for your home or office.

Attempting to upsell you more is a common practice of online stores, so offering this trading ability and integrating it with your back office seemed a natural extension. The basic premise was that once the trade was completed, you would use the newly purchased business application to receive the goods into inventory, pay for them, and do the necessary accounting, all under the one technology roof. This was a relatively new and unexplored marketing channel, but its potential for reaching this difficult market was too good to resist. Cost of sales to the IT vendors was far less. The online marketplace would become the *invisible* salesperson; the delivery mechanisms, the Internet; and the relevant billing could be done online. It seemed like the perfect strategy.

There were several open questions. Would SMBs actually purchase their back-office applications this way? IT vendors would need to make significant investments in R&D, sales, and marketing to upgrade their online marketplaces so that they could handle more functionality if software was to be efficiently deployed in this manner, going from what was traditionally sold as in-house. Billing, legal contracts, and revenue recognition issues aside, was the technology ready, were the investments worth it, and were the SMBs prepared to receive their business applications in this way? One big market with two potentially big opportunities was available, with equally big risks associated with each. As it turned out, at that time, for mission-critical applications coming from large IT vendors, SMBs were not comfortable with the security of the Internet, or, for that matter, with that of the ASP or the hosted model. So going the online route did not get anywhere near the acceptance that was expected, and even with the deals that were done, any profits were hard to come by, with vendors eventually abandoning the strategy and related investments.

Where Small Fits In

Thinking big and going big was not gaining big in terms of traction in the market, even though several vendors were able to mobilize their resources quickly and offer technology and services. In the end, a few online marketplaces were sold; the proprietors of some of these exchanges managed to stay in business long enough to start making profits or be bought out. The opportunity to sell business software did not take off, and most of the vendors' results fell short of expectations given the investments made. This example, spanning a period of four years beginning at the turn of the century, highlights and warns of the risks of thinking that a mass approach will bring about high growth and big profit. Both the global IT vendors and the incumbent vendors returned to their traditional methods of marketing, albeit, in hindsight, with a better understanding of the SMB customer. However, the challenge of getting to this market continued. In the midst of big ideas not working, a lateral thought occurred: *think small.*

The idea of looking at the market as smaller interconnected communities started to make sense, and tackling this market in this way, keeping in mind that the goal was to capture a large market share as the end result, created astounding improvements in generating qualified leads, a higher percentage of sales, a turnaround in customer credibility, and wider market awareness with much lower risk. Vendors using this approach ended up making more profit than the online marketplaces had done in the prior four years.

Over the last five years, thinking small to get to big markets has become a much more attractive alternative because of its manageability and control and its lowered risk. It also provides a good feedback mechanism if the strategy is not going according to plan, enabling the vendor to make corrections faster, with less disruption to progress and less risk of endangering the overall big objective. As vendors took the plunge into the B2B exchanges and time to market was perceived to be crucial for success, the vendors' quality assurance departments could hardly keep up with the software applications that were being released to the market. Furthermore, the initial releases of the B2B exchanges required several iterations to make them industry-specific. This was a good case of a situation where the attraction of a big market opportunity led to substantial investments in a disruptive technology in the hope that markets would be drawn to it and that their former patterns of buying software applications would change. We will come back to this later to gain a better understanding of how to discover whether there could have been small changes in strategy that would have helped us chart a better way forward.

When presented with a big market opportunity, it is not unusual for companies to go searching for a strategy that resembles something from past opportunities or challenges. Modeling successful strategies is a valid start, but there needs to be a brand-new way to map the current opportunity against those previously used methods. The mapping exercise highlights the extent to which this opportunity is different from the last.

In our case study, the presence of two marketing forces, the growth of the SMB marketplace and the emergence of the online marketplaces, led vendors to jump on the bandwagon and race to be the first to provide *the* environment that would enable software packages to be purchased online. This was similar to the strategy being used by other online providers and had been in place for several years previously as ASP hosting services. However, there were small but important issues that were largely ignored in the euphoria over the potential.

Small Differences Make All the Difference

In today's business world, it is better to know that you are exactly wrong than to think that you are approximately right, especially when you are going after large, highly competitive markets where large investments are required. On the other hand, looking for an absolute right answer that will guarantee the success of any initiative or project is like trying to find a foolproof formula for living. The basic think-small principle in this case is to define the big market that you are planning to get into as precisely as possible, then design a plan to get there, using the best knowledge available and allowing small incremental adjustments to be made along the way. Think of an airplane setting its flight plan to reach a destination. It has all the coordinates and information that it needs to get on its way; however, most people are not aware that for most of the flight, the airplane is off course as a result of wind and drift, and corrections are being made to get it back on course. This is the essence behind thinking small when a new project or initiative is involved.

As we touched on earlier, one of the key concerns of SMBs is the cost of the implementation and having the right level of resources available at the right time to ensure that the expected implementation of the desired software solution is delivered in a timely fashion. In their efforts to mimic the traditional software purchase, IT vendors were marketing innovative ways to download selected parts of applications, offer e-learning classes and user training, and even provide virtual implementation services where the system could be implemented and tailored via telephone or through online support consultants. Despite the efficiency of access, customers were still reluctant to buy business software in this way.

A + B + C = D

As a strategic overview, the focus areas for small incremental improvements as they relate to becoming bigger, better, or both can be encapsulated in this simple formula:

$A + B + C = D$, where
A = market
B = products and services
C = competition
D = scope

A = Market

It is important that you define the market as accurately as possible. There are market data out there that can be helpful, but there are also some very precise pieces of information concerning *your* addressable market that you need to know. The first element of the definition involves taking a look at the market as two-dimensional. One dimension is the size of the customer relative to its purchasing ability, resources, skills, and partner networks, and the other is the specific industry, subindustry, or niche the customer is in. The next element of the *discovery* process is to determine who and what are the vertical and horizontal business relationships of your customers within their related industries. Customer requirements play a major role. In the case of the B2B exchanges, these requirements presented a new opening for IT vendors; however, the requirements of the SMB customers did not all of a sudden change. The medium that was used to communicate and sell had changed, but the customers had not.

This slightly tilted view gives a different marketing perspective. It adds to the textbook definition of *marketing segmentation*, which is commonly defined as involving specific geographic, psychographic, demographic, and political criteria. The *alliances* factor is a small but important nuance involving the characteristics that bind companies together as interrelated communities or integrated segments and what those dependent relationships mean to those companies, given that they individually maintain a unique identity that distinctly differentiates their value to their respective customers. In much the same way that a supply chain links a diverse range of companies from different industries, the companies in an industry function and depend on a common set of customer requirements, but each adds value in its own way.

B = Products and Services

This is an interesting aspect. I am going to ask you a question that will seem basic, but you will need to think it through rather than giving the first answer that comes to mind. Is your company a product company or a service company? Let me help you clarify this: do you offer a product that you provide services for, or do you offer a service that involves a product? If you know this, then you are well on your way, yet for a surprising number of companies, it is a struggle to decide which element represents their core value to the customer. As part of the discovery process to figure out where the smallest incremental improvements will have the biggest impact, we need to find out where to start looking, and that process involves being clear about the type of value you represent today or can represent in the future.

C = Competition

Understanding the competition raises another interesting question. I am not going to ask the obvious question of who your competitors are, although it is important to know this and to rank them. The deeper question asks, is your prime competitor external or internal? Chapter 6 deals with this in more detail; the point is that as we locate areas for change, we need to decide whether the biggest barrier to growth is posed by outside forces or inside processes and systems. You need to identify your top four competitors and then rank them from highest to lowest, and you may include your own company as one of the four.

D = Scope

When we take A, B, and C and map them onto each other, this reveals the specific areas where the smallest changes will have the biggest impact. When we get deeper into the process and determine how to capture the relevant data in each of the three areas, we are actually moving our focus away from the things that are working well and isolating the areas for improvement matched against our objectives.

This becomes the real plan, which is further developed by determining tactical activities and reporting on them progressively. While keeping the bigger picture in mind, it represents tactical-level thinking, highlighting the most promising areas for small incremental improvements.

In Chapter 8 will look further into each of these areas and their application using the SMALL Tactics workshop, where these principles are employed to isolate ways of making changes that are different from the usual way. SMALL Tactics is a process for identifying and selecting the areas with the greatest potential. It is also about leveraging all those things that are working well and being precise about the small but meaningful advances to take. It is the ongoing process of making these minor but significant steps that gets you to big—whatever size big is for you. Naturally, thinking and executing big is more exciting than taking small steps; however, in the aggregate and in concert, the immediate feedback that small changes provide can be positive for morale and so motivating as to be considered even thrilling.

If we take a look at how companies that have stayed in business for 50 or more years have maintained leadership positions in their industries, interesting traits are revealed that are relevant to thinking small.[3] The following are extracts from a longer list of main points, with running themes of adaptation, continuous improvement, and focus on core business values:

- Very few of these companies started out with big ideas and market-altering strategies.
- Almost none of them had mission statements, but all had stated core values.
- Progress occurred through adaptation aligned with values.
- The new stuff came from trial and error and tweaks along the way.
- They focused on themselves with a "can do better" attitude.

The undervalued element that these companies have in common is the "can do better" attitude. Alignment with core values and adapting to meet objectives underscore the importance of staying the course. In a surprising number of cases, strategies that come very close to attaining their goals fail because management is impatient or uninformed. Through no direct fault of their own, managers commonly are unable to see how close the strategies are to success and quickly abandon them, moving on to other priorities or the next big thing. We often see this situation taking place in the workplace: something new is just about to settle down and meet the intended objectives, but it is stopped or replaced by something else, requiring people to reset their thinking and start afresh to make the new thing work—and then the next, and the next. After a while, companywide fatigue develops, creating burnout of key employees and management and inevitably leading to increased employee churn rates. This is one of the com-

mon reasons why companies get stuck in a dense fog of medioc-
rity, failing to spend more time exploiting what is working well
and prematurely replacing it with the next perceived big thing.

Prepare for Big

When they examine companies that were seemingly on the rise but
then suddenly fell short, management experts frequently report
that the problem was in large part a lack of internal preparedness
for the growth that they were about to experience. It is therefore
important for any company that is growing fast or that intends to
grow big that it makes sure that its internal systems are ready and
are fit for the heavier and longer workloads ahead. The knee-jerk
reaction of adding more resources to handle growth overlooks the
fact that adding more people who try to do business using inefficient systems and processes only makes things worse.

Oracle decided more than eight years ago to implement a continuous improvement strategy in its marketing function. The task
was huge. The scope of the strategy was global, involving more
than 40 countries, and it entailed improving the efficiency of the
day-to-day running of marketing as well as improving its performance and its contribution to the company, especially to its
sales revenues.

Like a lot of other large corporations, Oracle had had growth
spurts over the years, and during those periods the satellite offices
had been given the autonomy to make local decisions as they saw
fit. Over time, this type of independence from corporate control
can cause a veering off course from standard procedures and
guidelines, creating duplication, redundancy, and confusion both
within the company and among its customers, who see the same
company as having a totally different culture, attitude, and per-
sona depending on where they happen to be doing business. At
Oracle, the autonomy reached the point where international locations were designing their own Oracle logos for local use. As patri-
otic as this may seem, and I am all for localization, the fact is that

there were some very specific areas, such as brand consistency, that had to be returned to central control at the head office if marketing was to run as an efficient service for the company.

If we are going to embark on a process of introducing a culture and system that allow employees to make small incremental improvements in their areas of responsibility, it is essential that the overall business processes be running smoothly; indeed, small incremental improvements can be executed at this broader level of processes before setting the staff loose to improve their specific parts of the work.

At Oracle, a process had to be put in place that allowed incremental changes to be made in the way marketing was being done and that enabled marketing to be done better each time a similar program or campaign was executed. In order for this to occur, a carefully selected series of minor improvements in current practices that were suitable to become global standards was progressively made. This was, and continues to be, an ingenious way to enable big objectives by making small but meaningful and progressive changes.

Build the Engine to Grow

It's quite likely that there are processes in your company today that are slowing, choking, or blocking progress. How often have we heard inside our company that "we are our own worst enemy or competitor"? These processes are usually related to the interface that we have with our internal constituents and with our customers, prospects, trading partners, and key suppliers. Consider the launch of a new product. While the salespeople may be trained, what about the receptionist (who statistically speaks to more customers than any other single person in the company on any given day), or the support staff, or our distributor partners?

Small incremental changes can also improve the transactional flow from one department to another as long as there is a willingness to catch and run with the improvements. Now, what do we mean by the engine to grow? Like any engine, it is made up of a series of processes that are able to recognize and respond with appropriate execution when they receive signals from the driver (management) in the form of either data (content) or a goal (instructions). The closer to their optimum that the moving parts work, the better the performance. Where the engine is being driven is another matter. Before we embark on a process of small incremental changes, we need to make sure that all parts of the company are ready to make these types of changes. This is particularly relevant if your company is national or global or intends to extend its reach to become either.

Consider how long it would take for a newly branded product with a new tagline message to be rolled out across your company, including its subsidiaries and resellers. If the answer is more than six months, then the engine needs an overhaul. At Oracle, as a result of implementing small incremental improvements in key areas of the marketing function, a new marketing program can be rolled out on a global scale, with translations for major countries, in less than a quarter. This makes for a powerfully efficient engine that is capable of responding and deploying responses fast and positioning products against competitors and customer needs. Being faster to market is a key to getting big.

Small Is to Fast as Big Is to Slow

Aiming big requires being faster at taking market share than the competition. No company should forfeit market share because of lost time resulting from fragmented internal systems.

One way to get the maximum gain from small incremental improvements is to make these improvements reusable throughout the company. In my experience, when a company has several branches that are remotely located and are granted autonomy, it becomes almost a religious belief at these branches that they can run any way they feel is appropriate as long as they get the job done. What develops over time is a myriad of redundancies that reduce profitability. Upon joining IBM, Lou Gerstner found that the autonomy given to product areas created a chasm between product groups; they did not communicate with one another at any level, even though in a lot of cases they were selling and servicing the same customers. Small changes can be a powerful driver of breaking down intracompany barriers and promoting communication across lines of business while taking out as much redundancy as possible.

Getting back to the engine parts, what we need to address are the moving parts within the company that have a direct and indirect impact on growing the business. Sales are the company's front line; however, the rest of the company has critical support roles in helping the sales force to meet its and the overall company's objectives. Where internal processes are broken (for example, in flexible order entry systems that allow salespeople to process their sales), then clearly any ambition to become big is compromised. There are many other facets of the sales support process in many parts of the company that affect sales revenue more than people realize. A majority of the reasons why sales are either lost or reduced in scope and size involve internal systems.

The other ongoing challenge that we will specifically address is integrating sales and marketing, a festering issue that has been around for years. However, it is essential that the demand-generating machine parts and after-sales support systems are in place to serve every customer. There are many factors that affect whether a customer has a good experience, and it so happens that the small things can make the difference between customers' feeling that they received good or bad service, irrespective of the product or price factors.

We also look at accessing growth from a marketing point of view and then search for small things we need to change in order to get the desired results quickly and profitably, making the engine run optimally.

Let's walk through a traditional tactical marketing program to reach a target market. Assume that the marketing analysis has been done and that the target market size is 100,000 customers.

So, here is a typical scenario: we know the potential market size, and we have an approved budget to communicate to at least half of the customers in that market. We send out 50,000 e-mails. Based on previously run similar campaigns, we estimate that we will have a 1 percent response (this is high). That means that we expect about 500 customers to respond to the e-mails in a positive way. Again from past results, we estimate that a third of these responders will become qualified as prospects, meaning that we expect to pass on 166 leads to sales. The win/loss ratio for this type of product is 1:5 (for every five sales campaigns we win one), and therefore we estimate 33 closed deals. If we run this campaign once a quarter, we can forecast a total of 132 new customers.

Apart from the fictitious numbers and variables, does this sound familiar?

There is more to a marketing campaign than this; however, the example illustrates the point that the metrics used to measure success in marketing may not reflect significant growth in sales. The objective of marketing is to generate revenue—period. Brand equity, brand awareness, and brand value are all necessary and needed, but marketing has a core role to play and that role is to generate demand and increase revenues. Market share, mind share, brand share, and wallet share are by-products of what marketing delivers after you get *revenue share*.

Oracle learned that continued mass-marketing programs with generic marketing messages not only were ineffective, but were frustrating to some customers who could not understand how the full extent and range of the company's products applied to them. The trap that a lot of marketers fall into is transmitting messages to customers that do not articulate the value of the products and services well enough to make the association with the customers' specific pains or needs. Despite endless efforts and amounts of time spent on arriving at the correct messages and positioning statements, the focus is almost always on the product and the "value" it has for the customer. The small but important adjustment to this paradigm is to recognize that customers buy because of a complex set of company values. The basis for their buying decisions ranges from scientific to pragmatic, especially when a new product or service is being introduced. This is one of the fundamental differences between marketing to consumers and marketing to businesses.

Looking into the Problem

Several years ago, I was listening to a self-help tape by Brian Tracy in which he recounts the story of a truck that had gotten stuck under a bridge. The driver had misjudged the clearance, and consequently his fully loaded vehicle had become lodged, damaging the overpass above, and was unable to move forward or backward. Tow trucks and cranes were brought in to solve the problem by somehow moving the truck out of the way and freeing the highway lanes that it occupied, but the truck was so tightly wedged that they could not pull it out without causing more damage. After several hours, a 13-year-old boy, one of the bystanders who had gathered on top of the bridge, yelled out to the engineers below, "Let the tires down." They did so, and after the tires were deflated, the truck was able to roll gently and safely out from under the bridge and out of the way.

This simple story captures the essence of what thinking small is all about. It is not about approaching a problem by looking for that groundbreaking revolutionary new idea that changes everything. It appears as a blinding flash of the obvious—but only after the fact.

In business, we constantly encounter challenges that block our progress. When it comes to problem solving, whether at a tactical or a strategic level, we often assume that bigger problems require bigger solutions. There is an epidemic of "cut-and-replace" thinking and not taking the time to look into the problem, as the smallest of changes may be all that is needed and could be staring you in the face.

NASA was having an issue with its flashlights failing on liftoff because the vibrations would regularly break the bulbs, damaging the filaments. After several months of mounting pressure to find a solution, the program's specialists turned to bigger ideas, such as different materials like special glass compounds or plastics, which were much more expensive. In the home, a flashlight may be a convenient item to have if there is a power failure, but in space, it is essential. One of the scientists on the team decided to keep digging into the problem by looking at the existing bulbs. One morning he came back with some basic physics that revealed that bulbs are not needed at all. The reason the filament is encased is to protect it from burning out, which will happen in our oxygen-rich environment. As there is little or no oxygen in space, there is no need to have glass bulbs—problem solved.

If a company adopts a culture of small improvement behavior, where all employees come to work knowing that they are empowered to make incremental changes that benefit their job, their team, their business unit, their department, and their company, then ultimately the winners will be your customers, your suppliers, and your partners. When this happens, and when changes are consistent with the company's overall objectives and strategies, this model creates a powerful ripple effect of improvement throughout the organization. This approach, while alarmingly simple, has less risk and a greater chance of producing a successful outcome than larger cut-and-replace tactics, which historically have a high failure rate. When a companywide edict provides a systematic approach for allowing employees to take immediate action toward directed improvements, what is actually being developed is a rational and steady process of manageable evolutionary change that could possibly lead to a revolutionary change over time.

This is not a new concept, especially in Japanese business, where the methodology and process of Kaizen have been practiced for many years. In later chapters, we will integrate some of the principles of Kaizen techniques. Big change management goes hand in hand with revolutionary change; however, this is all about timing. Often the need for revolutionary change is noticed at a time of crisis or when there is a compelling event driven by the market or by competitors.

A powerful principle maintained by Vice Admiral James Stockdale, which has been popularized as the Stockdale Paradox, reinforces the idea behind the drive required to make small incremental changes and takes that emotional charge to the mechanical and technical processes. This profound quote reads, "Retain faith that you will prevail in the end, regardless of the difficulties—and confront the most brutal facts of your reality, whatever they may be."[4] Faith, vision, and looking for greatness are the core of thinking small. What is interesting to extract from Vice Admiral Stockdale is that he took day-to-day difficulties and tackled each one of them by breaking it down into small, realistic portions of what was within his control and ability at any time, building upon one success with another. He did not attempt large-scale radical behavior. He used the resources that were within his power, skill, and knowledge. When this principle is applied across the company, it shows what a unified approach to making small incremental changes can mean. Big is within reach—so in the absence of a sure thing, the alternative is to navigate through the economics and attain solid, sustainable growth—little by connected little.

The Big Fear Factor

How often have you come out of a meeting or presentation where company goals are being set for the new fiscal year, or where a new direction, product acquisition, or merger that is of "critical importance" to the success and/or survival of the company is being introduced? The objective of these internal communications is to motivate and inspire people, and to promote the company's strong and vibrant future. The aim is for employees to buy in, and to walk away feeling reenergized and confident of their long-term security and their career with the company. However, it seems that the opposite effect often occurs, as uncertainty sets in. It seems that the bigger and grander the plan, the more concerned people are about their job security and their future positions in the company.

Take, for example, the announcement of an acquisition or a merger. No one feels safe, as people do not know how their current job will be affected by the amalgamation; perhaps duplicate roles will be identified, or perhaps incoming peers may be perceived as being more highly skilled or better qualified.

In the following chapters, we will look at becoming smarter by taking carefully selected actions in specific areas of the company that will accelerate progress toward any big goals but that will stay within the framework of small but powerful incremental steps in which all employees participate and feel that they have a much more direct connection to where and how they fit into the bigger picture.

BIGGER BY
THE NICHE

Niche players think big all the time. They do not focus on staying small, even though they operate in smaller market segments. Instead, they work at being specific and significant, and they often seem able to capture market share more easily than their broader-based competitors. One of their distinct advantages over generalists is that their products and services have an appearance of specialization that acts as a protective coating, distinguishing them from their broader competitors by the way they are able to deliver service to a defined vertical market.

The advice for start-up businesses that is repeated in the entrepreneurial literature and promoted by market consultants is to find a niche and go from there. For established companies, what was a niche market several years ago may over time have become mainstream, and other niches may have emerged, especially when volume increases and a large number of competitors saturate the available market. Thinking small applies equally well to both start-ups and established companies; in fact, when a company has been able to obtain a solid position, growth by organic means usually remains steady, and big growth leaps are rarely made and are opportunistic.

The standard alternatives for expansion are to add more product lines and/or services, to merge or acquire, or to move into other new relevant markets. A key to doing this profitably is to focus on those areas where you can achieve the highest gains by making the smallest changes to the products and services that you currently have on offer to make them appropriate for entering the intended niche(s). Companies that already serve a niche market will admit that they are continually looking for ways to improve, expand, grow, and be more profitable. So there is nothing unique about this business model per se except that companies spend their time going deeper into specific market segments, with everything they do remaining congruent with the way they go about maintaining a position of exclusivity.

For niche players, competitiveness is about being distinctive to their customers. There are two main reasons why niche companies have higher customer loyalty than their corporate rivals and their adoption and retention rates are higher: first, there are usually a limited number of providers, and second, specialized products or services usually come with some level of personalized or proprietary specifications that others find difficult to duplicate, making it harder for customers to change suppliers.

Let us look further at the example in Chapter 2 of large global IT vendors targeting the SMB space and competing with smaller vendors that were already there and that had experience with the customers' distinct requirements. In the early stages, both large and small vendors saw this as a new and highly specialized market (resembling a niche), requiring a complete overhaul of requirements that were not part of their standard portfolios. The reality was that the vendors were better off than they thought. SMBs had been buying software in traditional ways since their inception; however, when vendors looked at this market more closely and compared it with customer buying behavior, the differences did not necessitate the organizational rearrangements and widespread changes that had originally been anticipated.

It is common for companies seeking entrance into markets where they have little or no experience to think that they are lacking and therefore need a unique specialization, only to find upon taking the leap that they had more in common with the new markets than they thought. On the surface, there often seems to be too great a distance to bridge from a functional point of view to enable them to properly serve these new customers and compete. On these bases, going into new markets is often wrongly discarded.

The other factor is the need to bring in special people skills that may cost too much to make the venture feasible. In the majority of cases, as long as the company has done its homework in selecting the niches, the changes required to achieve the measurable benefits are not as onerous as one would think. The key to sustaining growth and profit comes down to isolating those areas where the smallest changes are sufficient to enable the company to compete alongside the already entrenched competitors.

The Emerging Niche

As markets evolve and small communities grow, niches continuously emerge as viable market opportunities; the question is finding the right ones. "Picking your battles" is a saying that is particularly valid when it comes to niches. The opposite is also true: a market that starts off as a niche may become mainstream. There are, of course, many examples of this throughout history: the ballpoint pen was made popular by U.S. pilots, the typewriter by blind people, the Internet by students, and the zipper by the U.S. Army.

Interestingly, niches also grow out of niches, but what is common is for niches to emerge from broad markets and commodities. If we look at the technology industry, a saturated market for operating systems that run our computers was controlled by major IT corporations that thought they had cornered the market. Then along came the "open-source" movement with the idea that no one should own the operating system, and that it should be available to everyone for free. Furthermore, anyone should be able to enhance the system and share it with anyone who wants his or her new version containing the added functionality.

That is the story of the Linux operating system, which was made available to the public, at virtually no cost to the user, in a highly competitive market in which well-known companies such as Microsoft, Sun Microsystems, HP, and IBM were established. Originally popular within academia and among uber-geeks, over a period of seven years, Linux became mainstream, and its technology products were a staple of thousands of vendors. Despite public objections by Microsoft, the Linux user community continued to grow, and Linux is now one of the industry's de facto standards.

This emergence of new niches occurs in all industries, even in something as basic as food. For many years, organic foods were kept out of big supermarkets, as they were considered too expensive because of the limited shelf life of the produce; thus, they were available only in specialized health-food stores. Today, organic foods can be found in almost every major food chain, with some dedicating aisles to the category as loss leaders to attract customers.

Generic or Niche

In 1978, IBM released a midrange computer, the IBM System/36, for the SMB market. At the time, it was one of the finest computer systems on the market, renowned for its reliability no matter how brutal the environmental conditions in which it had to operate. Along with the IBM System/36 came a manufacturing software package called MAPICS (Manufacturing, Accounting and Production Information Control System [now Infor]). Developed by IBM and optimized for this IBM hardware, it was one of the first comprehensive but generic systems dedicated to running a manufacturing plant, one where it didn't matter what industry the customer was part of. Whether you were in consumer packaged goods or an automobile manufacturer, you could run MAPICS on your IBM System/36, with upgraded revisions available for the newer System/38 and AS/400 machines.

IBM was able to sell the same "box" and system to a variety of industries without the need for comprehensive changes. The market had not seen this specific set of functionality in one broad system before. Approximately 15 years later (about the time IBM sold MAPICS to Marcam, Inc.), MAPICS was being marketed with "industry-specific" solutions. The company started selling MAPICS and a host of other manufacturing software solutions to vertical "niches."

For many years the core base software code, delivered out of the box, remained virtually unchanged, with any industry-specific enhancements being done by implementers. Any modifications remained proprietary to the customer or the consulting company doing the implementation; however, the original software was carefully left untouched. In reality, these enhancements involved only a fraction of the standard overall base code that came with the system.

Marketing played a big part in the product's success by using discrete changes in nomenclature to incorporate industry-specific language in the sales literature for what was essentially the same software package. More time and effort was spent on developing marketing material to attract the target audience than was spent on developing the software code itself.

While marketing was doing its job, when it came to sales, customers wanted proof of the application's suitability and fit. This involved brokering a direct communication between prospective buyers and a peer company whose users were willing to attest to the software's functional capabilities; buyers made such a meeting a condition of signing a contract. While obtaining customer references to validate and add credibility to an industry-specific variation was seen as a potential barrier to entry in the early years, in fact this was relatively easy to do given that the company had for years been selling the generic product to customers from a wide variety of industries.

That was then. One might think that today, with more sophisticated buyers working in more economically complex environments, a single code-based system would not make the grade. Think again. Granted, business processes have become more streamlined with newer technologies; however, those same business processes remain fundamental, and systems such as MAPICS are still running and still being sold today, albeit updated with newer revisions. While the inherent functionality of the base code has been expanded to allow industry-specific nuances, this was done only after entering a target niche; as the demand increased, so did the functionality. Revisions of system programs for specific industries came over a longer period of time, and only when vendors could justify it economically. What is important to note is that the timing of entry into these markets was not stalled by a need to first assess *all* of the possible combinations of complex alterations or to completely rethink strategies.

A fast way to move into niche segments is to establish partner relationships with other solution providers who already have a presence and can credibly service a niche. This can also take care of the relevant skills and necessary experience issue and further remove the barrier to entry. As any seasoned salesperson would agree, industry experience should not be underestimated and is an important requirement that must complement the marketing efforts. The necessary expertise in sales within an industry domain is essential in understanding the product's value and communicating it to the target industry.

The MAPICS story illustrates the theme of this chapter and shows what getting bigger by the niche is all about. Creative deliberation and analysis are important when deciding to expand into new markets, but if you are in business today and have served a market successfully, chances are that you have a good base for entering more specialized areas. Unless you are serving a niche of *one*, it is highly likely that there is room for expansion, and with the concept of thinking small, the possibility of getting into a related and logical niche is greater than most people realize.

Finding Your Niche

There are, of course, many variables that need to be considered when entering any new market. The size of the market, incumbent vendors and their market share, customer requirements, products and services fit, legal or compliance issues—the list goes on. The starting point for finding a new market can appear to be relatively straightforward and can often be obvious. One naturally looks for related industries and identifies what one's industry has in common with them; a cursory measurement of the potential is made and weighed against the investment and return to determine whether the market is worth pursuing. Anyone can do that, and you can draw up a list of niches or related industries in a short time to get you on your marketing way.

A useful list for identifying related industry and subindustry categories is the Standard Industry Classification codes, or SIC codes. These are arranged in a *faceted classification*, meaning basically that industries are arranged in a logically related sequence. Every industry is listed under its official name, and the names are compliant with similar naming standards worldwide, making the SIC an invaluable reference; it is available on the Internet[1] and is worth downloading. However, to find the *right* niche, the one that requires the smallest change with the least impact on your operations, you need to ask a different question. This is where thinking small and drilling into certain specific areas come into their own. Thinking small is a complementary evaluation process that often introduces new and invaluable information, allowing course corrections and assisting with priorities.

Look Inward Before You Look Outward

When you are planning to enter a specialized market, you first need to be clear about the skills you have acquired over time and the strengths you have developed *internally*. Some combination of these is what will bring out the new value you will potentially represent to your newfound customers. The way to do this is through the framework of thinking small and applying it to finding a niche target, enabling you to discover any areas that are unique to your business and that differentiate you. For example, if you are in the printing business, then naturally you have a certain amount of skill and expertise in layout, machine printing, paper types, and so on;

however, in the course of building your business, you may have gained specialized knowledge in certain areas through your own learning and experience. For example, you may have expertise in mixing colors or ink types for certain mediums, special packaging, binding of special formats, or even the ability to deliver faster than your competition.

Look at the various areas associated with or adjacent to your business where you have specific qualifications (see Figure 3-1), and filter out the commodity part of what you do on a day-to-day basis. In other words, edit out the things that anyone else could do. Then you can ask yourself how these unique and differentiating skills could be taken to a similar niche market and delivered in an entirely new way; for example, you might provide an advisory or consulting service for printing on unusual surfaces or combining ink and medium for best results. What can be spawned or repackaged from the business that you already have skills in? Sometimes it may be a combination of skills and processes—for example, a design process or knowledge of packaging for special handling and delivery of certain materials. The results of this exercise of investigating or drilling into your unique values are reused later in developing your *core messaging and positioning* for marketing and outbound communications, as explained further in the next chapter. The next step is to look at your business network across your supply chain.

Referring back to the SIC codes, are there niches where, either by yourself or by partnering with one or more of your suppliers or customers, you could create a new offering that adds specific value? Your business alliances and suppliers are key relationships for your business today, and they may also be the key to expanding your business tomorrow. This is by no means a new concept. In Japan, for example, suppliers are business partners in the entrepreneurial sense of the word. In fact, it is not uncommon to see competing manufacturers in a joint venture using a common supplier as their sole business partner. This philosophy also extends to customers, who may bring complementary services to enter new markets. By looking into the intricacies of your business and

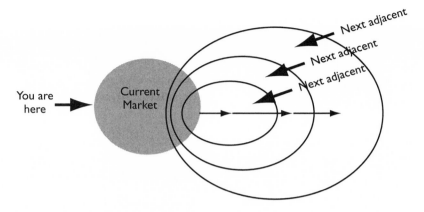

Figure 3-1 Finding Your Niche

looking at the internal value chain that exists in processes that you have developed, you may find that you have more marketable assets than you thought. Those specific areas of skill and uniqueness become the "raw material" needed to enter any new niche.

One Niche Leads to Another

Every time I have been part of a brainstorming meeting where we looked deeply at what we already had, as opposed to what we needed, I have found that we would uncover new talents and skills that were unique, repeatable, and scalable and that could be repackaged and marketed for distribution in other specific markets. Once you move into a niche and gain momentum, one of two things naturally occurs: either you find yourself moving quickly into other niches, or your customers want more variety or choices in what you have, pulling in more demand and driving expansion of the product or service, possibly into other areas that you may not have thought of in the beginning.

An example of this that I came across was a company called Phillips Seafood, based in Baltimore, Maryland. It had started as a small fish market with an adjoining restaurant that was open only in the prime seasons. Its niche and differentiator was very simple: it promoted the superior quality of the blue crab that it had for sale and on the menu. After seeing the demand for blue crab increase, the company decided to grow the restaurant and keep it open all year round. The problem was that blue crab is seasonal, and keeping up a year-round supply was a challenge because you cannot economically harvest this species of crab locally on a year-round basis. Other species coming from other areas did not have the same flavor once the crab was processed, and therefore serving them to customers was risky even though they were technically blue crab.

In its search, the company came across a plant in Southeast Asia that used a "fresh pasteurization technology" for seafood that was appropriate for blue crab. With this process, the restaurant was able to maintain the flavor and freshness that it had become known for. This solved the restaurant's problem, and it enabled Phillips Seafood to expand and provide fresh blue crab across the country. Today it supplies retail stores nationwide and has opened up six more restaurants. The change to being a full-fledged food-service provider led to other niches, such as supplying crab cakes, soups, and sauces to a host of food outlets, including airports.

Other examples can be seen in the nonalcoholic beverage industry, with giants such as Coca-Cola and Pepsi actually having started in niche markets. Coca-Cola was originally inspired by the French cocawine (a blend of Bordeaux wine and cocaine), and its creator, John Pemberton, later adapted it as a nonalcoholic beverage when his local market prohibited the sale of alcoholic beverages. He replaced the cocaine with caffeine and brought it to market as a uniquely different stimulant drink. Similarly, a brew concocted by Caleb Bradham and known as "Brad's Drink" was intended to cure stomach ailments such as dyspepsia (probably the origin of the name Pepsi).

Building on volume sales, the increase in mass consumption of the modified soda pops led to the great success of each of these companies. In recent years, however, smaller start-ups, aiming big but thinking in niches, created a disruptive market element in the form of sports and energy drinks, consequently stealing consumer share. These start-ups were able to quickly attract a significant portion of the normal soda-guzzling consumers to their healthier alternative, making a dent in the loyalty that the incumbent giants were relying on. Unprepared for the rate of uptake of this new consumer market, the incumbents initially responded in vain with domineering marketing fads. As this health-conscious market expanded, traditional cola sales seesawed from giant to giant, with nothing really moving the needle in favor of either, and the companies' marketing consisted of more of the same. For the most part, the products remained largely the same except for Coke's failed attempt to improve the formula, which required a reintroduction of the original product.

In their efforts to counter the trend, the incumbents were basically doing more of the same, rather than looking for something unique or distinctive that they could use to respond to their niche competitors. Energy and sports drinks soon became an official beverage category, and the vendors of those drinks, maintaining their niche positions, experienced bigger growth in relative terms than the incumbent giants. Once you gain a strong position within a niche, competitive advantage turns your way, and you can leverage it further by adding additional product choices and ramping up the marketing, which the niche marketers did. For example, while the category started in the health segment, it is now targeting new niches such as gender (with drinks such as Diesel Energy Drink,[2] Wellman High Performance,[3] and Go Girl[4]) and ethnicity (with brand names like Caball Nero;[5] Uno Mas,[6] meaning "one more"; and Tampico Energy, with the tagline "El Mas Bravo,"[7] loosely translated as "the brave one"). The point is that niche or small thinking gains momentum niche by niche. It creates a ripple effect that spreads into other niches; in this example, there is unlimited potential for creative niches, with likely candidates being amateur racers, hikers, or even tailgaters. When niche brands start to take share in incumbents' markets with recognized brands, the giants' likely strategy will be acquisitions.

In my experience, niche thinking within a company has an interesting effect on employees. Rather than seeing it as far-fetched or a barrier to normal business, there is a gathering of support and offers of innovative ideas. Employees welcome the expanding potential of the business, and being associated with something special or unique has a renewing effect on motivation, even though it may mean more work for some people. It resonates, giving an attitude and buzz akin to those created by launching a new product.

Finding niches by thinking small involves an inward search for the simple and obvious things that you can do day to day with the employees you have right now. The good news is that if you find the biggest opportunity that involves the smallest changes and impact on operations, you can take it to market—fast. No matter how complex your business is, the opportunities are out there. Take, for example, the technology business. It is a complex business. If a device or application is easy to use, most likely the technology behind it is sophisticated, and building it involves a high level of complexity.

When it came to moving into a market such as the SMBs, sophisticated businesses like Oracle Corporation used a process similar to that used by the relatively simple seafood business to "discover" the right niche, albeit with more criteria to take into account. Oracle's revenues had traditionally come from database products and services, complemented by a steady growth in business applications. As the Fortune 500 market was becoming saturated and growth was slowing, the company needed to find new growth markets, such as this huge SMB market.

An important point to be made here is that you need to know what type of relationship there is between the niche and the broader industry it is in compared with yours. This gives a sense of perceived distance (and therefore differences) that will offer clues to the extent of change needed to get into that niche. In other words, if you are a leather treatment manufacturer and you wish to enter the leather upholstery and furniture market, the distance is relatively smaller than, say, if you wanted to get into designer bags. This is not saying that getting into designer bags would be wrong; its reach may be close enough to your business for it to represent minor changes that would produce major gains.

As in earlier discussions, "small" is relative. What one business may consider a huge leap across different markets, others will find to be a small step. Our aim here is to first find what niches are available to us based on making the smallest alterations first. Often, the market or niche is only the starting point, and by the time the plan is developed, we may find that we have strayed too far across categories, straining the rest of the business and therefore defeating the purpose. Diversification and entering new businesses in different markets require a different business assessment, analysis, and approach.

In Oracle's case, SMBs were very much a related market, one that Oracle had in fact been selling into as part of its normal business for many years. Because of the upswing in the growth of this sector, as described in Chapter 2, it was a market that could not be ignored. However, before launching into any investments, a careful sequence of incremental analysis needed to be done to determine what would be the smallest changes with the least impact that would allow the company to enter this market and be competitive.

While a lot of companies start with the market assessment, this is actually looking backward. Energy is being spent on determining how to catch up with the trends and then deciding what R&D efforts, resources, and so on are required. The paradox of this process is that the opportunity governs the rest of the strategy and plan. Because there is no sure way to predict the future, even if you try to cater to it, your assessment often falls short. Why not reverse the process slightly and not only look at your readiness to enter a new market but also evaluate the line of least resistance within your company and make the necessary enhancements once you are active in that market by—again—making small incremental improvements along the way?

I have met entrepreneurs who do this naturally. They have an instinct for finding niches that they can grow into by offering seemingly new value but that require making only the slightest of adjustments to their existing products and services—in some cases not changing anything apart from their marketing and distribution channels. Most of us, however, do not have this instinct. We look at the opportunity and work back from there, figuring out what needs to be done inside the company. The thinking small philosophy works from the inside first. Unless you develop this acuity and reframe your approach to entering new markets in this way, you are merely doing more of the same. Most companies do not work this way because they do not identify or discover the equity in the unique value that they have built naturally over time. As much of a cliché as it may be, finding diamonds that look like coal is a powerful metaphor that is seen time and time again to bring about big results, and it is not dependent on company size, investment, or skill, or whether the product is a commodity or a niche product.

By going through the thought process leading up to the final development of a proposal and a marketing strategy, you will be able to appreciate the essence of thinking small as it relates to finding the right market to get into. The hope is that you can extract any or all relevant parts of this material from its context and apply the principles to your business, regardless of your company's size or complexity.

Finding the Niche within the Niche

Before we start, let's quickly profile the market. In the United States, there are over 5 million SMBs in various industries, of which around 620,000[8] have between 20 and 500 employees. This segment includes companies from almost every industry, subindustry, and niche that you can think of. These companies are widely dispersed geographically, with a few pockets of aggregation along the East and West Coasts, but otherwise more or less evenly scattered across the country, and over 75 percent of them are privately owned. Their business processes also vary, with smaller companies sometimes having complex businesses and larger ones very simple ones. Finding a meaningful common denominator that a marketer would be looking for was challenging, given that a large percentage of these companies were privately owned. What we knew was that the majority were looking for new computer systems.

Oracle is a facts-based company. While instinct and intuition play a part, business and marketing proposals that require any substantial amount of investment need empirical facts to back up and validate the strategy or plan. The challenge was obtaining quality data. Questions that remained unanswered were:

- What were these companies' top priorities and *business issues*?
- What was their buyer *behavior*, and where was the *purchasing decision* made?
- How and what were the *size of the budgets* that they allocated for technology?
- What was *their perception* of using corporate systems in place of their legacy systems?
- When and how was their last software *purchase experience*?
- Did they want *fully integrated* software, or more of best of breed?
- Did they want *modular systems* or *suites*?
- Did they want the software to be *in-house* or *outsourced*?
- What companies do they *trust for technology*?

While we had all the basic information regarding the size of the market, where potential customers were located, and so on, we needed to understand more about these companies, and any marketer would need this level of profile information to properly develop a business proposal or a marketing campaign. In pursuit of knowledge, we consulted industry analysts and asked them what their assessments were, based on their experience and research. While industry analysts like Gartner, AMR, and IDC provided many helpful missing pieces, the reality was that a lot of in-depth data were not yet available, as no one had spent much time researching this end of the market. Many of us were speculating. There really was no comprehensive information that we could rely on. We had no other option but to conduct the marketing research ourselves, surveying a handful of customers by telephone and asking questions we were not sure of. Spending time and effort on a simple telephone survey instead of attempting to piece together scant information and develop a hypothetical case can save you from making a big mistake and finding out about it later in the project.

Once we had collected the information, we needed to make some fundamental decisions regarding strategy. At first, there were basically three options:

- Go for volume sales, using mass-marketing techniques. Capturing a small percentage of the market would provide a significant increase in revenues.
- Group market segments based on estimates of the best match between the company's products and services and the customers' criteria or needs, and target those segments.
- Segment the market more deeply to find specialized niches that have not been infiltrated by incumbent vendors and expand within those regions.

You may find that you cannot easily access enough information to decide which of these techniques would provide the best return, especially when it comes to entering new or emerging markets. Any of the three options requires large investments of resources to create full-scale marketing campaigns, and you can end up with very little. Several companies that have gone to market with the intention of capturing a large market share have found themselves wondering why the acceptance of their products and services was minimal, even dismal, despite their heavy promotion of discount offers and branding campaigns. Why was this high-growth market not responding to these new offers? Ask the customers—don't second-guess them at review meetings.

When we spoke to customers, there was a mixed bag of responses. Some said that the perceived price was too high, others referred to the product's being too complex for their needs, and still others indicated that they were not skilled enough to manage the type of contracts offered by large IT vendors like Oracle. When they were asked whether they wanted a fully integrated business suite or specific modules focused at the department level, again a variety of answers resulted. The only common denominator was that all the customers were looking to buy within the next six months. This is a marketer's challenge that creates uncertainty—a hot market that wants to buy the type of products and services that you have, but that has many different reasons for not doing so. If you have ever faced a similar situation, then you are missing something—there is another parameter that needs to be found, or some other connections to the data need to be made. Information alone does not provide the answers—you need to bring in creativity.

The Small Things That Count

One idea was to group the customers by their responses. First, we put customers that felt we were too expensive in one group, those with product issues in another, and so on. When we did this, we found that there were no obvious correlations between the customers' industries and their responses. In other words, those that thought we were too expensive did not come from any particular industries, nor did those that made other responses. We concluded that these views were not related to the industry that the customers were in. Next, we looked at the products that customers intended to buy in the next six months to determine whether the perceptions were related to product areas; again there was nothing concrete that could lead us to a trend or common factors. After a process of elimination, we noticed that the *size* of the customer's company provided a pattern of responses. It was a light-bulb moment. It appeared that the smaller the company, the higher the scores on price issues were, but these companies also had a higher requirement for a fully integrated suite of applications, whereas the medium and large companies were less concerned about cost and more concerned about modular solutions.

The lesson to be learned from this is that you need to keep applying data to the problem until you find distinctive patterns that will answer the strategy-level questions. This is a key tenet of thinking small. Throughout the book, we talk about looking inward for the solution to a problem first. The same applies in strategy development, where the information brought in is traditionally at the macro level. You need to keep applying creative thought and follow the leads to the data until you find what you are looking for. In Chapter 1, we looked at how strategies are developed with visionary mindsets and high-level thinking. Small thinking does not negate that process; what it does is introduce a process for discovering specific data that may be glossed over at the macro level but that add to the bigger picture to allow us to proceed toward a plan that will have the biggest success.

The conclusion we were coming to was that the size of the customer needed to be one of the axis. Small customers were price averse but wanted packaged solutions that would cover their entire business operations, medium-size businesses wanted a modular approach but eventually would move to a fully integrated system, and the larger companies were concerned most of all with the suitability of the solution to their industry and the cost of implementation. Thus, patterns of buyer behavior based on their size were emerging. However, this still left some key questions unresolved. The size metric by itself was not enough to determine the correct strategy.

Before continuing with the rest of the process, let's summarize what we have said. You may have the idea that thinking small is nothing more than looking at details. Details are the small and important "bits" that can alter an outcome or conclusion, but small thinking is more than just facts or detailed data. Small thinking uses details to follow a path that triggers the discovery of another set of details, and so on until you find the answer. Think of it more as a forensic process of getting to answers by looking at and matching detailed information to create the course of action or plan to take. This process of small thinking can be scaled to any level. Whether we are looking at the design stages of a strategy or the full execution of a plan, small thinking inserts small pieces of important data to provide the *real* answers and direction needed.

The next phase of developing the strategy is to determine what market segment or niche to target. In Oracle's case, this came out of grouping customers' responses according to their size in terms of employees and revenues. What we found was that the smallest customers, those that had 100 or fewer employees, were looking for a more out-of-the-box packaged solution. Their business could not tolerate the cost of large-scale implementations, and their need for business process reengineering was minimal. They were willing to adapt to the "modern" processes that were inherent in most packages, and these packages were sufficient for them. Less than 25 percent were interested in a hosting option; instead, they wanted to keep the system in-house. Companies with 100 to 500 employees presented small but significant variations. They were looking for more flexibility in the system. Important features included a need for the solution to be integrated, with a suite of modules that interacted and shared common data, but it was also important that these modules be able to have a level of personalization or tailoring that reflected the companies' matured business processes. Unlike their smaller counterparts, they were not willing to give up specific ways of carrying out certain business processes that they believed were part of what made them nimble and able to compete with their larger rivals. Customers in the third group, those with 500 or more employees, were very particular concerning their needs and would often develop detailed functional specifications of their requirements and invite vendors to respond with formal RFPs (requests for proposals) as part of the buying process.

Advantages of Niche Thinking

Thinking in terms of niches, therefore, includes the notion of thinking in specialized but lower-risk ways. After all, being in a niche implies having a particular strength that makes you stand out from the rest. Niche thinking and small thinking go hand in hand, because to become a niche company, you first need to focus on a well-defined demographic or segment with distinctly tailored products or services that set the segment apart from broader consumer market categories or commodities. Because this usually means belonging to a specific subset and having the appearance of operating in a somewhat unique segment, you start with a strong competitive position. This is why it is harder to compete with niche vendors than it is with generalists.

Looking from the inside out and matching the unique value you can bring with related niche markets enables you to stretch out to new markets faster and more frequently than is typical when a radical market-shifting product innovation comes along. The cost to market is much less, and the risk is mitigated by the scope of entry. The lower overall cost of offering a unique product or service that is a small adaptation of what you already have provides a shield against having to reinvest in cases where the analysis missed the mark. Because the new offering is a revised version of what you already have and know well, the internal skill training and learning curve are drastically reduced. This also holds true for other areas of the company, such as sales, support, and production. The approach is alarmingly simple and obvious; however, few companies take the time to look deeply enough and appreciate the value they produce, mainly because they do not look beyond the surface.

The other benefit of niches is that they invariably create a *ripple effect*. The ripple effect is a consequence of entering a specific market or niche; other related markets or niches are attracted to the product or service but want a further modification. As in the cases of Phillips Seafood and the sports and energy drink vendors, adjoining markets that have a link somewhere in the supply chain open up. Phillips Seafood expanded from selling cooked packed blue crab to producing a range of condiments for salads and dips. The ripple effect can take you both horizontally and vertically, not only presenting the products and services so that they take on new shapes in value but also moving across industry borders and distribution channels, both locally and internationally.

When you start with small-scale projects, you can take steps to manage success more quickly than is possible in large-scale projects, and the reaction to corrective changes is more immediate. Furthermore, if moving into new niches is seen as part of the company's overall growth strategy but is kept separate from the mainline business, then disruption of normal business by the new venture can also be controlled. The urgency to launch is also not a factor. A radical product innovation that has had a great deal of investment put into it usually has a deadline to meet, with stakeholders demanding to see returns as soon as possible. This leads to compromises in product footprint and to market preparation being sacrificed to meet the all-important launch date. When a company takes the approach of looking inward and carefully assessing the niche markets that would most benefit from its products, there is no pressure to get to market at any particular time. The idea of pilot-testing the new offering in a sample market is sensible and is encouraged, unless doing so would give competitors a target. A great deal can be learned in test or pilot marketing. Again, the beauty of picking niches is that the feedback is immediate, with go or no-go decisions able to be arrived at quickly.

Once we set an external view of looking at small or differentiated markets on the outside, this must be translated to what needs to happen on the inside of any organization. Niche thinking within the company can be a supportive agent to the company. These niche principles can be applied to a department or business unit as a way of thinking and behaving. Thinking in terms of moving into a niche is an opportunity to communicate to employees the company's commitment to becoming *bigger* or better and sends a message of promoting innovation within the company at any level. Thinking small is about getting bigger in a steady, safe manner through incremental steps that are directed toward being uniquely better at getting bigger. Irrespective of whether your company operates in a broad consumer-based market, there is an opening for specialization that can add to current revenues. By not considering niches, you may be missing opportunities to produce potentially big gains with relatively small investments.

Niches Build Volume

If you are in business today, you can appreciate that going into niches can provide a complementary revenue stream coming from smaller deals. A lot of businesses facing a high cost of sales are putting pressure on their salespeople to increase volume—to do lots of big deals and fewer small deals. In reality, most sales pipelines have a combination of large and small opportunities. Assuming these potential customers are all qualified, this is normal. When competition increases, there is an impact on the win/loss ratio, with decreases in the probability of wins. Therefore, if the target market remains the same and nothing else in the company changes, the reliance on the larger deals, and therefore the risk of not making quota, increases. In short, the more competition there is, the more the risk of not making quota goes up. This does not argue against making a lot of big sales; on the contrary, if growing bigger in terms of revenues is the company's aim and need, then looking at niches in any economy is being recognized as a way to fast-track growth that will complement and increase volume sales that may lead to bigger deals.

Niche vendors are not limited to small market segments. Consider Boeing and Airbus. They are definitely big dollar value businesses, and they are in specialized, difficult-to-replicate markets. They also have a volume-based business, with the necessity of covering costs, profit, growth, and so on. However, they are acutely aware of the importance of differentiating their products and services in very specific ways, especially in the commercial airline business units. For example, Boeing differentiates itself in areas such as delivering training programs for new aircraft using multimedia techniques, offering industry-compliant certifications, maintaining networks of examination centers, providing pilot and crew self-service simulators over the Internet, and the list goes on. Airbus responds with similar programs, manuals, and simulators. Boeing's approach, however, is slightly different from Airbus's in that Boeing gives each department the responsibility for building, developing, marketing, and delivering these services. What this means is that Boeing's customers develop a relationship directly with the departments that provide the services rather than having to deal with corporate bureaucracy for attention, as Airbus's customers do.

The next section is about finding what market you are really in. It looks at what your value is relative to what your customers are looking for. Determining what market you are in may seem trivial, but it isn't.

Becoming a Niche the Small Way

Before you look outward to find a niche to grow into, you need to look inward at what you do well. That means starting by asking what are the component parts of your business that differentiate you from your competitors today. The reason this is an important first step before assessing the viability of any other market is that it is possible that your niche may not be the same as the core business you are in. For example, if your customers see on-time delivery as setting you apart, and if this is one of the factors that keeps customers loyal, it is possible that you have mastered distribution to such an extent that you may be able to launch a new service as an offshoot of this acquired expertise. Now, that is not to say that you should get into the logistics business; however, the processes and systems you have in place could be what are marketable. This is an example of becoming or expanding into a niche the small way. Extracting a uniquely differentiating part of your business, repackaging it to form a different product or service, then deciding how to bring it to market is what this is about. The process starts with *identification*, followed by *elimination*, or narrowing the possibilities down to those things that require the smallest changes, and then *evaluation* to find the most viable market.

Identification

The process of identifying how value is created within your organization, which has been built up through necessity to compete, involves looking for skills and innovations that you have developed or unique qualities that would be difficult to repeat. Consider these as units of value (single marketable components) and see if one of them or a series of them in combination can be repackaged and resold. Value creation can be identified as either a process, a set of unique experiences or innovations brought to a common process, or a service that comes from a process or product. If there is a process that adds value (for example, the ability to deliver faster), it is important that you identify and document the elements that create that process (in this case speed).

The significance of doing this is that it helps you articulate how the value can be transmitted when it comes to marketing. The more specific you can be about how the value is created, the easier it is to develop the message for customers. Faster delivery resulting from better scheduling is the surface statement. Drilling deeper into the core reasons *why* this makes you different from the rest is what is needed. As you arrive at each of the facts of your differences, ask, "So what?" For example, faster delivery is the result of specific changes in your computerized scheduling system that only you have made—so what? This will take you deeper still; your unique scheduling system provides faster delivery because the minute the customer places the order, the system assigns that order a priority and determines the best carrier to use based on when the customer needs the order and the customer's location— so what? This means that customers get their orders faster—so what? It means that they save money and are more efficient if they do business with you. You can see that the last statement gives you more to work with in developing a new marketing strategy.

Elimination

Finding a niche is a process of determining markets that are adjacent to the center of your core business. What that means is looking for related industries that are within an already existing niche or in one that can be created with identifiable new value sets. Taking the elimination route has proved to be easier in picking potential niches. Either the SIC list or the North American Industry Classification System (NAICS) list is useful in this process. Once you have a list of candidates, then it is a matter of prioritizing them to determine which would be most appropriate in the initial phases. Bear in mind that in almost every case, you will find yourself being pulled to other niches, and the list may change depending on where the demand is. Referring back to the SIC list provides a reality check and helps you decide whether the opportunities coming from another niche or market are one-time situations or could represent growth. This final list can also be incorporated into your business or campaign plan.

Once you have prepared this list, you are in a position to conduct research to determine the status of each niche or market. You need to find out such things as who the competitors are, if any; what the size of that market is today; the trends in the market; how the pricing regime that is used compares to the one you use; and how customers buy, whether directly from the supplier or through resellers and distribution agents. Finding the characteristics of the market, comparing them with those in your business, and determining the biggest opportunities lets you identify your target markets. If the list is long even after the elimination process because of the versatility of your product or service, then break down the list into phases, grouping common industry types. The idea is to think of going to market not in one big blazing spectacular, but through a series of incremental and precisely guided launches where you can receive feedback and build up knowledge as you go, making incremental changes along the way as you enter the next market and the next.

Evaluation

Once you have identified the internal value sets (potential products and services) and listed related industries (markets), you now need to evaluate what changes in your product, service, business, pricing, distribution, and marketing are necessary to make your entry into the new market a success. There are a number of areas to evaluate. The aim of this planning cycle is to determine what changes to your existing core values are needed so that you can easily represent your value to the target market as precisely as possible. The closer the focus of both, the greater the chance for speedy acceptance and for the ripple effect to take place. Once the ripple effect starts to move across other industries and niches, you will find the evaluation process to be critical, as the temptation to accept all and any business may take you outside of the small incremental changes when you make a decision to launch a new business. It's not necessarily a bad thing if this happens. Our aim here is to provide a method of growing that involves the least risk, lowest cost, and minimal impact by finding the easiest to enter, least competitive markets fastest, and in the most manageable way possible.

The evaluation process involves a cost and risk analysis plus a time frame for breakeven. While the definition is left to you to determine, time to market should not be in years, but in quarters or months. This should help you get a feel for how small is small when we say that the changes should be kept to a minimum. More time should be spent on repackaging and repositioning, either through the direct sales team or by finding partnerships with existing suppliers or customers, than on R&D. Another condition in the evaluation process is to determine whether there are any legal considerations to be taken into account in the niches that you have as targets. For example, in the faster delivery example, are there certifications or levels of experience required to handle hazardous materials? This should be part of the research into the market. Determine if there are any government or industry certifications or validation processes that the industry enforces. Even though we are targeting niches, those niches may be subject to a governing or regulatory body that has certain controls in place, and you will need to become familiar with those controls. The importance of this is that it may add enough of a burden or require a sufficient investment to take this niche out of the small incremental advances category. If so, it may be either deleted from the list because of the compliance issues or moved to a later launch phase.

In upcoming chapters, there is a format and template to document not only this process but others as well.

The other activity that is valuable in the evaluation process is establishing a consortium of customers and suppliers that are in the niches you are targeting. Once you have identified your value sets, you are in a position to outline your plan for going to market. This blueprint can be the basis for setting up an informal advisory group with a charter to provide feedback on your initial ideas for further refinement and future buy-in. I have found that people are willing to contribute to your ideas in this way. The forum need not take a lot of their time, and with the variety of communication methods available, it can easily be done. If you have determined that you need to collaborate with partners to go to market, their contributions will be invaluable in bringing market-ready experience into the development and execution of the business plan. Customers are particularly useful, as they will be able to tell you their expectations, point out the shortcomings of their current vendors, and help you shape the differentiating messages that you wrap around your offers.

CHAPTER 4

DRILLING TO THE CORE

Fat chance and slim chance mean the same thing, but only one is preferred.

—Anonymous

If you ask a business to define its value proposition, most will rattle off a trite spiel that is no different from those of its competitors. Distinguishing a core business and a core value proposition is no trivial matter. Failure to do so can immobilize a company and even escalate its problems until they come to the attention of the board of directors. This is not an easy question, either: in many a company, there is outright dissonance between the definition of the core business and the reality of what the business actually does well.

Remedying this disconnect requires the business to rediscover itself, not by grappling with the question of what it *would like* to be, but by tackling the question of what the market *wants and needs* it to be. Let's say, for example, that the company's core business is printing. What is valuable to the customer is what happens behind the scenes. The fact that there are color experts, layout specialists, designers, and packaging and distribution capabilities is what gives the business its value. Anyone can print something. The real differentiator is found in the backroom processes. In the print example, it may be something like expertise in color mixing. The fact is that it is along the internal value chain that strengths, differentiation, and stories are found. The beauty of this analysis is that even the most basic business will have acquired unique competencies that not only add value to the supply chain but instigate the internal process of incremental change.

Consider a transport company that delivers goods from one place to another. What could this company have learned that would allow it to differentiate itself from anyone else, let alone build its market share in a competitive industry? The answer might be maintenance management—the science of fleet efficiency aimed at keeping its trucks on the road longer and minimizing cost. How much value does this produce for all other logistics suppliers and transporters in the related industry? Could one sell this "product"? Of course. That is what this chapter is about: finding a company's core business, which may very well be different from the company's existing mission statement.

Messages That Matter

What is important is that you develop a message that in both oral and written form is consistent across the company. If you want to build up your brand, then a consistent look and feel for all your outgoing content is essential. While these may seem to be basic marketing fundamentals, and they are, too often they are overlooked; the importance is placed on simply getting the materials out there instead of having a dedicated focus on making sure that the materials do some work. It is actually far worse to send generic marketing material that adds no value, such as a piece of direct mail, than to not send anything at all.

The area that we will spend some time on will be the Internet and your Web site. Everything should look and feel the same. Even if you are in several different lines of business and have a diverse range of products selling into multiple industries, your brand needs to be consistent, and the way you show that consistency is to have everything look and feel the same—it is as simple as that. How to get that to happen is what we will be covering, and we will specifically look at those areas where the smallest changes with the lowest cost will produce the biggest impact and highest gain.

There are two types of message development that we will examine in this chapter. One is the development of a message from scratch, and the other is refining your existing messages to ensure that they do their job properly. Drilling for the core is finding the value statement that you want to project from all levels of your company and determining how that translates into a superior customer experience at every point where your customers interact with you. *Every* interaction with customers (or prospects) has an impact on your message, your brand, and your continued commitment. The mantra I preach regarding branding is this: when I am asked what I think is important about branding, my response is, "everything." Brand is a holistic concept. It holds together and builds power (or equity, if you like) through the accumulated consistency of quality and through recognition given to it in the form of earned loyalty from customers. That's earned loyalty, not forced or bought or trapped loyalty—loyalty that's freely, willingly, and voluntarily given.

Your message is your key pathway to loyalty—what you say needs to be what you stand for. The challenge with developing marketing messages is that you have a lot to communicate to people with short attention spans and a myriad of past experiences, and you have only words to do it with. This is, of course, true of any communication, but when you are attempting to transmit an important and sometimes complex value message across multiple media, the situation becomes more involved. By the time the members of your audience have the materials in their hands, or on their screens, they have already been subjected to hundreds if not thousands of messages from other people, some of whom are competitors of yours who are thinking exactly what you are: "How do I get my message through?" The answer is simple, but it takes some work.

Start by removing all the adjectives from your description of your products and services. This comes as a surprise to most people, as the normal way to develop a message is to *add* as many adjectives as possible to make the product or service sound wonderful. Note that you remove the adjectives, not the descriptors. Describe what you have in detail—keep going, even if it means including the obvious, until there is nothing left to say. Lay everything out in lists and tables, and then correlate it with what your customers talk about. You are now approaching the real value zone. This exercise has surprised everyone I have ever done it with—they think that certain features of their product are cool and that *all their customers* are using them, but they discover that their customers are not emphasizing these features and may not even be bringing them up at all. This situation is particularly common in the technology industry, where the latest is thought to be the greatest, and where there is an internally held view that customers will always buy the latest thing in order to gain the competitive edge they are looking for. Even if you are planning to sell that latest thing to only one customer, everyone will have it before very long—and away we go again.

The fact is, whatever customers are saying about *your company* reflects the products and services you sell and deliver to them. Make no mistake: the way your customers see your company is determined by the service that is delivered by you or your staff. A mediocre product can compete with the latest and greatest if the customer service is better. The opposite is true as well—there have been exceptional products that did not reach their full potential until the service aspects were addressed, and there have been cases where those aspects were not dealt with and the "great" products involved went away forever. Remember Harvard Graphics, 20/20, or WordPerfect? If you don't, it doesn't matter; if you do, you know what I mean.

Finding the core of your business, therefore, requires understanding what you do on a daily basis that is different from the things that anyone else does, and discovering the unique competencies that you have that you can leverage further by focusing on making continuous, small incremental improvements in them. In order to do this in a way that highlights the differences immediately, you need to understand the ecosystem that the business is in and the environment operating around it.

Drilling for the Core Business

How, then, do you get started on developing a message that represents your core business? First, do not attempt to do this by yourself. Bring in people from a cross section of the company: R&D, sales, marketing, production, and delivery. For optimum results, bring in business partners, resellers, distributors, and selected customers as a second step. They do not need to be part of the development phases, but they will be invaluable in fine-tuning your message and adapting it to its specific requirements. Do not be concerned at this point about whether the message is for online or offline use. What is important is that you gather information and have it all in one place for the purpose of building and correlating the points you want to make.

Developing your core message is not unlike drilling for fuels. The surface picture gives telltale signs, but it is not enough to let you determine what is really underneath. Different types of maps and data in different combinations are required to accurately define the terrain in a way that gives you the optimum information for taking further actions. Similarly, formulating a core message requires aggregate information from multiple sources, not just sources inside the company. The combination of internal and external information will highlight the areas where value is perceived. Until you get to this external/internal comparison, you are not in a position to know how to highlight your strengths and manage your weaknesses. The process starts with the products and services (*what*), then looks at the industries (*where*) you sell into, and then finally identifies key customers (*who and why*). Figure 4-1 provides a template that can be used for gathering the information required in this step of development.

Message Development Phase 1:
Products and Services

The process starts with the products and their features. Do not list any features that you know are mandatory or standard. Next, list

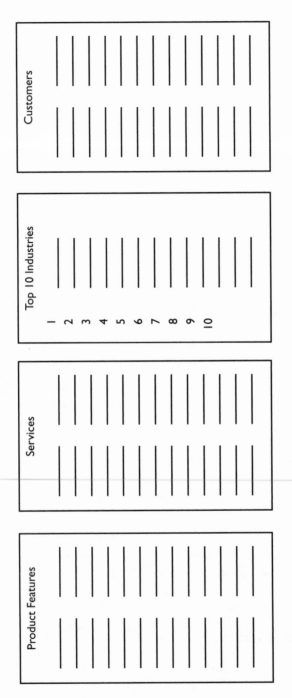

Figure 4-1 Drilling for Core—Message Development

the services that are product-related and those that are not. List the two types of services separately. The reason for separating product-related services from other services is that customers may highlight product-related services without mentioning the products. Also, this forces you to think about the differences. Features and functions are not the service; they are the reason the service exists. Therefore, mixing these elements together will not help you unbundle the ingredients that will later make up the message. This is why a lot of messages on company Web sites and in literature highlight the products up front, with services being buried several pages down. This is common in the technology industry, where the engineering advances are seen as the value and are placed at the front of the presentation. Your customers should be the ones who decide whether they want to see product first or not.

As a general rule, the level of service capability is based on the products. Products in and of themselves do not provide *service*—they provide features and functions. Think of the multitude of devices packed with features and functions that are available in the wireless telephone business today, yet the number one reason that customers change their telecommunications provider is—customer service. Therefore, when developing a message, one of the small but significant differences you need to incorporate is to list the product attributes separately from the services.

Message Development Phase 2: Industries

Once you have made these lists, the next process is to identify the value you provide to the industries that you are selling into and the customers within those industries that you serve. List the industries in which most of your customers operate. (You may need to refer to your customer database for this information.) Limit this list of industries to a maximum of 10. Even if you have customers in more than 10 industries, you should determine the 10 industries in which most of your customers can be found. We will look at the rest later; for now you need to establish a framework in order to develop and bring out the core of the business.

Using the SIC or NAISC codes can be helpful in maintaining a standard nomenclature while the lists are being discussed and documented.

What we are doing is preparing an inventory of what you have, what you do, and where you do it. There will be obvious trends developing as you start to appreciate where your business is focused and exactly what it is that you are delivering. When these lists are compared, unit managers have sometimes been surprised by the breakdown of customers by industry. I have seen R&D managers make comments regarding their plans for the future that were not aligned with enhancing functionality for the industries in which most of their customers happened to be.

Message Development Phase 3: Customers

No doubt you have a fair idea as to why your customers buy from you, and this is valid input; however, you need to record it from the source. The best way to find out why your customers buy your products and services is by asking them to pinpoint the value they receive from your products and services and to express it in terms of what they were able to *increase* or *decrease* as a result of doing business with you, and by how much.

This is the toughest part of this assignment. With the advent of compliance and governance issues, companies are becoming sensitive about giving out empirical numbers for savings or cost reductions without official audited numbers or legal sign-off. In this phase of message development, it is recommended that you assign someone the task of handling the administration of the see-saw process that may be needed to get final approval of some customers' statements or comments. Customer testimonials give anything you communicate the highest form of credibility, and it is important that you reflect what your customers say when you reach out to new or existing markets. Unlike the phase of producing lists of products and services where you eliminated adjectives, when it comes to customer feedback and testimonials, you should *highlight* the adjectives and make a list of them.

This exercise becomes interesting when you combine your list of product functions and your inventory of services with your customers' statements and adjectives, categorized by the key industries you service. When you have done this, *you have reached the core*. This is one of the best pictures you can get of your business in terms of the comparison between the value *perceived by your customers*, the value you think you are providing, and the value that you can still deliver. When you look at the lists together, you have the necessary reference materials to enable you to easily construct statements and sentences that match products and services with the customer's benefits. This is a good representation of the perceived value you represent to customers, and it is significant in building your story. One of many lessons that marketers, myself included, have learned is that you should sell and market what people want to buy.

The Message Tree

This information, when gathered together in one place in this format, is the raw material for the next phase of message development. A concept that I have called the Message Tree allows messages to be built for any level of the company or for any single product or service. In fact, this concept can be used for the development of press releases or special events where there are various separate segments and locations, all of which need to be consistent. The principles are simple: a hierarchy of messages is built based on either the different broad levels of audience that you need to communicate with or a targeted audience.

Selling requires communicating at different levels; therefore, depending on what your products and services may be, it is possible for you to be selling into your customers' or prospects' organizations at three or more different levels. Salespeople know that this is often necessary in order to close deals. Marketing knows that the messages have the same job to do.

There are two main uses for the audience hierarchy. One is for the situation in which your products are aimed at a specific functional or operational department within your customers' or prospects' organization, and the other is for the situation in which a single product that you sell affects multiple levels of your customers' or prospects' organization. In either case, the hierarchy is essential to ensure that the messages are fine-tuned for what that audience wants to see, hear, and do. You need to have a consistent message that is personal and relevant to different levels of the organization, and the Message Tree allows you to do this very simply; however, the homework we have just done is a prerequisite if you wish to arrive at as close to precision positioning as possible.

The Message Tree is also useful for the different industries that you are in or want to move into. There will be specific nuances that will distinguish one industry from another; some of these are big differences, and others are minor. If you follow the strategy of looking at adjacent markets that have a relationship with the markets you are servicing today, the differences in messaging are not likely to be vast. In any case, you need to make your messages resonate emotionally as well as be strong pragmatically. You can achieve this with minor language changes that use industry-based jargon.

The core message, once derived, must be consistent and must be supported by messages at the other levels. When changing industries, you may develop the bad habit of rehashing the high-level messages. Think of the messages you send to different industries as being dialects of the same message. What is important to note is that once key messages have been derived, you should stick with them for at least a year, unless there has been a major milestone within the company that warrants a complete revamping of the core message or the company has taken an entirely different direction. Other benefits of using the Message Tree include the provision of a very useful briefing document for marketing, press relations, industry relations, investor relations, sales, R&D, employees, and so on. The Message Tree is an excellent resource that can be used as a foundation for any internal communications in company literature, such as newsletters and announcements.

When building sales collateral, you will use this documentation as a central reference for maintaining consistency. In fact, this process begins to set the groundwork for your brand. The reason this process works so well is that the foundation for the brand and any messaging and content that is produced comes from the core of what the company represents. That means that you are able to live up to the expectations that arise from what you say you are. What happens in a lot of situations where messaging is developed for a company is an overemphasis on the embellishments and self-gratifications, so that when it comes to aligning these messages with the reality of what the products can actually do, there is a friction between development, production, and marketing.

Bringing the R&D and production folks into the message development and creation phase opens a dialogue and allows everyone to realize the importance of being "on message." This reduces any tension when marketing launches the message to sales and the marketplace. The age-old friction between sales and marketing also results from R&D and marketing not being aligned. That is, of course, an entirely different subject; however, one area of alignment that can be readily achieved is in the design, framework, and structure of the message. The actual final creative and content production remains within the domain of marketing, which can proceed with some confidence that it has buy-in for the core message.

Message Constantly, Consistently, and Consciously

The Message Tree has a versatile framework that can be used as a reference point for standardizing and maintaining the consistency of the message throughout the company and for communicating it to both the internal constituents and outside suppliers. It is especially useful if you do business in international locations; the core message can be kept intact while the local nuances based on culture, language, or political influences are considered. Messaging specialists will tell you that the most powerful message occurs when the company speaks with "one voice" to the market. The Message Tree provides the structure and format to allow the company to have many stories and one voice, with that voice being the core themes and value statements that underpin what the company represents.

The information collected in the previous exercise is used to build the Message Tree. It has a hierarchical structure, where the top of the tree represents the company's key message (see Figure 4-2). The branches are the messages that support the top-line message—they are the evidence, if you like, that substantiates the core message. The information gathered earlier will provide the subject matter that you grow the branches from. If your customers have received value because of their ability to reduce costs in certain areas, then this is a second-level message. Underneath that, there are specific factors related to a business process or flow of work that has improved, leading to the customer's receiving those benefits; this is the third-level message. This level identifies those features that were used at the product level.

Target Audience

At the top of the Message Tree, there is a provision for tailoring the message for a specific audience. The first time you do this, it will be at the companywide level. However, the versatility of the Message Tree allows you to use it in a multitude of ways. Suppose you are planning to send a communication addressing a specific target audience, such as chief executive officers (CEOs). Extracting the top-line and second-level components will provide the key messages appropriate to their level of appreciation and understanding. The ease of use and versatility of the Message Tree allow you to use it to address other target audiences as well—for example, chief information officers (CIOs) or shop floor managers in production; all you need to do is use the top-line message followed by a selection of second-level elements (those that resonate the best with that audience) and the corresponding third-level items (as these audiences are more detail-oriented).

The power of this method is that no matter whom you are sending the message to and no matter what format or medium you are using, the message will be consistent, will focus on what the

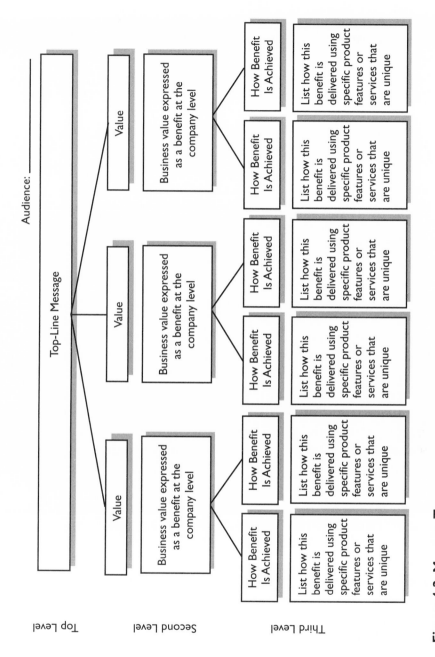

Figure 4-2 Message Tree

prospects and customers want to know about, and will have the credibility provided by your customer testimonials. The Message Tree is dynamic to the extent that small changes can and should be made periodically; however, the core message at the top and the messages at the second level should not change very often; they should remain consistent for as long as is practical.

The Top Line

The top-level message is a concise, simple statement like a tagline or headline, the basis of which has come from what your customers have indicated. It should be thematic, catchy, simple, and memorable. It should be a single sentence with fewer than 10 words, if possible. This is not as easy as it sounds. Think of this message as the company tagline. The statement is broken down by a set of value components that underpin the top-line message. What different areas of value does your company provide that make the top-line message true? You can have as many value items as you feel are appropriate, but you should limit them to the values that your customers have articulated and those that you want to highlight.

Supporting each value statement is a list of the business benefits gained from this value. For example, if the value you provide is quality service, then what business benefits do your customers receive as a result of your product's providing those higher quality standards? Following this, there will be further specific areas where benefits can be seen in tangible ways, again referring back to the customer data. There may be productivity gains resulting from the quality of the products that you deliver; if so, under productivity gains, articulate what features or services you provide that allow these efficiencies to be gained. For example, a product feature could be that you provide automated validation checks along a production process. List these as features or services.

What you are building is a comprehensive map of the value that you represent. Once you have drawn this map, it becomes the basis for all other literature and marketing collateral. It is also an excellent briefing reference for public relations and for your Web site developers and designers, who are often struggling to understand what your business actually does in "real" terms. Furthermore, this map becomes the basis for your internal communications to the company to align everyone in the organization with the message. There should be no excuse for anyone not being able to give a concise "elevator pitch" on what the company is about and what it does.

The Second Level: Value

The second level is where you identify your value statements. Each of the value boxes (see Figure 4-2) has a header portion and a supporting table portion. You should be able to describe each of the key values that your customers have indicated that they receive, plus those that you want to further expose them to, and you should be able to do this in three or fewer words in the header portion, supported by short statements in bullet form in the business value table area underneath the header portion.

The key point in developing this part of the tree is that the statement and the value headers are at the *business* level. There is no mention of the product's features or functions. It is clear now why collecting the customer information is an important part of this development cycle. Examples of second-level value statements include the following:

- Quality
- Reliability
- Accessibility
- Simplification
- Efficiency
- Usability
- Security

The supporting statements should reflect the way in which the value in each of the headers is derived and delivered. Using security as an example, supporting business statements might be these:

- Reduction in security system costs
- Management controls available across all divisions
- Compliance with government regulatory standards
- Increased employee productivity with secure remote access

The Third Level: Benefits

The third level drills deeper and includes the product's benefits. Each benefit header box contains a short statement regarding one of the benefits delivered by the value. This is followed by the evidence that supports the claim for the value item. This section may have multiple branches for any one value statement. Using the security example again, the benefits headers may include the following:

- Security controlled by user access codes
- Self-managing firewall protection built in
- Alert systems available at department level
- Twenty-four-hour support available

Underneath each of these statements, the ways in which that benefit is delivered are itemized. Product features and functions may be included here if they directly deliver the benefits. In the following examples, features and delivery methods are intermixed. We will take the "Security controlled by user access codes" as the header line and expand on that benefit with the following:

- System login identifies and controls the resources that each user has access to.
- User passwords are matched to Human Resources files.
- Protection of user data is provided by storage at remote facility inside firewall.
- Senior management approval of all new user profiles is mandated by the system.
- Encryptions of codes are unique and specific by location or department.

Include as many boxes as required for each of the benefit areas. Notice that the descriptions are also becoming longer, although they are still brief and concise. This is a discipline that eliminates superfluous wording and that maintains a focus on useful words.

Speaking the Language

The other way of using the Message Tree is to target a specific niche or industry. By making small changes in the second- and third-level messages, you can "flavor" your core values so that they resonate with a particular industry. The values you have in the second level remain basically the same; what changes is the way they are achieved for that industry. In other words, quality is a value that everyone wants; however, the application of quality to a bank may be different from the application of quality to a manufacturer. If you supply a way to get better quality to customers, then the second-level header value is always quality, but how this value is achieved and the way the product is used change. You will be surprised at how small the changes required to accommodate other related industries or niches will be. If the selection was done using the process in Chapter 3, the changes can be very small, and a lot of the initial work done up front will be reusable.

Still another use for the Message Tree is for an individual product or service line. The tree is particularly useful when you have a new product launch and the product needs to fit in with other existing products or when you have a new release or update for an existing line of products. The top-line message becomes the tagline or headline regarding the product or service. Second- and third-level messages drill down in the same way that they did at the company or industry level.

Message for Business

Now that you have a good understanding of what your products and services represent to your customers, you need to bring this understanding to the world so that it can work for you to generate more and more business. Therefore, there are two other dimensions that you need to consider; the first is the competition, and the second is what your potential customers want to buy.

The previous exercise has given you a good understanding of the value you have been providing up until now, but I am sure that there are items on the products list and the services list that your customers are not utilizing—or that your competitors have and you don't. The importance of completing the message development phase before you use a message inside and outside your company is that doing so lets you know where you stand with regard to the next two elements of information, which will tell you what small but significant areas you need to address in refining the message to pitch it exactly where you want it. The two remaining elements are these:

- Customers' pain points and current-day issues
- Competitors' offerings that are different from yours

It's the Small Things in Life

Building and refining your message can be one of the most beneficial small things you can do to improve your business without changing anything else. Perhaps more than at any time in the past, communicating value to customers is a challenge, partly because so many messages are being sent out by advertisers (direct mail, e-mails, and so on), but also because companies do not spend enough time developing the right messages, positioning them, and keeping them relevant and fresh. There are three key ingredients in developing your message to your customers:

- The perceived benefits of the products and services you deliver that are important to your customers, without regard to what you may think is important or whether others consider your products and services to be state of the art, expen-

sive to build, leading edge, or in possession of some other favorable quality
- Points of differentiation that are important to your customers that you provide and that others cannot duplicate easily or simply do not have
- Evidence regarding the benefits you offer and how you are different (not just better), provided by engaging your customers, business partners, industry commentators and analysts, and influential associations

In the last chapter, we formulated a list of values that you developed over time that included people skills, product enhancements, processing excellence, customer service, or any combination of these. It is with this list that you begin to further formulate what the core of your business is and how its value can be transmitted in a way that can make a big difference in terms of attracting more business. We have already covered the problems with sending generic messages to mass audiences, and you need to make sure that if any of your marketing material is generic, abstract, overly strategic, or otherwise vague, you have made a plan to retire those items to the archives or the company museum. Whether you are in a niche of specialized goods and services or selling a commodity, you need to connect to your customers in such a way that they are able to appreciate at the emotional level what you have and how you are better than anyone else who supplies the same thing.

What People Say

There are two sources that will bring out the "remarkable," as Seth Godin put it in his book *Purple Cow*.[1] In order to figure out the customers' pain points, you need to go to these two sources. The first is the customers themselves, and part of this has been brought out in the profiling exercise outlined earlier. The second is other useful resources, such as industry thought leaders and commentators who watch the economic impact of events on various industries. Their data will vary from broad-range forecasts and trends to specific customer issues and pain points. Correlating the customer feedback, industry analysts' opinions, and your instincts gives you a good basis from which to produce a list of "customer pains."

There is a distinction to be made here with regard to the behavior of different types of buyers, and these are often confused: when you are selling to a business, solving the *pains* outweighs selling the *gains*; in a domestic consumer market, selling what customers *want* wins over selling what they *need*. I have been in branding and messaging sessions where the structure has been to find out what "the customer wants to buy," then to set a course toward creating a need for that product. Several years ago I attended a sales and marketing training seminar where the session leader opened with, "You need to create an environment where the customer wants to buy." That is doing it the hard way. Find out what the customer wants—period.

Connecting People with the Message

If you have invested in the development of your messaging and positioning and you feel that it is all there, but your message is not resonating as well or as powerfully as you would like, this may be a symptom of common mistakes that need only minor adjustments to bring better results. The most likely problems with messages are these:

- Too wordy
- Too vague
- Too complex
- Too much jargon
- Too impersonal
- Too much tooting (of oneself)
- Too brief

On the positive side, a lot of the creative work that has been put into developing your message can be very useful. All you need to do is put the messages and statements that have been created through a process of refinement. This is something that is rarely done; if it is done at all, it is usually rushed through to meet pressing deadlines. The fact is, in most cases, some basic changes in the materials that you already have can make a huge difference in their impact. Remember, what is important is not how outlandishly creative you can be, but how you apply focused creativity to produce the desired reaction and feedback from the audience. Going over messages that were created some time ago, updating them for currency and the latest themes, and using some of the message development tools have produced a lot of fresh material in a relatively short time.

An understanding of the way people experience their world is useful when it comes to developing messages. One method based on the study of the structure of human behavior and the way we model our experiences is known as Neurolinguistic Programming, or NLP.[2] NLP is widely used in many applications, including sales and marketing. The understanding of how people experience information that NLP provides has many benefits on a personal level, and it also can be applied to the development of materials designed to influence and inform. NLP requires a certain respect for the audience your messages are aimed at. The audience rewards this attention by connecting with the content and materials and associating with the messages they deliver at a more personal and deeper level of comprehension.

How does this all work?

It starts with the way *we* work. In our daily lives, we have experiences that affect each of our senses. We see, hear, feel, smell, and taste, and although we unconsciously use all of these senses all the time, *consciously* we rely on one sense more than on the others. In NLP, these most-used senses are commonly referred to as the visual, auditory, and kinesthetic senses (VAK). There's nothing new in this so far; however, while we all use the same senses, at some stage of developing into adults, we subconsciously decided that one of these senses was a favorite way to *store* and *recall* experiences. Evidence of which sense is favored can be found in our *language*.

In other words, if we have decided that our favorite way of experiencing the world is visually, we will express our views in visual terms. For example, you may have heard people say, "I don't see what you mean." Others will say, "That doesn't sound right" or "I can't grasp that concept," the last two being auditory and kinesthetic responses, respectively. Therefore, if you are developing a story regarding the way your products and services are being used and you introduce these VAK modalities into the content and context of the story, the readers will associate with the story because they will appreciate the language you used.

There are other factors to consider when you are using NLP techniques for persuasive writing. These are known as meta-programs, and they are based on the way we perceive and process information. It should be noted that a more comprehensive study of NLP is recommended. The focus here is on identifying the small things that can make a big difference in the way we create messages to influence and motivate people. The abridged versions of NLP concepts given here are specific for this purpose.

As we matured into adults, we learned many things about ourselves. For example, we learned how we are best motivated, how we like to make decisions, what we like in people, whether we prefer being with people or being alone, whether we like to lead or follow, and how we are influenced. Consider the following traits when you are developing messages and related content.

Proactive–Reactive

Some people prefer to take action rather than sit around waiting for something to happen; this is the *proactive* group. These people are known to be "go-getters." They like to get the job done, and when you talk with them, they will be interested in finding out about project specifications and how the project was accomplished.

People with *reactive* behavior like to wait for others to make a decision, and then they want to know all the details regarding how and why the decision was reached. It is important for them to know how many others have already used the products and services and with what result. They view pioneering as a risky behavior compared with waiting and learning from others.

Toward–Away

In a motivational context, there are people who are motivated *toward* a goal; achieving it becomes their focus. These people like to know what was accomplished in relation to the initial objectives that were set. For these people, messages need to describe benefits in terms of achievement.

The other type of behavior is based on avoidance. These people want to be achievers, but for different reasons. Their motivation is to get as far *away* from failure as possible. Messages that attract people with this trait discuss how others have avoided problems by using certain products and services.

Sameness–Difference

People with a *sameness* style of behavior prefer things to stay the same. When meeting people, they get along better with those who are most like them. A common expression used by people with this behavior is, "It has always been done this way." Aiming messages at this type of person requires highlighting the things that do not change.

Then there are those who see change as being necessary to achieving success. Progress is a result of doing something *differently*. Radical change is fine as long as the rewards are greater than the risks. For these people, messages should give information about big improvements and cite metrics.

Specific–General

Some people like to delve into the finer details and build the bigger picture from many *specific* pieces of data. These people enjoy knowing how something works. In order to do this, they like to take things apart (sometimes literally).

Generalists can work at the big-picture level. They understand broad, *general* statements, and they appreciate theory and models. Economic simulations and what-if analyses work well for people with this trait.

External–Internal

For people with *external* behavior, the approval and opinions of others matter. Messages to and correspondence with these people should contain quotes from customers, industry analysts, and influential leaders.

People with the *internal* trait are opinionated, show their skepticism of anything new, and believe they know better than anyone else until proven otherwise. These folks are proof-loving people. All the data you give them need to point conclusively to the answer you want, but you must leave out the answer because they want to find it for themselves.

Options–Procedures

People with *options* behavior like to know that there are many choices available to them, and they enjoy exploring alternatives, especially in the buying process. These people tend to ask for substitutes on menus, even when the substitutes they request are not on the menus. Rules are basically conditions that allow for possible alternatives. Messages that are attractive to these people are those that indicate flexibility, choice, and mixing and matching.

Someone who likes to follow orders has the *procedures* behavior trait. Breaking the rules is out of the question, and solutions must always be found within stated policies and processes. These people find integrity in well-defined procedures. Information to these folks should include methodology, setup steps, assembly information, and so on.

Competitive Messages

Information regarding your competitors complements and further fine-tunes your messages. It can be useful to show that yours is not simply a "me too" product. The danger with competitive analysis is that it pulls you toward a response strategy, where you feel a need to counter, better, or negate your competitors. Once you start this journey, it usually begins to affect other areas of your business.

Business is not a game or a war; it is business, and you are in business to make a profit through a complex reward system that involves exchanging a consideration for a perceived value. If the perceived value is greater than the price you charge, you have a sale; if you deliver what you promise, you have the beginnings of loyalty. When your customers pick up the phone and call you to do business again, you are on solid ground for growth.

Competitor obsessive disorder occurs when your focus on the competition is equal to or more important than your focus on your customers. The result may be that your attention becomes centered on building competitive strength, leading to aggressive behavior that creates a culture of winning deals at any cost, affecting and potentially lowering margins. The other problem that this leads to is a lowering of customer loyalty if the relationship was created purely by outselling the competition (meaning that the value of the transaction may have become more important than the value provided by your company).

In today's economics and in almost every industry, it is a reality that pressure to close the deal is paramount. A trend that I have seen emerging in recent years is that whenever a customer is acquired by using a tough and aggressive competitive sales process, more than the usual amount of attention needs to be given to after-sale support. Customers buy from companies; they do not buy products just because of their price. Therefore, keeping abreast of the competition involves identifying where and how you are different. Considering your competitors to be better based solely on their products may create a mental parity, resulting in your losing sight of the reasons why you are the leader—your company's attributes, culture, integrity, and so on.

After taking an inventory and determining the things your competition does that are the same as what you do, you should consider those attributes as areas where you can change the level playing field. The key is to identify what you do that is different. Being different is often confused with negating the competition; the word *different* comes from the Latin *differre*, meaning "to set apart." Therefore, when constructing messages involving competitive positioning, you should focus on how you set yourself apart from the others, not on negative information about them. It is what you highlight as the differences that makes you better, the subtle distinction being that just telling everyone that you are better does not differentiate you effectively.

The attributes that are most effective in developing your competitive differences are found at the company level. Playing feature/function poker with your competitors is another form of the "game" syndrome. In later chapters, we will discuss in more depth finding who your real competitors are; however, for the purpose of creating your message, you need to identify those things that you do that are different at the *company* level, not just at the product level. What can your customers and prospects expect when they build a business partnership with you, including the ways they will be treated that will differ from the ways your competitors will treat them?

If your value comes back to a particular product that you have, your message should tie in with how the product supports your values as a company rather than focusing on product superiority alone. For example, when it comes to products, most have similar functions, but some have more functions than others; for these extras, explain why time and effort was spent on developing each function and how that means better value for the customer. In short, anything you have that is different or extra needs to be related to the value provided by the company, not just by the product.

Once you are in the sales cycle, you will have ample opportunity to expose the particulars of the product, but when you are communicating to gain mindshare and attract your intended audience, where you stand from a competitive point of view is about how your company differentiates itself. Identify those things that are the same and consider them neutral. Look at what your competitors have that you do not, and rate those features in order of importance; then list company-level attributes that you have that are different from those of your competition and expose those differences.

A simple and quick way to determine the strength of an attribute or function compared to the competition is by charting it in a simple format, as shown in Figure 4-3. The horizontal axis of the chart takes into account the industry, segment, or niche in which you are operating. It is important to include this parameter, given that the priorities and uniqueness of particular functions will differ depending on the targets you are addressing. The top right-hand quadrant is the most highly differentiated position and the one that any of the messages that are being developed should highlight. The usefulness of this quadrant can be seen when you are having difficulty deciding whether a particular item should be emphasized in the documentation that will come out of the message development process. This is a fast way to determine an item's ranking relative to the other items that you may have on the list.

The relationship that each quadrant has with the Message Tree is that the reference to "functions" here relates to third-level messages. The way in which these three pieces of information are integrated becomes a powerful tool for determining what you will go out with in order of priority by target market. The tool you have now enables you to accurately access this.

This process is disarmingly simple, yet it is so powerful that not using a methodology of this type limits you to gut feeling and guessing most of the time when you are attempting to decide, "What are our most powerful messages?" At the third level of the Message Tree, the bullet points in the supporting boxes under the benefits headers will have functions or features. Take these functions and test each of them using the chart in Figure 4-3 to determine if, in fact, that function represents a true differentiator.

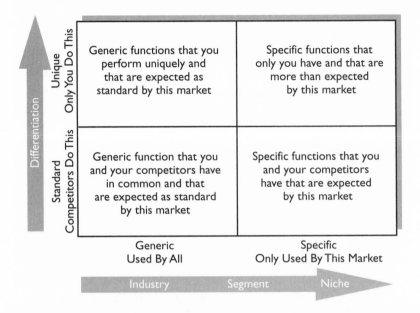

Figure 4-3 Differentiating Your Message

Consider the chart a measuring stick to which you bring each function (or group of functions, if applicable) to determine its competitive value. For those that are determined to be in the top right-hand quadrant, follow the *branch line* of that function in the Message Tree upward to arrive at the value boxes.

You have found the areas that will tell the most competitive stories. Match those with the customers that gave you the insight into that value from the first activity, where we collected the information from customers. These are the customers that tell the strongest story according to your value.

Tell the Story That People Want to Hear

Now that we have the messages that represent the core values of the company, supported by customers, partners, products, and services, we need to construct a story that stands out. A good source of reference material for this is the survey data you collected when you spoke with customers. Competitive data will be useful also, but only as a cross-check to make sure that you do not sound the same. This part of the communication development process often gets bogged down, as the company tries too hard to come up with a big story. In actual fact, the story needs to be simple, authentic, unique, and worth remembering. It is aligned with the opinions and attitudes of your customers and prospects or within the industry or niche you wish to target.

The presentation of the story includes fashionable ideals. It addresses the question of why people wouldn't buy, as opposed to why they should buy. Take, for example, the apparel industry and the reasons people buy designer clothes instead of basic clothing at a fraction of the price. Fashion marketers make sure that their product tells a story. They focus on the connection to the opinions that people have (or want to have) about themselves.

In the late 1980s, SAP told a story that everyone wanted to hear. It came out with an "out of the box" fully integrated business software solution called SAP R/3. Up until then, people had to buy their computer applications for different parts of their business requirements from different vendors—for example, a financial system from one vendor, a manufacturing system from a second vendor, and a sales system from yet another vendor. The problem with this was that all these systems needed to "talk" to one another to allow data to flow across them. This was not only costly but it was also a burden on computer departments, which were stuck with having to maintain the different systems and keep them connected every time one of the vendors introduced a new release or product.

The industry was craving a single-vendor system that had the connections in place to remove that overhead. SAP's story was about *integration* and its importance for business—and everyone wanted it. Other leading vendors either followed SAP's lead or made sure that their systems would integrate with SAP's. The offer by SAP was so compelling at the time that it opened new lines of business for consultants and partners who could teach the world about integrated systems and how to implement them and maximize their benefits. It responded to what was on everyone's mind.

Your story does not have to be on such a grand scale (although it could be), but it should focus on the generally held beliefs that people have with regard to their industry and how you as a company address these beliefs through what you have to offer. The story is best told using customers and influencers within the market. This type of communication, often called buzz marketing, is becoming more important.

No matter how mundane, commoditized, or bland you feel your product or service is, there is a great story to be told. The owner of a new 7-Eleven told me about the press release he sent out when he opened his store and how surprised he was at the number of customers who came into the store as a result of it. The news article in the local press had him pictured outside his new store next to a water drain and throwing the front door keys down the drain. The caption read: "Our Doors Are Always Open." There's no need for keys if that is the case. People remember something as simple as that.

No matter how simple or complex you may think your business is, there is a story worth remembering that encapsulates what you stand for. The story needs to be fact-based, have an innocence that people relate to, and be memorable. It represents the value you have to give and how you give it.

The Online Presence

In this era of digital trade, business-to-business and business-to-consumer transactions take place online by the millions, and it is clear that unless an effective online presence is part of your business model, you are at risk of losing not only revenue but also the opportunity for branding and being considered an equal among your peers and competitors. It is a well-known fact that businesses go to the Web to find suppliers before taking any other action.

Irrespective of the quality of your product or service, not having a useful Web site sends the message that you are not really in the game. Furthermore, your Web presence needs to be fashioned in such a way that it is informative and intuitive enough as to have a "selling" function.

Every company wants to do things right the first time, do them now, and do them better than the competition. When it comes to what defines success, most will attest that it has everything to do with execution. One recognized measure of good execution is a company's Web site demonstrating its ability to bring products and/or services to market more efficiently than its competition. The scale of the launch is not the measure of success.

With today's technology, it is much easier than it was a few years ago to launch just about anything on a grand scale. The Internet has made it cost-effective to reach and communicate to a global audience when relaunching and repositioning a company's image, introducing new brands and logos, or providing an innovative software release. Still, even with this access and potential coverage, any business message needs to expose the costs and benefits while capturing a moment of competitive glory against those of a shorter-term business goal.

Where Branding Fits In

The *2007 Brand Marketers Report*, based on Interbrand's Annual Survey on Brand and Branding,[3] ranked the top 10 aspects of successful branding as seen by 299 respondents who were responsible or made decisions for their company's brand. The results are revealing and are useful for understanding how important the message is for success. The most critical aspect of successful branding was *consistency*. It was by far the leader over all the other areas, with more than a third of the respondents mentioning it. The other areas, in order of importance, included *understand the customer, the message and communication, creative design, relevance,* and *differentiation or uniqueness.*

The least critical factors, starting from the bottom, were *advertising, marketing, people, public relations*, and *delivering on promise*. It may surprise you that advertising, marketing, and public relations are ranked the lowest when it comes to branding. (The reference to people had to do with the people working for the company.) Clearly, the message you create, adhere to, and send will create brand equity. Brand management is important; however, there is often too much emphasis on exposure and awareness related to the image rather than on building the brand by supporting the value it represents. This process starts with the communication of evidence to your customers and prospects.

CHAPTER 5

GETTING TO BIG THE SMALL WAY

Small opportunities are often the beginning of great enterprises.

—Demosthenes, 384 B.C.

In earlier chapters, we touched on the ability to make small incremental improvements and how these improvements can ripple across the organization and lead to significant changes over time, especially when taken in the aggregate. This is an empowering process for most employees, who often feel hamstrung by the bureaucracy, especially if the company policies and procedures that they must adhere to are outdated. There is no question that there are legal reasons why certain in-house rules are necessary in conducting any business, but in this chapter we will not be dealing with company policies that management has laid down to ensure integrity and standards. Iinstead, we will be dealing with the processes that are directly related to increasing revenues and profits and the effectiveness of those processes.

In every business, there are certain processes that are there for the purpose of performing tasks that enhance or increase the company's ability to grow. These processes have been handed down by management to possibly generations of employees, and the current employees continue to carry out the same activities even though those activities are fragmented and broken. As a result, a lot of the employees' time is taken up with temporarily repairing disjointed sequences in order to get their jobs done.

To be more specific, the problem involves the way transactions related to the service that is provided to customers and business partners are handled within the company. Together, these activities represent the overall experience that customers and partners receive in the course of doing business. The way a sales order is processed is an example of the many conditions that need to be met and challenges faced internally before the company can come close to providing any level of customer satisfaction. People in every related function within the organization, from the front to the back office, seem to face challenges when it comes to doing their everyday jobs in a streamlined manner, let alone in an efficient one. If we take a hard look at the barriers to growth, there are only a handful of areas involved, and the internal workings and flow of business within a company is one of them.

The Structure of Growth

As organizations grow and develop, their internal complexities grow as well, and what were once simple processes often require variations. This increased complexity may occur in any area, from processing customer orders to following accounting procedures. Companies deal with the larger array of possibilities by introducing additional layers of control, and with those layers comes the need to supervise their compliance. This, of course, means more middle managers. Over time, the number of middle managers often increases out of proportion to the need for them, and before you know it, it's time to "clean out the attic," with rightsizing strategies and RIFs (reductions in force) taking place.

The issue with regard to growth is not about eliminating processes and protocols, but about the effectiveness and efficiencies of those policies and protocols. The organizational structure you support today is a reflection of the processes that you harbor, and, in some cases, protect. It is entirely possible that the way you handle transactions within your back office today is stunting your growth, or that functions that were put in place years ago have become redundant.

The issue regarding inefficiency is that things do not become better by themselves; if your company is geographically dispersed, inefficiency spreads infectiously across the locations, taking on a culture all its own. I once visited the branch office of a large textile company based in Austin, Texas, where the logistics manager indicated that it took two days to get the inventory count input into the system after the count was complete. He admitted that it could easily be done the same day (leading to a cost saving, as larger reorder quantities could attract better discounts, and potentially affecting customer back orders), but as the head office was so slow at getting back to him on important issues, he concluded that this was "just the pace of the company." He never received a complaint about his tardiness or a bad performance review in the seven years he was there.

Companies experiencing growth realize that it is the quality of interactions between and across the layers of the organizational structure that plays the most important role, irrespective of the size of your company. Management consultants and business scholars agree that it is not the structure per se that is important. The good news is that it doesn't matter whether your organizational structure is built around product owners, business units, or territories. The issue with any structure is the ease with which business is conducted and whether the model allows the company to scale bigger.

Having made that statement, it is entirely possible that there are layers of bureaucracy that originated because of the need to manage processes that were unnecessarily complex. This is not to imply that reducing staff is a quick and easy way to get big; rarely, if ever, will a reduction in staff accelerate a company's drive to become bigger. Growing big, therefore, is not just a function of how well you are structured to allow for growth, but of how the business runs within the framework you have.

The action that has the largest impact on becoming big is breaking down the walls within the structure you have and introducing a culture of access, knowledge sharing, and communication. Frank Diassi, chairman and CEO of UnicornHRO, a leading payroll and human resource services provider based in New Jersey, advocates, "You can never overcommunicate." This is only one of several actions that are required if you are to break down the barriers to growth. Knowledge and content need to flow actively through the organization, with access by employees and business partners made easily attainable. The only caveat is that proper security controls must be applied where applicable. This goes beyond the corporate newsletter.

In the next section of this chapter, we will look further at processes; however, when dealing with structure, the two are interrelated, and what is relevant here is that the processes within the veins of the operation need to respond to the information being sent and distributed. For example, if you are truly going to become a bigger organization, then information and knowledge need to flow quickly throughout the organization, *and* the receivers at every level must know instinctively what they should do with the information or knowledge that they receive. *This is at the heart of what thinking small and the small way attempt to accomplish*. A process to openly share knowledge has the ability to remove any blockage and allow the flow of transactions, information, data, and instructions to everyone in the company. Once the information is received in whatever form it comes in, it should trigger a signal for action by the appropriate people.

You may be thinking that this is about sending a lot of e-mails to everyone and having everyone pick up on what he or she should do next. It's not just e-mails. E-mails are relevant, but they are low on the effective communication food chain; their place is at the very tactical and basic information level. A great deal of what goes on in a growing company is strategic and requires a different set of activities—for example, localizations for pricing, translations, market readiness, sales training, legal and accounting adaptations for compliance, and so on.

This goes beyond effective internal communications or quality standards and initiatives for continuous improvement such as Six Sigma, Total Quality Management (TQM), or Kaizen. Open access and shared knowledge create a downward flow of strategy, ideas, outcomes, and results to all corners of the organization, along with the resulting upward feedback, making any or all initiatives work more effectively. Thinking small or the small way therefore complements those quality instruments and is all-encompassing. When Six Sigma is done in isolation, for example, within a common group connected by a product line or geographic territory, the excellence awards handed to this group from a companywide perspective are irrelevant unless the rest of the company receives some direct benefit from the work.

In a more simplistic way, thinking small involves breaking down the silos between departments and organizations, allowing individuals to behave freely to perform their specific tasks with full knowledge of how and where they fit into the bigger picture and the extent to which their roles are dependent upon others. In fact, even if someone's instruction to perform an activity (for example, to execute a marketing campaign) is exclusive to that person's domain, the fact that it is fully visible to others in itself plays an important role. Too often, individuals are blamed for not sharing and communicating initiatives directed by the head office with others, resulting in their feeling ashamed and inadequate even if their unit of work was executed to perfection. The fact is that unless the entire organization has an inbuilt culture of making communication available in the first place, any e-mails sent by a small group of employees will be futile and short-lived.

Thinking small, therefore, is enabling people at every level of the structure to understand that their small part not only is important but also is a link to the business's success. The question is, how do you arrive at this, and how does thinking in terms of small incremental improvements get you closer to developing the company to be as big as it can be? We need to get small and think of the units of work that occur along the lines and across the links of the structure. Big companies have taken the time to address the internal fragmentation starting in three broad areas and then drilling deeper into those areas—specifically, where processes connect with customers, partners, and employees. Representing the company as three related and active components makes it easier to identify where thinking small does its part for improvement. These three areas can be summarized as follows:

- The corporate structure, representing the operational flow and how everyone interacts with everyone else
- The performance of the company, representing how everyone interacts with the customers
- The strategy, representing how the resources and skills are deployed for growth

The Customer's Experience Starts Here

The major impact of internal fragmentation is that it has an adverse effect on your customer's experience. The quality of the customer's experience can be traced back to the seamlessness of the internal processes in the back office and the systems supporting them. For example, take customer hotline support services. After listening to the menu options and making a guess as to which one best fits your inquiry, you have most likely already been asked to give up personal and account information to verify your identity. When you finally make contact with a human, it is likely that you will need to be transferred to a different department, at which point you will again need to input your details and most likely retell your story. This can occur multiple times on the same phone call. If you are wondering why, it is because the organization has fragmented, disconnected systems.

Another example involves direct mail. How often have you received the same promotional piece from the same company multiple times—perhaps, worse still, with your name spelled incorrectly on each item? The waste created by duplication and inaccuracy is obvious; however, the opinion of the company that the recipients are forming is even more costly. In many cases, employees at their jobs have the best vantage point for offering suggestions and ideas that can improve processes and make life easier for all. There are three basic aims of process improvement:

to be more efficient, to be more accurate, and to be easier to do business with. The last is the most important. The notion of being business friendly is important to your business partners and suppliers as well.

Information Is More Important Than Integration

Another side effect of fragmented business processes and the computer systems that support them is that consolidated and companywide information is difficult to come by, especially when historical data are involved. Over 60 percent of most technology budgets for business systems is allocated to keeping the systems "glued" together. CIOs have the daily challenge of ensuring that all applications are somehow updating each other with relevant transactions and then keeping the data in a database that can be used for reporting purposes on a companywide basis. Company leaders need information at the macro and micro levels to determine the status of the business in order to make good decisions. It is difficult to know what direction the company should be taking if the data are coming from different places and a snapshot of each department or location is the best that is available.

The cure is an alignment of the business functions; this is a critical step in obtaining good-quality data about the business. Unless there is companywide visibility, especially in terms of being able to cite developing trends that indicate where the growth is coming from, it is difficult to determine the direction of any future investments that are needed in order to grow bigger. Volumes have been written on the dangers of using piecemeal information and of relying on past experience when making strategic decisions. The irony is that while managers are spending more and more money on business applications and maintenance, which largely mirror fragmented internal processes, in return they are getting a lower quality of information to use to do their jobs. Under the forceful hand of higher regulation and control regarding corporate governance and compliance, the need for better information has reached urgent status on any to-do list.

Become Easy to Do Business With

There are several positive by-products of taking on a mission to simplify the inner workings of the business. Simplifying is included as a think-small strategy because a great deal of what can be done starts with minor alterations, the proper solution is generally obvious to the employee involved, and the results usually have a bigger than expected positive result. A culture of incremental improvement with the objective of simplifying is sufficient to uncover inefficiencies in any organization that otherwise would never have been thought of.

Another benefit of simplification is that it has a definite ripple effect across other parts of the company, extending outward to customers and partners. Look at any customer satisfaction survey and you'll probably find that at least half of the reasons customers are disgruntled involve a lack of timely access to the right person, the right information, or the right product. If you disassociate yourself from the analysis for a moment, you will be left scratching your head and wondering how getting company or product information can possibly be a problem when there is so much of it out there. This will coincide with wondering why people aren't returning customers' calls quickly enough, and how we can be shipping the wrong products given our new computerized system.

The common issues that you will find are the result of inbuilt complexity. Complications creep into the systems: Web site navigation, call tracking disciplines, escalation procedures, procurement and payment processes, overall approval processes, and so on. Your internal business processes, therefore, affect your image in the outside world. This is an inescapable relationship that you cannot mask even with a Web site as your storefront. Customers will at some point come into contact, directly or indirectly, with the inner operations of the company. This will happen either before, during, or after the sale. Therefore, the impact of streamlined processes on growth cannot be underestimated. The critical areas that can retard growth are scalability, partner relationships, and customer satisfaction. There is an impact on employees, too, and although we will deal with employees to some extent here, they deserve to be treated as a separate topic.

Scaling Small to Big

When you are looking for *small ways* to become big, a good starting point is to address the business's ability to scale. I have been in companies that have experienced growth spurts and found that they could not handle the incoming business effectively because they could not scale fast enough. The short-term cure is to add more staff; however, much to the surprise of management, the additional staff does not seem to move the business any more easily—in fact, it may exacerbate the problems. The reason this happens is primarily because the internal systems are already stressed to capacity and are subject to overload when more people try to use them.

When resources are added before adequate systems are in place, it leads to a new set of problems, mainly involving users attempting to bypass policies and procedures just to get the business done. I have even seen situations where layers of approval processes are put in place specifically to deal with the circumventions that have occurred. This attempt to plug loopholes increases paperwork, and therefore delays, and therefore bureaucracy, and presto—there is more complexity. A telltale sign that this cycle is getting out of hand is that the answer to any problem is, "We need a process to handle this." The reality is that rarely do you need a new process. If you have been in the same business selling to the same group of customers for years, then the issue is more about loosening up the system and allowing some flexibility than it is about tightening up and attempting to control every variable that comes along. What is often needed, therefore, is quite the reverse of adding a new process: parts of processes should actually be eliminated or simple repairs made, either as one change or as incremental improvements over time.

A wholesaler of paper and packaging products once told me that it had a paper trail on file for every purchase it made. Not for every supplier—for every purchase. The reason was that because of the number of inquiries the company received from its suppliers regarding payment, shipments, back orders, and so on, the only efficient way to operate was to keep track of every transaction. This procedure had evolved over time; it had started with purchases from the major suppliers, but it had gradually been extended to everyone and every purchase, no matter how big or small. The transactions were filed in purchase order (PO) number sequence; this was done because suppliers needed to have the PO number available to follow up on the inquiry.

These purchase orders were kept in the main office until the goods were received and paid for. A supervisor would go through all of the files weekly, selecting those to be archived in alphabetical order at the company's document archive storage facility; they were then sent to a data entry service that would key the data into a separate inventory system and scan the related documents for future retrieval purposes. The time from receipt of goods to their placement in inventory could be as long as 10 days, and customer service calls would often be routed to the purchasing department to determine when the stock would be available (assuming that the documentation was not en route to the archiving service, in which case purchasing would have to get back to the customer). Imagine what would have happened if the business this company did had doubled in a quarter.

Clearly the right computer system will solve a lot of the issues related to this problem; however, this extreme case makes the point that complexity is compounded when more processes are added to fix an already inefficient process that *appeared* manageable when it was originally implemented. In this case, the root cause of the problem turned out to be that the PO numbers were too long for the company's computer system, so the comments field was being used to store the longer PO number, and this did not permit an easy search or retrieval capability. It was suggested that simply adding an alpha prefix to the PO number on the printed forms would make the number of possible combinations exponentially greater so that the company could use a more efficient field. (This suggestion had been made by a purchasing clerk but had been ignored.)

The fact is that managing complexity requires a lot of time. In this case, the convoluted process had an adverse effect on supplier relationships and on customers who could have gotten their orders earlier had the stock number reflected more accurately what was actually in the warehouse. This example highlights the fact that you need to fix the small things in order to make the big things happen. By the laws of attraction, small impediments will attract more issues; the resulting temporary repairs will usually create a new set of small issues, and so on. The cycle needs to be stopped and reversed so that any change leads to excellence, rather than being merely better. Better is better, but it's not good enough for bigger. In the majority of cases, those companies that experienced the highest growth did not rely on large opportunistic deals to bump them to another level. They did it by sustainable growth strategies that, in turn, attracted large deals. How, then, do we find the areas where small incremental changes can have the biggest impact on the ability of the company's processes to scale and allow for the sharing of knowledge and the transfer of communications and ideas throughout the company?

Small Ways to More Sales

Complexity can arise almost anywhere within the operations of a company, and there are ways to simplify the units of work within a process by using small changes; however, you need to start somewhere, and if you are looking to grow bigger and increase your profitability, you need to focus on increasing demand, generating revenues, and doing these things as profitably as possible. We are therefore centering our attention on the marketing and sales functions, as it is here that the smallest changes with the largest impact can be made.

The role of marketing has matured over the last 10 years; it has become a change management agent for companies that want to make directional changes or to implement new cultures. The *small way* introduces techniques and offers tools that can be used within your company in a variety of ways and that are easily adaptable to whatever industry you are part of. These techniques also apply to companies of any size and can be expanded over time or as resources permit. Along the lines that we have discussed already, the marketing and sales departments operate within an organizational structure in which transactions are created and moved from the different functional areas.

It is along the *lines* in which activities are performed that the small but significant changes make the difference. Take, for example, the handover of leads generated by marketing to sales or reseller partners. There is continued debate over what constitutes a "lead." If sales and marketing are one department in your organization, then the issues will be related to the quality of leads. If they are separate departments, one responsible for generating sales leads and the other for executing them, it is highly probable that the definition of a lead will differ between the two. An agreement on exactly what is a qualified lead needs to be established. Marketing departments often will argue that it is not their job to process leads—just to create them (the "bums on seats" syndrome, as it is sometimes called). As long as they get the predicted number of people to attend the event and get those people's names and telephone numbers, marketers consider that they have done their job. Sales, on the other hand, will protest that the salespeople may be wasting their valuable time chasing people who are just kicking the tires or are not thinking of buying for a long period of time. Therein is the crux of the issue.

Another factor that contributes to increasing revenues is the way leads are transmitted. This issue has two parts; one is whether leads *ever* reach the sales department, and the other is the timeliness of those leads if they *do* reach it. In other words, if the details taken from prospects attending a marketing event were in fact recorded, do they ever reach sales and, if so, when? The reality is that if a prospect attends an event because he or she is attracted by and interested in the content, unless a follow-up is done soon after, you should consider that "lead" stale or gone unless the prospect has called you.

This problem is a big one when you consider the number of marketing events that may take place and the aggregate investment that goes into making these events successful, especially given the noise and haste that marketing needs to compete with. The solution can be found within the innards of the business flow that takes place between the moment a campaign is activated and the time the leads are passed on, and, in fact, all the way to the time the customer signs or buys from you. We will look at the complete cycle.

There are two types of marketing, strategic and tactical. While this is an overly simplistic view, for our purposes we will isolate the two types and define them as follows: strategic marketing is where trends, market analysis, and research are done to formulate a marketing strategy; this strategy is eventually handed over to the tactical marketing groups, which will design and execute a plan. Each of these functions involves a flow of activities that may be one and the same or, depending on the size and needs of a company, may be performed by different groups within the overall marketing department. In any event, what is constant is that a planning process kicks off an execution process. To keep this simple and add clarity, we will follow the path of a typical campaign and identify the specific areas where small changes can be made along the way to produce better results.

When a campaign is being designed, there are several elements that need to be taken into account. The objective of the campaign should always be to generate more revenue. If the objective is anything other than that, then what you have is not a campaign but a program, the distinction being that one is a component of the other. Launching a new logo or brand is a program, not a campaign. After you launch the logo, you will want to make money from that program, so you will need to carry out a campaign. Campaigns are specific in nature, are targeted, and have measurable results. The acceptance of a new logo or brand is very difficult to measure until there are signs of increased revenues. Both campaigns and programs are important and both are needed; however, we will focus on the events that are intended to produce revenue in the short to medium term and that can have an immediate effect.

In the development of the campaign, the first small and meaningful change is for marketing to brief sales *before* the campaign is fully developed. I know that there are marketers who flinch at the idea of presenting any unfinished work to a group, especially a group of salespeople, as this leaves them open to criticism and rejection. However, one of the key issues in integrating the sales and marketing functions more closely is communicating early. Marketing should brief sales as soon as the concepts are pulled together and the design has passed the drawing board stages, but while it is still in a preproduction and execution mode. This is marketing to sales. There are two important aspects to this communication: it needs to be done live, and it needs to be prepared.

This is an important step, and it is useful for a number of reasons. One of the biggest problems in maximizing the return on marketing investment is that sales does not get on board with what marketing is doing. This problem arises because information on marketing's tactical activities is not communicated early. For a lot of companies, the norm is that sales finds out about marketing activities when it is too late for sales to adequately take full advantage of them. When prior notice has been given but sales has not been involved in some way in the creation of the marketing activities, the response is usually skepticism concerning the validity and purpose of the marketing activities and their usefulness to sales in terms of generating leads. The fact is that a marketing campaign in and of itself may be a masterpiece; however, without sales, it will produce little more than a venue for providing company information to the outside world.

The way in which marketing presents the campaign to sales is also important. It needs to be done with passion and excitement, and it needs to link the overall objectives to the numbers. Reference to the overall company objectives is valid, but the emphasis needs to be on how this campaign and the associated activities will assist each of the salespeople in making his or her quota. The campaign outline should include fresh new content, and any messages and positioning (what we learned from the previous chapters) need to be part of this communication. Samples of new materials can be handed out as a reference for the salespeople to look over and to serve as a good reminder. Present as much of the detail as possible, including event dates, venues, speakers, and so on, and include what the salespeople's participation needs to be. Ironically, some of the best prospects that attend marketing events come from sales.

Another small but important change that can be implemented in the design of the marketing campaign is to provide a quota of leads for sales to invite directly. In order for this to be successful, given the limited time that sales should spend or want to spend on developing any content or collateral, especially invitations to marketing events, the campaign materials should include blank invitation letters or cards that salespeople can easily use to send personalized invitations to marketing events. The design elements for the invitation will thus be aligned with the theme or message of the event and will provide a look and feel consistent with the other materials that the prospects will be exposed to.

In later chapters, we will look in more detail at a format for specific components of this communication, but as part of the planning process, marketing should allocate time and effort to exposing the intended campaigns to the sales organization and producing a calendar of events with a view toward soliciting feedback and making any finer adjustments that will ensure the sales organization's buy-in and therefore cooperation. The follow-on effect of this preliminary work is that sales now *expects* the leads that are generated by the campaign, and this expectation topples many barriers to their acceptance.

Visibility to future campaigns is a small addition relative to the larger investment that goes into marketing and is a proven technique that will increase responsiveness and return more revenues per event. The briefing may take place in one or multiple locations, depending on the size of the company and whether the sales organization is dispersed or centralized. Telesales and telemarketing are being introduced into campaigns, performing a lead qualification function, and therefore they need to be included as part of the sales briefings as well. Successful telemarketing services companies will attribute their success rates to the quality of the briefing they received from their clients' marketing departments.

There are challenges in doing this type of briefing in an effective manner if this is a new concept for your company. Getting the attention of salespeople is difficult in the best of times, and asking them to attend and listen to a marketing presentation is harder still. Thoughtful planning is in order, and holding the briefing at a time when their attention will be at a maximum will pay off in the long run. Quarter- and month-end periods, conferences, and other clashing events should be avoided; however, there are times when marketing can get a good hearing. Regular sales meetings, internal sales kickoff seminars, and sales achievement venues and events are just some situations where you can capture the undivided attention of your sales group.

The Extended Family: Partners

The same goes for business and channel partners who resell or distribute your products and services. Depending on the number of partners you have and how they are geographically dispersed, face-to-face or live online media can be used to perform the same type of briefing. The go-to-market aspects and elements will need to be adapted to this audience, but many areas of the campaign should remain the same—for example, the message and positioning, agenda format, and event content. Although logistics, lead distribution, and access may be different from those for the internal sales organization, the objective of the briefing is to provide an opportunity for partners to prepare in advance for the campaign, to contribute to the invitation lists and have those invitations personalized, and to provide feedback based on their on-the-ground experience of what customers are looking for at the detail levels.

The more preplanned campaigns your partners are aware of, the better. A marketing calendar is an invaluable tool that you should distribute to all sales and channel partners in confidence, and you should update it regularly. One way is to allocate an area of your

Web site that sales and partners can access in order to obtain the latest information from marketing, including an updated calendar of events. Setting this up is a small task, but it is of enormous benefit to everyone in the sales and marketing ecosystem. There are excellent examples of Web-enabled resources for partners. IBM, HP, Cisco, Oracle, and SAP are some of the industry leaders when it comes to using an online Web service to provide resources for their partners.

The next area where small and useful changes or additions can be made involves the transmission, processing, and maturing of leads. A useful philosophy regarding leads is that anyone who has had even minimal contact with your company is, in fact, a potential deal and therefore a lead. Some of these people may not be "ready" for the sales department, but marketing should look at those who took the time to make contact, either online or in person at an event, as being a deal in the future.

As we touched on earlier, one of the most contentious issues between sales and marketing is this question of leads—specifically, when is a lead qualified enough for sales to consider it worthy of follow-up. The tension is valid when you take either point of view. Marketing will argue that part of its role is to attract interest in the company and its products and services, and it will measure its success by the fact that an action has taken place as a consequence of its efforts. Salespeople will reply that they have a limited amount of time in which to make their quotas, and therefore they need to ensure that they focus their activities on prospects and customers that are ready to buy in the short term.

Ironically, both marketing and sales are playing a numbers game. The underlying idea adhered to by both marketing and sales departments is that more is more. Marketing departments rely on mathematical probabilities, assuming that the greater the number of people that come to an event, the higher the probability that these will include interested parties. The arithmetic is correct, but these are not the numbers that salespeople are paid for. They want more with less—more leads with less time required to close them.

In order to highlight potential small improvements in these areas, we need to tackle each of them individually. First, let's look at the timely transmission of leads from any event that a prospect has attended to sales. In general terms, if a prospect who attended an event has not been contacted within five business days after the event (and the sooner the better), that person's interest (if he or she had one) has faded or gone, and this has become what is known as a "stale lead." If this happens, you will find that when and if the prospect is contacted, too much time will need to be spent on refreshing the prospect's memory of the event rather than on communicating your key messages and selling points.

Therefore, it is imperative that some form of contact be made within that five-day window, and this contact needs to be more than a thank-you e-mail, letter, or postcard. The contact needs to be person to person. We have established that salespeople are rightly not interested in talking to anyone who is not qualified; therefore, this follow-up activity falls into the domain of marketing. Telesales is a useful tool to use in this case, and we come back to the reason why, of all sales-related parties, a precampaign briefing is the most essential: unless the attendee has checked the box on the feedback form (which I recommend be made available at every marketing event) with "I am ready to buy today," marketing needs to initiate a follow-up call to determine the person's level of interest. During this call, a qualification process can be performed without being intrusive.

So far, this is fairly standard marketing practice, but there is still a small change that can make all the difference. Instead of asking the prospect if he or she is thinking of buying in the short term (a question that prospects hate to be asked and one that is used as the key indicator for lead qualification), ask whether the prospect wants to receive information about the value and benefits that other customers who have purchased the product or service have received, and whether the prospect wants this communicated via e-mail or through some other method of follow-up. This works best if the customers whose information you send to the prospect are in the same industry category.

Looking back at Chapter 4, this is one of the reasons that having customers who are willing to provide testimonials concerning the value they received and noting the industry they are in are important in maturing leads. It is up to you whether you add this question to the telemarketing script or replace it with the "When are you planning to buy?" question. The problem with the "When are you planning to buy?" question is that prospects often do not know for sure when they are planning to buy. There will be a few who are actually shopping, and for decades this one question has been the criterion for certifying that a lead is qualified. However, in most cases where a prospect is followed up solely because of the timetable to purchase, you will be late in the game and will be entering somewhere in the middle of an active competitive sales cycle. Any seasoned salesperson will agree that it is better to come in early in the sales process and in the buying cycle than in the middle or, especially, toward the end. The intermediate step of sending customer information *is* a sales call. If telesales is not part of the campaign's activities, another way to achieve the same result is to have a feedback form that prospects can fill out.

This simple change will increase exponentially the "hit" rate of converting leads to prospects and prospects to deals. You may find that you are running out of things to send, and you need to ensure that the material you do send is fresh and current. Giving a prospect something before you ask for something increases the chances that you will develop a relationship. An online tactic that is widely used is the promise of a white paper, article, or book in return for giving all contact details and answering a few questions. This is becoming a standard practice (if you Google on "white paper," you will get over 207 million sites that offer a downloadable document of products, services, or expertise), however, as some people have received poor-quality content, this technique is not working as well as it did when it was first used. A small variation is to offer not just flat content but "alerts" when interesting information comes along. An e-mail address and contact details are required in order to send alerts. This technique is becoming increasingly accepted and is more effective in gaining a response than is baiting with a downloadable offer.

Back to lead transmission. Once you have prospects who have agreed to receive information, be sure to send it to them and, if possible, in a personalized way. This has unobtrusively changed the lead to an interested prospect, and with the lead's approval. The *level* of interest is still to be determined; however, the urgency of timing is less because you have made contact and the prospect will be receiving materials from you. In reality, you have made two sales calls. The big advantage of this small interception is that by passing these types of leads to sales, marketing has created an environment in which the customer is expecting a call.

The main thing to note is that when passing lead information to sales, it is important that sales keep a record of what has been sent to the customer so that when the salesperson places the call he or she has the most up-to-date information. I have seen increases of as much as 200 percent in leads converted to prospects by using this simple technique. If you are in an industry where customer information is not available or for legal or other reasons cannot be obtained, then offer industry information that you know will interest prospects. The other refinement of offering information in this way is to tailor the information to the role the prospect plays in his or her organization. These small nuances of specificity create a personalized touch that makes all the difference to the leads-to-prospects ratio.

Leads Never Die—They Become New Opportunities

There are plenty of other small ideas that can come out of this process. What generally happens is that small thinking kicks in and incremental improvements continue to provide creative ideas for offering customers many other forms of value before they are given the hard sell. By introducing this step, what you are starting to create is a closed-loop marketing process. This is often confused with sending prospects information and e-mails while monitoring their reactions. In *closed-loop marketing*, customers' specific requests are monitored, and content is changed based on those requests. In other words, when a customer is interested in a product category, you ask a question at the next specific level of detail, then the next and the next, and so on. For example, when a prospect is interested in buying a software package and is looking at manufacturing systems (as a category), you would ask that prospect whether he or she would like more information regarding manufacturing systems for a specific industry. If the answer is food and beverage, then you send information regarding process manufacturing. Next, you offer information about customers who use that same system, but this time you ask if there are any specific areas of process manufacturing that they is interested in, where the choices are supply chain management, production scheduling, and so on. The purpose of this is to maintain a dialogue of offer and ask, in that order.

When you use this method, some prospects will move toward being qualified leads faster than others; however, the process will ensure that prospects develop a relationship with your company in a nonconfrontational manner. When the time is right, there will be strong indicators that the prospect will take a sales call. Remember, big companies are very selective about selling to customers who want to buy. It is possible that you may need to "feed" information to a prospect (in accordance with that prospect's request for specific personalized information) for long periods of time. What this tells you is that if this prospect had been passed to sales as a lead, it would have been a waste of time.

The ideal scenario, and something to build up to incrementally, is to keep a database of all the touch points that the customer has with your company and the information that is sent. If you do not have a customer relationship management system or marketing system that allows customer interactions to be tracked, then I recommend that you get one or get access to one; this is a worthwhile investment. In the interim, with modern development tools it is a small task to create a database that will hold this valuable information for your company.

The Web Storefront

The importance of your Web site cannot be overstated. Statistically, it ranks as one of the top five places that professionals go to identify potential vendors for most categories of products and services (commercial and domestic). There are millions of online sites that provide services to assist in the evaluation process and that cater to different types of buyers. Several of these sites offer search criteria to help narrow the choice of vendors; others have conducted evaluations on behalf of buyers and may post their findings, with a prepared report on a selection of vendors being made available for a fee. Most of these sites have links back to their companies' Web sites. While it sounds like a cliché, your Web site represents your storefront, and it makes an impression. Regardless of the size of your company, if it is to become bigger, your Web site needs to expose certain characteristics of your company, and you have about six seconds to do it in (the average time visitors take to decide whether to stay or leave a Web site). Before we look at small things that will make a difference, we need to cover some of the basics to ensure a positive initial experience.

Fast and Clean

It is essential that the site be fast. Pages that load slowly are unacceptable in today's broadband world, and they leave the impression that you are lagging in terms of technology. Whether you provide services in technology-oriented markets or not, a slow site means fast exits by visitors. Rarely if ever will they return for a second attempt. Web designers will be able to optimize your Web site to ensure that it loads quickly.

Looking at cluttered Web pages with lots of scattered pieces of information that serve many different purposes may seem like entering a flea market: there is a lot to see and do, but no logic to the layout. Think of the way supermarkets and department stores are designed and organized. The site needs to provide the same experience. Clean is about layout and content categorization and information indexing. Multimedia with videos and flash screens makes a good impression. A word of caution: if the site is slowed by having multimedia, reconsider its use. It is better to have a fast response than a sophisticated site that customers may never see because they hit the back button and move on.

Look and Feel

This is about consistency and navigation. Consistency means that all the pages are organized in a similar way so that the visitor can become intuitive very quickly. High-quality resolution for pictures, especially for company logos, signage, and taglines, is essential and should be the same throughout the site.

Navigation of the site is one of the most important areas to consider, as this is where things can get confusing even for the seasoned Web surfer. Where the visitor is and where he or she has been at any time while clicking deeper into the site needs to be clear. The content needs to be logical and carefully sequenced. The site needs to be experiential, with plenty of opportunity for the visitor to do something when he or she arrives at the next page.

Information and Access

Consider the six-second response time when developing information. Avoid the habit of reproducing your brochure online. The Web is a selling tool; therefore, the information needs to articulate the benefits to the customer in clear, short sentences and provide the visitor with the opportunity to drill down for more information. Access involves providing areas of the Web site that are exclusive for a particular community of users. For example, you could provide an area for customers, business partners, resellers, distributors, and agents, where they need to log in to access their unique materials and content.

There are small additions that can improve the visitor's experience and increase the likelihood that he or she will become a contact and eventually a sales lead. Consider the following.

Customers First

The home page can make a better first impression if it has some of your customers speaking about your products and services. This can be challenging, but it gives your customers free advertising and tells your story with greater credibility up front. It also increases the chances that the visitor will drill deeper to find out more at the product level.

Action Items

Every page should provide an opportunity for the visitor to take another action. Such opportunities are in addition to the index and tabs on the page; they need to provide a way for the customer to access you. You should give visitors the ability to call you or open a chat session on *every* page and always on the same part of the page. I am amazed at the number of Web sites that force visitors to search the site to find out how to contact the company. The "Contact Us" tab does not work effectively because it takes the user out of the current page (where the thought originated) to a different area of the site. Capture the inclination to make contact at every page.

Resource Site

Apart from the standard company and product information, add content relating to the industry you are servicing. Providing the latest news, current legal information, research information, thought leadership materials, industry news, and other such material encourages the visitor to bookmark your site and return to it in the future.

Online Support

If you have a product or service with a warranty period or a maintenance or support agreement, then providing an online support resource will be beneficial to your customers as well as a huge savings in support and repair costs. A support system can be as sophisticated or as simple as you care to make it; either way, it will save you time and money. Many support calls are directly related to customers' knowledge of how the product is used or the scope of services. A small percentage of calls deals specifically with either product failures or fixes. Therefore something as simple as a "frequently asked questions" (FAQ) section on the site, with the answers to questions that are commonly asked held in a database and made available through a simple search engine, is a good start. Building on this, and using the small incremental improvement philosophy, the support site can provide downloads of fixes, user manuals, and even online training.

Partner Resources

An excellent way to update business partners and provide them with resources for sales and marketing is to allow them access to the main site. There is no need to have a separate Web site for customers and another for partners. Allocate specific pages on the Web site where partners can access all the latest company information, sales and marketing materials, and contact names of relevant employees, and where they can tap into your supplier network if appropriate. Another way to add value for partners is to provide functionality for networking, where partners can contact each other and communicate, much as they would if they were hosting a blog. Partners can register their companies and provide brief details of their expertise, services, and support.

Online Store

A service that is often overlooked and that has many benefits for your customers and for you is selling over the Web. The Web is a very cheap salesperson. If you sell a complex product or service that requires a formal measure and quote or analysis and consultation before it can be purchased, then having an online store where people can buy your core products and services directly is not appropriate. However, as most of the profits from products and services come from accessories and add-ons, you can have an online store where existing customers can obtain these things. It will be ideal to have a customer login process to identify what products the customer has and suggest possible add-ons or compatible accessories that can be purchased. These are usually high-volume, low-margin items and not what you want your expensive salespeople to be focused on.

Personalized Views

Personalizing Web sites for individuals was once an involved and complex process; however, with the modern tools available today, that is no longer the case. With a simple login request, usually an e-mail address and a nominated password, sites can provide specific content tailored for the visitor. This goes beyond just having the visitor's name on the first line of the Web page. Pages of content can be built dynamically based on the visitor's requests. The good news is that recent research regarding what constitutes personalization of an online medium has found that less than 20 percent of the total site needs to have tailored content for visitors to feel that the site has been personalized for their needs.

SMALL WAYS TO GAIN COMPETITIVE ADVANTAGE

The competitor to be feared is the one who never bothers about you at all, but goes in making his own business better all the time.

—Henry Ford (1863–1947)

Anableps are extraordinary fish. They are known for having four eyes. They do not actually have four eyes, but each of the two eyes they do have is divided to allow the fish to see both above and below the waterline. Each half of the eye has a separate pupil, iris, and cornea, and, amazingly, the lenses correct for the different behavior of light when the fish is looking at objects in the air and in water, with the underwater lens being more strongly curved. The underwater half of the eye projects an image to the upper half of the retina, while the part of the eye that is above water projects to the lower retina. This gives the anableps the ability to be alert to predators from below and seek out food from above at the same time. This chapter deals with how to remain focused on your business and on finding and dealing with your real competitors much as the anableps do: by keeping an eye on both.

The word *competition* conjures up a wide variety of definitions. The language that people use reflects their perception of what competition represents for them as individuals. Common themes are being at war, playing a game that needs to be won, or needing to be successful in order to survive. These are all motivating concepts; however, the danger with these sentiments is that devoting our attention to the competition can be so seductive that we steer the business based on competitive response, and this can take away our focus on our own success. As Edward de Bono, the pioneer of lateral thinking, puts it, "The paradox is that you cannot truly be competitive if you seek to be competitive."[1]

If we come back to economic basics, competition is allowed to exist in order to benefit consumers and provide a regulated environment in which everyone has a fair and equal opportunity to trade. Government regulators see competition as both necessary and positive for trade and the economy. Business leaders facing competitive pressures see it from a contradictory point of view. In their view, there is always too much competition and too many government restrictions, and these generally have an adverse effect on their business. This self-centered view is understandable, as the less competition there is, the easier it is for organizations to increase their own business, but this can harden into an attitude that competitors are "taking away our business." The net effect becomes an overintensified focus on competitors. The modern interpretation of *The Art of War* by Sun Tzu[2] reminds us that the best way to compete is not to compete, but to render the opposition helpless without fighting. Some people dismiss this concept entirely or consider it an abstraction that is out of reach.

In sales, there are many different strategies that can be used against competitors. It is possible to contain, divide, confront, surround, block, neutralize, stall, change the game, and so on. At some point in the sales cycle, however, you must take one of two basic stands: either to strengthen your position by clearly communicating where your products and services are uniquely better, or to weaken the competition by highlighting where its products and services are worse. The latter approach sometimes invites attacks, and it often draws attention away from value items and toward the manner in which potshots are being taken, with any consideration of or attention to the substance of the arguments being rare. Customers are more likely to be amused by fights between competitors than to take any serious notice of what is actually being said. The reality is that when it comes to denigrating the products and services of others, there is less and less to shoot at, as product differentials in most categories today continue to narrow, making it harder to find any impediments that will make enough difference to change customers' minds.

A generalization regarding competition could be that it is anything that prevents or reduces the ability to win deals, and in that context there are other competitive forces coming from other sources, such as suppliers, industry analysts, the media, and unsatisfied customers. They may all contribute in varying degrees to businesses staying away. A symptom of this occurs when the differentiation that a company markets is superficial and cannot be substantiated. This is another reason why competitive strength must be built from within and not be left in the domain of unsupportable spiel.

The time for becoming more competitive is today. Every day provides an opportunity to be more competitive. It is futile to plan to be competitively positioned in, say, one to three years and embark on projects to improve products, channels, sales, and so on, in the hope of becoming better positioned. Readiness is within reach today, and using anything other than short-term plans focused on a steady toning of competitive muscle may result in missed opportunities. In looking at short-term and small incremental advances, there are essentially three areas where building a competitive profile can be done within an organization. While other strategic endeavors should not be ignored, the following are areas that can be addressed easily and in the relatively short term to increase competitive clout.

- Differentiate by uniqueness
- Reduce internal competition
- Target open markets

The techniques we will be adopting are tactical in nature and will initiate an ongoing process of incremental changes that with only small effort will improve your competitive stance. Noticeably absent from the list is "develop competitive strategy"; this is important in another context, but it is deliberately omitted here, as it usually involves a broader companywide review requiring further analysis and study. Although competitiveness includes all parts and all employees of the company, sales, marketing, channel partners, and R&D have central roles because of their proximity to customers and competitors. The ideas presented here, therefore, have specific aims to build a strong competitive position from the ground up rather than the top down. This does not preclude management's support, as that support is crucial to implementing these ideas and making them a success.

Differentiate by Uniqueness

When we look at ways to differentiate the company, small things are often enough to make it unique. The task is to find those small changes that will make the company special, to carry them out, and then to communicate them widely. Using the criteria for making small changes, there are a number of things that can be done in the short term that are within reach of the skills and competencies that the company already has. The key is to identify areas where, while the change or addition is small, the benefits are lasting and not easily duplicated by the competition. The competitive focus will center on those areas that are customer facing and influenced by competitors' behavior: sales, marketing, customer service, product development, and channel and reseller partners. If we examine these areas first individually and then collectively looking for changes that we can make, we find a few meaningful tasks that, once executed effectively, become useful as springboards to communications with the outside world.

Sales

As the company's front line, sales is important in creating the perception of being unique. The sales materials that you use create an impression, and small but significant changes in these materials can have a big impact. Prior to any sales call, an understanding of the customer is, of course, essential; however, while you need to have done this research, it does not show up in the course of the call. Therefore, any materials that you generate for the purpose of presentations, promotions, or proposals need to be *personalized*, both at the company level and for the individual. There are several small ways to achieve this.

Sales Collateral

Presentation materials should reflect the prospect or customer's industry. The terminology and examples used should be those that are common within that industry. This goes also for brochures, white papers, and other collateral material that provide information regarding your company or its products and services. You can achieve this by having soft copy templates of the standard sales materials, inserting the appropriate industry flavorings, and printing the material on high-quality color printers. Proposals need to be based on a standard template that can be easily modified to insert the specifics regarding the prospect's unique requirements. Where appropriate, insert the actual names of the people involved and their roles and titles if project-related information is included.

Company Success

The point here is not to brag. The successes you mention should be related to accomplishments of your company that will be of benefit to the customer. If these are carefully selected, this is a much better way of indicating your superiority to your competitors than using direct attacks. The small nuances to select here are those that are focused on customers' pain points that you have overcome. For example, if customers are experiencing high growth and need to put systems in place to help them handle it, tell them your story of how that happened in your company and how successful you were.

Verbal Communication

In any sales call, either in person or by telephone, making a connection or establishing rapport quickly is essential. Often salespeople interpret this as being ultrafriendly and accommodating. While there is nothing wrong with that, its overuse may come across as sleazy and may actually put the prospect off.

A small but powerful way to increase the probability of establishing rapport is to listen to what customers say and *how they say it*. In Chapter 4 we identified in detail the modalities as a tool for developing and refining a company message to connect better with a broad range of people. The same concept applies equally at the personal level in verbal communications with prospects and customers. The objective of building a single message that resonates with a mass audience means including a variety of modalities. The objective at the verbal level is the same, but its application is different in that it requires tuning in to what is being said in order to isolate the prospect's or customer's preferred modality and mirror it accordingly. By listening to the way the prospect answers your questions or describes a situation and by using the same *language* in return, you establish a deeper understanding of the prospect's experience, thereby gaining a much better chance for rapport. The idea is not to use exactly the same words, but to use the same modality; for example, if the customer says, "I can't see what you mean," then answer, "Let me shed some *light* on that." You can use the same technique for sounds and feelings, choosing words that are related to those senses. You are literally using the same "sense" as your customer or prospect when you speak. (See Chapter 4, "Connecting People with the Message," to review the VAK modalities useful for one-on-one verbal communications.)

Unique Reputation

After a sales call in person or by phone, have a letter prepared that you can send *within an hour* of your call. If you have indicated dur-

ing your sales presentation that timeliness of delivery and customer service are key attributes, then you should find small ways
to prove it aside from your written materials.

Marketing

Marketing plays an important role in positioning the company as
being more competitive because many important messages are
developed and transmitted through various types of media. Marketing is a balance between being an art and a science in support
of company strategies. Fine tuning these messages is one of the
small but significant changes that can increase marketing's effectiveness and therefore its ability to help the company, and specifically the sales force, to be more competitive. It is here that the
perceptions of the company and its products, people, and culture
are created in the minds of the viewing public. Here are some
tools and techniques that can be easily adopted to improve marketing's ability to display the company in a more competitive
position.

Collateral

The first thing to do before making any small improvements in
marketing materials is to take an inventory of all the materials that
exist within the organization. Once you have done that, you
should remove from circulation anything that is more than a year
old. What you have left is what can be refreshed with small refinements. There are obvious improvements that you can make without using outside consultants:

- Inspect all the current materials and make sure that the com-
  pany or product logos are consistent.
- Make sure that the naming conventions for your products and
  services are consistent.
- Categorize the materials by their purpose and their audience.
  Some popular categories are sales, events, Web, public

relations, analysts, and earnings. Cross-reference them to the audiences they are intended for, for example, C-level executives, managers, end users, customers, prospects, industry analysts, financial analysts, channel partners, and internal users.

- If there is any company information in the materials, revise the information to highlight the things that are *unique*. This includes brochures, customer presentations, white papers, and so on.

Sales Support

One of the most important functions that a marketing department can perform is to produce high-quality sales support materials. Often so much time is spent on the outbound marketing functions that this area is not given the attention it deserves. Sales materials should support each of the steps of the sales function and process. What this means is that marketing has to have a clear understanding of the process that salespersons use to sell. If you have a discipline or methodology for sales, then marketing needs to support this process by providing materials for each stage of the cycle. Start with the cold call and follow the process all the way to the final proposal, looking at what would make a salesperson more effective. One way to do this is to produce materials that save time. Here are some ideas:

1. *Cold call.* Build a sales call information package that is current and that salespeople can easily access when visiting a prospect for the first time. Once you have done this, the next phase is to modify the information packages by product and audience.
2. *Competitive cheat sheets.* Determine who your main external competitors are and produce a printable sales briefing document that includes publicly available information. Organize the information in a structured format that the

salesperson can refer to quickly. A simple way to keep this type of information current is to include recent press articles, product announcements, and earnings call data that will be relevant. As this information is constantly changing, it is recommended that this type of material be placed on an internal Web site where salespeople are able to refer to it and print it as required; this makes the task of updating and distributing the material much easier.

3. *Categorize sales materials.* These materials should be in the same order as the steps in the sales cycle and tailored for the products the salespeople are looking to sell and the people they are going to sell them to. The next phase is making the materials industry-specific. This invaluable set of materials for salespeople to use will increase their productivity many times over. Make sure it is kept current.

4. *Customer information.* Useful information regarding customers can be obtained from *external* services such as Hoovers.com, Dun & Bradstreet.com, and OneSource.com. These services profile many companies both within the United States and internationally, and the profiles are readily available for a monthly or an annual fee. A small addition that will add more value to this generic information is to include *internal* information, specifically the products that the customer is already using; contract information, including renewal or expiry dates; debtor and payments status; recent support calls; and complaints filed.

5. *Competitive alerts.* Using tools that are readily available on the Internet, it is possible to provide the sales organization with real-time communication of competitor announcements that can be personalized for individual sales teams or territories. The small addition to this is to provide the information in the form of e-mail alerts that salespeople can pick up with handheld devices and mobile phones, *and* to categorize the alerts by product/service and territory order.

Web Site

The Web site is increasingly becoming one of the most important sources that prospects use to select their short lists or to find out more about your company and its products. It is a sales tool, and just as a salesperson must understand how important it is to make a good first impression, the Web site faces the same challenge.

Home page

If your home page provides all your product information, then it is likely that unless there is something outstanding about your products or services, it will look the same as your competitors'. A good exercise is to visit 5 to 10 of your competitors' Web sites, list the products and services that each has, and count the number of times the same words are used on each of the sites you visit. This use of the same words, sometimes known as "buzzword bingo," makes it harder to show any unique qualities. Therefore, the small but important change to the home page is to reduce the amount of product information to less than 20 percent and to make the Web page more about your current customers and the way they are deriving benefits using your products.

In the context of being more competitive by your Web presence, there are some things that you can do to your home page that will increase your chances of being considered a viable vendor:

- Put the detailed information regarding your products and services on a secondary page that viewers can drill down to. The value of putting product-related pages deeper into the site is that there is a higher likelihood that viewers will stay there, increasing the chances that they will take *action*. There need to be as many actions as possible on every page. The Web experience needs to be a kinesthetic one. Actions include downloading information, registering for events, requesting more information or a return call, viewing online demonstrations and Web seminars, taking training classes, and obtaining pricing information. A small but significant

action is to add the ability to find and contact a sales representative within the logical sales territory.
- Design the site so that the actions become more "intimate"
and specific the farther viewers drill down. If they are at a
product-related page, provide actions that would answer naturally occurring questions.
- Avoid the use of "free" or "limited time only"; people don't
believe it, and it reeks of some hidden commitment. Instead of
"free," use "exclusive," "invaluable," or "updated." These are
competitively powerful words that suggest your uniqueness.
- Segregate the content of the Web site in such a way as to
encourage visitors to register (only once and on their first
time) to become part of an exclusive community. Offer specific
content *and* the opportunity to network with (1) peers in their
industry or product categories, (2) people within your organization in sales, development, production, customer service,
and accounting, and (3) your resellers or channel partners.

Welcome Kits

A way that customers can identify you and also become potential
references for you at a later time is to develop what I call welcome
kits. These kits may have a number of different things in them,
including *useful* promotional items, how to access resources, contract obligations, warranty information, service and performance
levels, and so on. Anyone can do this; however, to make your relationship special, add a certificate or plaque that commemorates
the customer's being part of your company. There should be two
copies, one for the new customer and the other for you to display
on your company's premises.

The welcome kit is most effective if it can be presented to your
new customers ceremoniously at their premises, with staff from
both companies attending. It is an opportunity for a press release
and also a valuable addition to your Web site, to internal newsletters, and to internal communication, especially to your sales force.
Depending on the nature of your products and the way they are

delivered, the presentation can be made at the time the deal is signed or when delivery takes place. If you are in a high-volume business, make this a special piece of correspondence, and perform the ceremony and press announcements for a group of selected customers at special events. In any case, this is a small addition that has many competitive benefits:

- It emphasizes your unique qualities.
- It regularly communicates customer successes to employees.
- It sends messages of your success to prospects and industry watchers.
- It frustrates competitors.

Playbooks

Surprisingly, in the many companies across the wide spectrum of different industries that I have dealt with, I have heard a recurring frustration on the part of the salespeople that they do not have a good understanding of all the products and services that their companies actually make and sell. With the increased levels of mergers and acquisitions, it is easy to see how information on what products to sell, how newly added products and services are to be positioned against traditional ones, and what to sell to whom can blur. This situation presents open opportunities to any focused competitor and leads to lost sales.

While proper training and integration strategies need to continue, their timeliness may leave a vacuum for sales out in the field. A relatively small project that can greatly assist as an interim tool is a *sales playbook* in document form that clearly articulates how every product fits in, with all the segments and customer profiles being addressed. It needs to contain schematics of the rationale for each product so that salespeople can easily decide what products are the best fit for each customer and why. It also assists in the integration process when two or more sales organizations come together, eliminating confusion where there are similar products or overlap.

Given the nature of this type of sales reference material, it will inevitably undergo frequent revisions; therefore, it is advisable that the document be available from an internal online source. See Figure 6-1 for a generic layout for a sales playbook that can be used as a starting point and adapted to your specific requirements. Depending on your particular industry segments, customer profiles, and product mixes, there are some mandatory items listed here that may help in the creation of this resource for sales:

- *Products and services.* A comprehensive list of products and their official names, itemized and identified as existing or new.
- *Key selling points.* A list of key features and overviews, including any competitive differentiation, how the product is being used, and examples of customers who are using it.
- *Best buyer profile.* A concise description of the optimal customer who will purchase the product, including size, the industry the customer belongs to, the size of a typical budget requirement, and any skills or training needed as a requirement for using this product.
- *Add-on opportunities.* A "what-if" list where the salesperson can easily identify whether and where this product can be sold as an addition or whether there are any prerequisites.

Customer Service

This is a wide-spanning area of the company, but, for the purpose of introducing small ideas, we will narrow the focus to situations in which customers request some type of support, either by telephone or by e-mail. It should be noted that customer service is provided either directly or indirectly by almost everyone in the organization. The small ideas presented here relate to people who have a high touch-point frequency with customers and can quickly engage in activities and behavior that make you unique and therefore more competitive.

Product Name	Key Selling Points	Best Buyer Profile	Add-On Opportunities
List product names of existing and new products.	• Key selling strengths • Unique value • Specify where this product is best used • Competitive differentiation • Links or references to more detailed product information	• Profile of customers who always buy this product • Size of customers; segment or industry they belong to • Budget requirements • Skills customers need	List products that are a natural add-on based on what the customer has, including competitors' products and if there are any product-related prerequisites

Figure 6-1 Sales Playbook Reference Guide

Customer-Centric Teams

Support organizations and departments of large companies are almost always organized by type of inquiry. For instance, support may be required for a financial matter, a product issue, a sales-related question, or simply a general request for more information. Customers are routed to the specific group that is best trained and skilled in answering the query. In the case of product-related support, customers should be put through to a pool of experts with specialized knowledge where they can get their specific issues addressed. This is a good arrangement, as it provides the best way to resolve customer queries; the only problem is that depending on the way they describe the issue, customers may have to repeat their information over and over again.

Assuming that you are using some form of technology to retrieve customers' information when they call, a small and hugely differentiating way of organizing your customer service is to allocate a subset of customers to each member of each of the support services departments. (Customers may be allocated in equal proportions or based on territory, zip code, or some other logical grouping.) In other words, if there are 100 people in four support departments—20 on the sales staff, 50 in product support, 10 in accounts, and 20 people in general support—divide your customer base by the number of support people in each group and make those support people part of a customer's team as long as they remain employees.

For example, if you have 500 customers, each sales support person will be assigned 25 customers (500/20), each product support person will have 10, and so on. Over time, the support people build up a history and develop a familiarity with the customers, as the same "customer team" is speaking with the same set of customers all the time. For training purposes, some rotations may be valid; however, what you are doing is getting back to good old-fashioned one-to-one customer service, without any investment other than a reorganization and routing policy within the department. I have seen customer satisfaction and loyalty ratings increase by as much as 300 percent using this simple, easy-to-implement technique.

How does this become a competitive weapon? It goes back to sales. It sets you apart by the fact that you have personalized customer service that does not go away when the salesperson leaves or changes. Within this model, you will be able to provide opportunities to upsell new products, communicate upcoming company information, share knowledge across teams, and take many more actions to increase revenue in a cost-effective way. Once you initiate this customer-centric team approach, you can incrementally add and introduce new ideas that continue to make you unique and differentiated. Furthermore, this policy should be promoted as widely as possible by sales and marketing.

Management Pickup

Another small but effective idea is for senior management to spend several days over the course of a year in the support department speaking with customers. (In cases where support is largely outsourced internationally, management can easily be integrated into the call routing and sequencing, although it may require consideration of time zones.) Knowing that the senior executive management of the company is prepared to speak with them as a courtesy will make customers feel important. What naturally happens is that the incoming callers will tell their work colleagues about their positive customer-support experience. Reporting that they spoke with the president or CEO makes a great story.

Acknowledge Individuals and Reward Teams

Nothing motivates like motivation itself, and front-line staff such as those in telesales or support roles require internal support. Rewarding employees is always fraught with danger, especially when complicated compensation and bonus plans are in place, so the small change here is in addition to any current company incentive schemes. On some occasions, certain individuals in customer-centric teams will give exceptional service to a customer. Typical evidence of this excellent performance is a memo of some type from the customer.

When this happens, a nonmonetary reward should be given to both the individual *and* the other members of the customer's team. Send the information along with any customer correspondence to marketing so that it can build a story around the incident, the level of service, and the customer's experience, and create a broad market communication. At times you will notice full-page ads in national newspapers and magazines showing one customer's letter of thanks. This is a powerful story—tell it as a unique experience that is available only from your company.

Product Development

If your business has the ability to decide how your product is to be developed or has an otherwise influential role, then the importance of your future product development plans to customers is whether your product or the services surrounding it will someday become so specific for their needs that they will not have to make any modifications when they buy from you again. Their future needs can be found in the product specifications or in the related services that come with the product.

Most manufacturers and developers of products will attest that they build based on the requirements of customers and markets. In reality, most generally available products are rarely able to cater exactly to individual customers' needs. Flexibility is built into the base products, allowing customers to tailor and modify them or to select the features that they want or need, but there are costs associated with the amount of tailoring or customization required.

The way a product's fit is assessed by customers is a detailed analysis of the available functionality. This often plays out much like having a hand in feature-function poker showdowns between vendors, and it is used as a differentiating factor during intensely competitive sales cycles. The assumption is that if one vendor has more flexibility or functionality than another, the one with more flexibility is better. While this is a valid argument on the surface, the reality is that the sale does not always go to the most functionality-rich product. There are valid reasons for this disconnect; the first is that customers are also buying a relationship with the company, and the second comes from the realization that while a product may have a lot of functionality, there is a question of what percentage of that functionality will be specific to customers' needs.

Let the Customers In

A way to become highly competitive and to strengthen customer loyalty toward you is to provide a means by which customers can participate in the development process, and in some cases in the design of future product and service offerings. Their actual level of involvement and how deeply they can participate remain under your control.

There are various forums that can be set up where customers with common interests can form a consortium that functions as an advisory committee, offering input concerning product development and enhancements. This is more than market research and should not be viewed as such. The purpose behind it is to have customers collaborate with you and propose what they would like to see in future investments and direction of the products. The extent to which the recommendations will be used can be outlined in the group's charter. In those places where I have seen this in operation, it offers invaluable input and feedback. More important, it makes you stand out from others even if they do the same thing because what *you* are doing is offering a system to create unique value based on your products. The unique value proposition for new customers is that if they buy from anyone else, their competitive advantage will be compromised. This is because, while they can buy similar products or services from your competitors, if they buy from you, they will receive built-in functions specific to their needs.

The practical reality is that a lot of the features and functions built into products, especially in the technology industry, are not used immediately or are never used at all. Think of any popular software product—for example, Microsoft Word[3]—and think of all the thousands of functions available and how many of them are actually used on a day-to-day basis. Only a fraction of them are used. However, what is valuable, and in some ways unique, is that all of these functions are there. Microsoft does not differentiate Word at a product level with all of its many functions, but it maintains uniqueness by including what its customers have asked for over the years. The result is that the single program now caters to just about everyone's needs.

In some industries—for example, in specialized manufacturing or construction—everything is done according to specifications dictated by customers. This is not the same as having an advisory group from the customer base that engages in discussions regarding how customers can be better served. In cases where there is a one-to-one specificity around the end product, the idea behind the forum is still valid. What changes is the subject matter. In this situation, the topics will center on such things as project management, material handling, skill levels, and cost-reduction strategies.

I have seen forums set up specifically for the purpose of developing training programs and curricula for a product. Customers are open about their typical usage of their business systems, disclosing the skill levels that they have and need. This leads to designing courses for your products and services that optimize training, standardization, and documentation. I have also seen situations in which customers welcome the idea of integrating training classes for vendors' products into their own in-house programs, combining process and user training and making user manuals available. If you are looking for customer loyalty, being able to tailor customers' internal operating manuals to include your product usage manuals is a step you can take to fence off the fiercest of competitors.

Integrated Customer Collaboration

In terms of publicity, there are many ways to exploit your customer's point of view to the fullest, as it touches on so many different variables. It speaks to the idea that you are a company that not only listens to its customers but allows them to become part of the company. It is an authentic act of partnering with your customers and a definitive display of long-term relationship building. The spin can genuinely assert that customers have a hand in directing their investments with you by sharing in the strategic direction of the company. You can also highlight that this goes beyond the "user group" membership concept, where participation is restricted to newsletters and annual conferences; this offers customers a place at the decision-making table.

This is a powerfully simple attribute that is easy to implement but difficult for anyone else to duplicate in its exact form. There are several beneficial by-products that come out of this process.

- It provides unique insights that will allow your product's development and enhancements to become more aligned with customer needs.
- It produces a creative input that allows you to expand into new markets.
- It makes a unique but authentic offer to become "partners" with your customers.
- It advocates a long-term relationship.
- It provides a sound basis for telling the market that you are customer focused.
- It gives the perception that customers have influence over their investment with your company.
- Even if your competitors copy you, they will never be able to duplicate the information that you get from your customers.
- It provides a platform for customer advocacy and loyalty, as customers will stay with you if they know that their unique needs will someday be part of your base offering.
- Value creation is collaboration *with* customers, not *at* customers.

Development as Part of Sales

During complex sales cycles, very specific questions regarding product specifications and futures may often become important weapons to use against your competition. The answers to these questions and the timeliness of the responses speak volumes to prospects, giving them a glimpse of how they may be treated if they select your company as their vendor. It is in these situations that the doors of the development labs need to be wide open and easily accessed by sales.

A simple way to do this without disrupting the operations of either R&D or sales is to make each of the development leaders or managers available for the initial sales inquiries. The development heads can then decide who on their staff is best suited to tackle the presales requests. Depending on individual circumstances, there is a spectrum in terms of the level of development's involvement. It can be as formal as assigning development managers a set of customers for which they are "executive sponsors" (based on product and industry) and having them build a personal relationship with those customers, or it can be as informal as allowing access to development only by phone and e-mails. In either variation, this arrangement is not difficult to set up and adds another nuance that reinforces competitive strength.

Product Roadmaps

Product roadmaps can be a powerful way to slow down the competition's sales. Usually generated by the development organization, these roadmaps, sometimes referred to as statements of direction, announce future enhancements and releases of products to existing customers and prospects. Product roadmaps are particularly useful where the prospect has short-listed its potential suppliers or is about to make a decision, as it can create a stalling effect that may work in your favor. Rightly timed and properly executed, this technique has a strong competitive effect. Some of the typical outcomes are:

- Waiting for one of the milestones from the roadmap to be delivered delays making a decision to buy a competitor's product or service.

- It locks in existing customers who may be thinking of replacing your product or service until the milestones are met and delivered.
- It moves the competitor's focus away from any current issues during a sales cycle and toward your roadmaps, therefore potentially changing the game.

In each of these scenarios, there are more benefits for you than against you in a competitive sense. Small tips in communicating a roadmap for future product enhancements are (1) do not provide unconfirmed delivery dates, (2) place the emphasis on the enhancements and how they address what customers have been wanting, (3) make the milestones significant enough for people to wait and see, and (4) be sure that everything in the roadmaps is realistic and deliverable.

Simply Unique

Differentiating by uniqueness can also be done in other ways. Being unique means that you are the only one who has a particular thing. There are simple things that you can do to find attributes that only you have. A good reason to hunt for unique things is to be able to use them for marketing. A way to start is by asking questions beginning with "We are the only ones who . . ." Complete the sentence with as many things as you can possibly come up with. There are some guidelines that need to be adhered to, however. The statements need to be true and fact-based, genuine and easily proven, credible and official.

Of the listed items, what are the things that customers will care about? Once you have narrowed your list down to those, write a story around the individual items. For example, if you are the only print shop in town with 24-hour service, then that is unique. In your story, explain how and why you decided on that level of service. In the past, when working with companies to identify unique value, I used this technique: I included groups of people from different parts of the company and asked them to think for a few days about the things that made the company special. Next I had each group generate a list of their thoughts, and then I consolidated the lists. Often something that may be obvious to everyone in the company is, in fact, a unique quality to customers.

Channel and Reseller Partners

Channel and reseller partners have valuable experience in selling and distributing your products and services; are well informed with regard to what you need to do to be more competitive, especially at the point of sale; can be integral to finding what specific attributes customers are judging vendors by; and can help pinpoint why customers choose certain vendors over others. (This concept was first introduced in the late 1940s and is known as the *unique selling proposition*. Marketers used it to determine how advertising campaigns could change customers' minds from one brand to another.)

Customers will have a perspective from the point of delivery. The channel partners' view complements and rounds off the way you position your products and services within the sales cycle. This can be just as important as your overall company's message, but it is often overlooked when all the attention is on the product quality and features and there is little regard to understanding how those actually differentiate your company in the market. The point here is that you are able to tout a unique aspect of your company in the way you build relationships with channel partners. They become an integral part of your product sales and marketing process, and their specific requirements are heard and acted upon. The small but important difference you can make is to include the channel partners in the development of sales and marketing activities as well as of product requirements along the lines we touched on in Chapter 5.

Differentiation Is a Perception

Differentiation is important to the extent that it presents a unique value to customers, and you must create the perception that this unique value can be readily obtained only from your company. The key word is *perception*. Internal competition relates to the internal barriers that uselessly waste energy, resources, and assets on in-house battles that can evolve into a culture and become deeply entrenched in the company's DNA. Market making is where you seek market segments within your competitors' gaps and enjoy free air space for a limited period of time, and where you are constantly on the move into new segments and niches, causing competitors to follow your lead. The common denominator for each of these areas is that they exist in some form in your business today, and therefore an opportunity for small thinking exists.

Reduce Internal Competition

One of management's roles is to build a culture of competitiveness within a company and to instill a positive attitude in employees so that they are proud of the company's achievements as they relate to winning business from competitors. This feedback should be given on a regular basis and should highlight the unique values that customers found when they selected the company over others.

There is no competitor more powerful than the one that has entered the veins of your company. No, I am not talking about some undercover agent masquerading as an employee who got past security and is impersonating the janitor. This silent but powerful force was created from within and can be anywhere. It moves and manifests itself in all the important meetings when decisions need to be made or projects need to be approved. It flourishes within the bureaucracy, and evidence of it can be seen in delays, low morale, and lack of motivation. This competitive force is more powerful and smarter than your external competitors.

This inside operator is independent of company size, and it conspires to reduce sales and growth. You know how to recognize this invisible competitor whenever there is a conflict between parties within the company's operations that makes marketing, selling, and delivering to the customer difficult. If you have ever heard yourself or anyone else say, "We are our own worst enemy," then the invisible insider competitor has just visited you. How did we get this way, you may very well ask. It is difficult to answer this question specifically for every case; however, there are common traits that can be addressed without major overhaul.

The first symptom of insider competition is the *fiefdom*. The term *fief* originated in feudalism, where a more powerful lord would be the ultimate protector of the land of his vassals (nobles) in return for military service if it was needed; each large landholding, or fief, was then ruled by a noble and worked by serfs (peasants). Sound familiar? Competition lives inside companies because people become protective of their roles and maintain a loyalty to the agendas of their managers, irrespective of whether those agendas are hindering the progress of others.

Competitive Analysis

Competitive analysis can bring a lot of information to the table, and it is useful input when you are developing a strategy or tactical activities for sales, marketing, or R&D. No amount of understanding your competitors, however, can set you on the path to becoming a bigger company; it just makes you a better-informed company. The danger is that once you feel you have figured out what "the others" are doing, counteractions on your part may cause an imbalance of resources, with energy being spent on unproductive work. As with the anableps, a balance between food and foe is required.

In previous chapters, we looked at how to make fine adjustments in order to strengthen the relationships between companies and customers, and how profits will soar when we do so. The next chapters provide practical guidance to prepare the company for growth and identify what specific things can be done in the short and medium term.

CHAPTER 7

GETTING READY
FOR BIGNESS

Don't be afraid to give your best to what seemingly are small jobs. Every time you conquer one it makes you that much stronger. If you do the little jobs well, the big ones will tend to take care of themselves.

—Dale Carnegie (1888–1955)

Where are all the best ideas for making small changes in the company that will allow growth, and how can we find them and put them into action—today? That is the question. The answer is that these ideas are in the minds of the employees, and they present themselves each and every working day. I bet that if you asked 10 different people who work in your area to name something that they do that seems futile, protracted, or just plain nonsense and that they can't justify other than "that's the way it has always been done," you'd get an immediate answer from each. However, before you embark on a policy of letting all the people in your organization loose to make free-flowing changes as and when they decide, you need to spread an important message in a way that makes people feel comfortable and reinforces the importance of their roles. Ironically, what we are dealing with is learning that has already taken place and that has actually reinforced *not* doing anything, but instead leaving things as they are.

Building systematic structures leads to patterns of behaviors that condition certain responses to events. We spoke in earlier chapters of "active inertia," or the condition in which people believe that it is their job to maintain the status quo. In Peter Senge's book *The Fifth Discipline*,[1] he elegantly explains how this conditioning of "mental models" could create learning disabilities for change. The remedy is to introduce a new way of learning, reinforced with feedback promoting the idea that it is OK for staff members to take action. Making your job easier is within your control and *is* part of your job, so employees up and down the organization should feel free to make improvements. The ultimate aim is to unlock the company's ability to achieve growth without the need for reorganization and to leverage existing systems and structures and make way for new changes in small, manageable steps with the resources already present.

Oracle's Billion-Dollar Baby

At Oracle Corporation, it became apparent that the company's internal systems and the way the company had come to be organized were inefficient and potentially stunting growth. There was a history of autonomy across the regional offices, and while growth was steady and sustainable, it became clear that duplications and redundancies were cutting into margins and indeed stifling growth. A corporatewide initiative to centralize and standardize the internal operations of the company worldwide was mandated by senior management. Further, management also required the use of Oracle's business application E-Business Suite (the same one it sold to its customers) during this transition.

To tackle a project of this magnitude, it was decided to start with the back-office operations and systems first and then work out to more customer-facing systems over time. The first systems to be consolidated were the financial systems, namely general ledger, accounts payable, accounts receivable, fixed assets, and purchasing. Different accounting systems and processes were being used in several regions around the world. Thus, it was necessary to get the business ready before any of the new systems could be implemented. This meant that processes and procedures that were different in almost every region needed to be standardized, localized, and centralized. The biggest issues came not from the inability of the technology to respond and handle the task, but from people and processes that needed to be undone and relearned.

After a lightning-speed rollout of these applications worldwide and centralization at the head office, the aggregate savings in the first year amounted to in excess of $1 billion, or almost 10 percent in bottom-line savings. The magnitude was so overwhelming that Oracle's customers wanted to know how it was done so that they could benefit by similar proportions. Jeff Henley, then Oracle's chief financial officer, toured the world presenting Oracle's results and the methodology used with Oracle's technology, processes, and people. Over a period of two years, the incremental rollout moved to other parts of the business, including payroll and human resources, sales, marketing, alliances and channels, telesales, and so on. The success was repeated in the following year; another billion dollars was saved and, just as important, the processes were in place to enable Oracle to scale to any size and at any rate, evidenced by the fact that since 2005, the majority of the companies that Oracle has acquired have been integrated into those same systems and technology. While the payoffs were enormous, all this was done incrementally, using a series of small changes across the globe in unison and aligned with corporate objectives.

This meant that every detail of every process and function within the company needed to be adjusted. In order to do this effectively, managers were empowered to make changes at their individual locations in accordance with their specific business needs and to allow operational staff to implement those changes as required. However, the key success factors remained a clear understanding of what Oracle's objectives were and an agreement that the change process was not to be left to a select small group while others were bystanders; instead, everyone in the organization had to participate.

This case study reveals a number of key ideas necessary to prepare a company for growth, no matter how big:

- Communication of corporate objectives needs to reach every person in the organization, along with an interpretation of what these objectives mean for the individual and how he or she is to participate in making them a success.

- It is possible to make changes fast using small increments.
- The model is applicable to any size organization, as some of the offices in the regions and international units were small, while others in major cities and countries were large.
- There is a built-in framework and process allowing any magnitude of growth to occur, either organic growth or growth through acquisitions; both types can be accommodated by and integrated into the same systems.
- The model uses in-house skills, and training, where necessary, can be conducted in small steps.
- Projects, whether large or small, are executed rapidly across all or selected locations.
- There is a comprehensive ability for all employees to share knowledge and access resources to perform and execute tasks as required.
- The potential savings can be huge, increasing profitability even during the process of preparing.

Not Another Mission Statement

In Oracle's case, the objectives were not communicated as yet another mission statement. It is important that objectives be conveyed in such a way as to make everyone feel that achieving them will become part of the daily work routine. The importance of this simple message is that it helps prevent employee negativity, especially if in the past, whenever something "different" was implemented, it turned out poorly. Buy-in at all levels of the company is essential in avoiding the situation where people nod their heads, only to move on without doing anything new. This is a typical fear-of-change issue. Employees need to understand that this is *not* a radical change—at least not in the traditional sense. This approach creates an inspiration for them to feel free to make those little changes that can improve their lives at work.

Implement a Small Change Behavior Culture

The next question will be, "What do you mean by small?" Finding the small changes that will have the biggest impact is a matter of determining where in the company's operations these changes will create the least disruption but the maximum benefit. In order to *release* those changes, there needs to be a clear definition of the scope of each employee's ability to effect changes in his or her day-to-day job. This will involve invigorating rather than reviewing everyone's role and attempting to outline the ideal in the job specification. The balance is to allow employees an increased ability to make changes where they see benefit, with established parameters for accountability that are accepted by all. The most effective way to do this is to charter managers to encourage their staffs to make incremental changes and for line managers to supervise and manage those changes. Therefore, the empowerment of employees to initiate changes needs to come from the top. However, before any of this can happen effectively, and to avoid random changes, there needs to be a clear alignment of the company's goals and objectives.

The implementation of small change behavior requires business unit managers to create an environment in which staff members are encouraged to feel free to make changes according to predefined objectives rather than rules. These objectives at the business unit or department level are aligned with the corporation's objectives and thereby become the manageable scope within which employees understand that they can perform their jobs. The task of business unit managers is to break down the corporate goals and translate them for their area of responsibility. For example, if you are planning to become bigger by doubling in size in the next two years and by increasing profit margins by 30 percent in the same period, each business unit manager will need to know how his or her department will contribute. He or she must also understand that all employees should be involved in the accomplishment of the goal *with* permission to change things that they believe are impeding its success. The subtleties here are what make all the difference. Contrast this with what generally happens when new mission statements and corporate goals are declared: the employees go about their normal jobs unchanged, assuming that there is nothing that they can do from where they stand to make any impact.

If you are thinking that revising job descriptions and making this type of change a mandatory part of people's jobs is the solution, let me point out that I have seen this done, and the results are scant. This is because people mostly brush it off as management's way of increasing the workload, giving them yet another responsibility they need to perform to secure their quarterly review and bonus. Instead of making it a function to be used as a scorecard for performance, implement it as a culture and an attitude that is rewarded outside of and in addition to existing compensation or incentive plans. Rewards need not always be monetary in nature, but they do need to have certain qualities that for some people mean more than money. You will recall that the 3Rs at school were reading, writing, and arithmetic; at work, I believe the 3Rs change to (in priority order) recognition, respect, and remuneration.

The Talent Lies Inside

To implement this type of behavior, it is important that the business be well understood, and that is why, in earlier chapters, finding the core of the business was described as an important step and one that is often surprisingly challenging. When you service an industry or a niche, the fact is that there is a built-up talent pool that may have evolved over time into something different from the business that was initially created. This is actually a good thing, as these newly acquired and necessary skills are raw materials for growth. It is recognizing and harnessing this talent that is the key to building a bigger and better business. The other thing that is needed is to have a good understanding of the type of people you have been hiring in each area of the organization. Skills are one thing, but what is often overlooked is whether the people hired fit in with the culture of the growing company.

Where to Start

If you are going to look at developing a strategy to implement in your company that will maximize its output, you need to look at the areas that are most important. In most cases, these are the touch points with the customer. In second place come the interactions you have with your suppliers and partner alliances. If your business relies on distributors, resellers, or value-added dealerships, then clearly they are included, as they too represent your customers.

A good place to start in clearing and preparing for growth is with internal transaction processes that engage and affect customers. We have seen examples where small things can have a big positive impact on the back-office functions of the company, and such changes should continue in parallel as you focus on specific areas to increase effectiveness through small changes, moving across different parts of the company over time using a list of priorities. The ideal is to initiate a sequence in which you focus your attention on certain specific functions and processes for a period of time and then move on to the next area, with the priorities determined by assessing the scope of small changes relative to the revenue and profit they will produce.

Reenergizing Business Processes

The aim of preparing for growth is operational excellence. In earlier chapters, we touched on the importance of the entire organization sharing knowledge, with the linkages between the corporate structures representing lines of communication, where everyone responds according to his or her job whenever implicit instructions or signals of change are recognized. Volumes have been written about business process reengineering, which is used as a catchword for implementing change, usually by introducing a new technology.

In order to implement a culture of small change behavior, where we are specifically isolating those things that can be done in a short time but with great impact, the idea of business process reengineering doesn't entirely fit. Business process reengineering usually involves large wholesale changes or replacements of existing processes and functions supported by technology. When it comes to small, we will tackle effectiveness and efficiency using a more revolutionary approach, and that is to do as much repair work as possible and make changes that are within the means of existing systems.

It is perfectly reasonable to decide at some point that it is no longer possible for further small changes to rectify a process or a problem, and that replacement is the only answer. This is a valid approach, and one that I am not arguing against here. However, even if systems substitution is decided on, using the small incremental approach has a place in introducing the new systems. In fact, a number of the adjustments to the business that will enable and sustain growth may require eliminating some current practices. Our focus will be on processes that are in place today that need to accommodate a bigger company.

The issue most often encountered is scalability. The biggest concern of any company on the brink of growth is whether the internal systems are able to scale and allow new business to be processed properly, no matter how much of it there is. What we are dealing with, therefore, are those processes that are not flexible enough to allow for expansion. Our focus will be on the areas of the business that have a direct impact on customers, revenue, and profitability.

The Marketing Function

The marketing function is connected by a number of integrated processes that reach from within the organization and out to the marketplace, including channel partners. The preparedness of marketing as it relates to being big involves its ability both to execute according to strategy and to be flexible enough to allow for opportunistic situations. In both cases, there needs to be a high degree of operational excellence, with the execution having a military discipline. The best way to identify where small improvements are to be made in order to allow this efficiency is to isolate the main areas and take them one at a time.

Campaign Design, Rollout, and ROI

Campaigns or marketing programs are the investments needed to generate demand and therefore aid in growth. Budgets aside, there are two things that require attention. The first is to ensure that there is an integrated approach to any campaign, one that involves a number of other related activities, and the second is that each activity meet the demand and scope of the market being addressed. The weakness that is being eliminated involves demand-generation activities such as direct mail or tactical events, which by themselves do not achieve anywhere near the results that can be achieved if the same campaign has associated events that occur before and/or after it. It is therefore important that a minimum number of interrelated activities always be included each time an investment in a campaign is proposed.

Often what happens is that sales, relying on marketing to create demand, applies pressure to load up pipelines, and marketing responds by executing mass mailings in the hope that an adequate number of responses will come back to pass on to sales. A benchmark test of whether you have an integrated approach is if marketing is able to produce a calendar of events that includes internal and external activities that are linked and leveraged. Here are a few examples:

- An advertising campaign is linked with a telemarketing campaign that is leveraged by a series of Web seminars that invite attendees to "breakfast events" conducted by sales.

- A third-party conference at which you have a booth and a speaking session is followed up by a direct-mail campaign that refers to a press release regarding a new product launch.
- A channel partner's direct-mail campaign is integrated with a call to action for events that you have planned throughout the year.
- A telemarketing campaign is followed up with Web demonstrations that are used to generate leads for a specific product range.

There are, of course, many more possibilities; however, you can get a sense of how the campaign design needs to integrate all the elements.

Branding

This is a broad subject. While there needs to be a branding strategy in place, the one significant area where small change will improve brand recognition involves *consistency* in the way *all* outbound materials look and feel; this includes logos, advertisements, product names, Web pages, and even legal documents and signage where they are used.

Communications

There are two types of communications to address here, marketing communications and internal communications. Both are important, and both need to be integrated into the overall marketing campaigns. Press releases, for example, should have activities around them to leverage the "moment." Internal communications should include notifications to the rest of the organization, especially to sales, of all outbound communications. Centralizing these communications is a good process improvement; a unit can serve as a clearinghouse to ensure the validation and consistency of messages and their alignment with corporate objectives.

Telemarketing

The telemarketing or telesales function can be one of the most cost-effective business units. It can both generate leads and prospects and also close deals. There are several areas where small improvements can vastly improve performance:

- *Shared services.* These are allocations of shifts or rosters made according to either inbound or outbound duties. In other words, other departments are able to book telemarketing time for very specific purposes, with time and resources being apportioned for purposes such as creating demand, generating leads, inviting prospects to events, following up on mail campaigns for marketing (provided telesales is integrated into the campaign), and performing specific customer relations duties such as satisfaction surveys.
- *Sales tele-tory.* When a broad market is serviced, a very cost-effective and high-margin change is assigning the telemarketing department a sales territory that is based on segmentation criteria or a customer profile. One simple example is allocating to the telemarketing department a cross section of small customers. This reduces the need for direct salespeople to handle smaller, less profitable deals, giving them more time for strategic opportunities. Whatever the territories, when it comes to compensation and commissions, these must be clear and understood and should avoid as much as possible the need to compensate both direct salespeople and telesales representatives for the same deals. Therefore, territory allocations are a subject where both business units need to agree on the arrangements.
- *One-with-one sales and marketing.* Here a telesales representative is paired with a direct salesperson. When salespeople need to maintain a large number of accounts at any one time, having a sales support person in the telesales department who can take sundry calls and follow up frees the on-the-ground salespeople to tackle complex and relationship-building

issues. Again, the compensation criteria need to be considered in order to avoid paying double commissions, as this defeats the purpose.

- *Value-added sales.* If contract and warranty renewals are within the domain of either the support or the accounting function, there is a benefit from reallocating this role to telesales. Telesales personnel are usually better equipped to take advantage of opportunities for add-ons to existing products or upselling when making the renewal calls, and they are able to spend more time in follow-up calls if a sales cycle is initiated.

The Sales Function

The main areas to focus on when it comes to the sales organization are integration and alignment with marketing and the channel partners. The common issues are related to the way in which leads are generated, processed, and sent to the sales department. There are always areas for improvement between sales and marketing that will have an impact on the effectiveness of both. Some remedies where small repairs can make a big difference are these:

- *Centralized leads.* One of the simplest ways to help prevent leads from getting lost in the system or not getting attention and follow-up in a timely manner is to mandate that all leads for the entire organization be stored in one central location. Classifying the leads based on their origin, location, sales territory, and product group makes for easier retrieval. Access will need to be restricted to authorized users.
- *Pipeline status management.* One of the issues that occurs most often when managing sales pipelines and accounts that are in a sales process is the temptation to leave stale and dying opportunities on the sales reports. Since hope is not a strategy, a simple but effective system for qualifying sales opportunities is to assign a *status code* to each opportunity. The way this works is that accounts are judged based on where they are in the sales cycle, and a code is assigned accordingly. The

opportunity can remain at a particular status for only a fixed amount of time before moving up a level in the cycle, meaning that it has moved closer to closing. If it does not move, it is eliminated or downgraded. For example, using an alphabetized system:

A = *Contracts in hand.* The customer has decided, and the contract is awaiting signatures.

B = *Selected from short list.* The customer has made you the final selection.

C = *On the short list.* The customer has added you to the short list.

D = *Qualified in progress.* The customer shows genuine interest.

X = *On hold.* The customer is interested; more work is required.

In each case, the opportunity can stay at a given status only for a limited time before it either is upgraded or downgraded. For example, if the time limit is 90 days, an opportunity with a status of C that has not advanced to a B status within that time is either downgraded to X or taken off the list. This is an excellent time management tool for sales. The role of marketing is to keep the pipeline adequately filled with D status opportunities.

- *All for one and one for all.* Sales organizations are among the most interesting and complex organizations in any company, irrespective of the products and services being sold. This is a group of people who are motivated by individual gain and see the company as their vehicle for obtaining success, and at the same time know that what they do is the most important function for everyone in the company. This may create a competitive culture among the sales teams and individuals, and this culture may be anywhere from healthy to corrosive; in any case, a useful agenda item to include at sales meetings is for salespeople to pick one account that they are having difficulty moving to the next stage in the sales cycle or status code, and open it up for colleagues and peers to assist. Rules are required for this assistance barter system—everyone must help at least one other salesperson on the team with at least one opportunity. (It may be more depending on workloads.)

- *Win of the week/month/quarter.* Communicating sales successes to the rest of the company regularly—weekly, monthly, or quarterly—has a wide impact on morale and motivation for the rest of the company. If possible, the communication should come from senior management and in particular should include the nuances that made the sale go in your favor. I recommend that there be two types of communications:
  - *To all employees.* These should include wins of the week outlining the customer's company name and industry, the size of the deal or what it means in overall revenues over time, who the competitor(s) were, and specific reasons why the customer selected you.
  - *To the sales and marketing employees (and sales partners).* A detailed description of the sales process, including every nuance and complexity and how they were dealt with, who was involved, and so on, is to be provided in a transcript-style report. One of the best ways to obtain this information is by conducting an interview with the salesperson who made the sale and his or her team. These interviews become internal case studies and are excellent as training resources if they are filed logically and are easily retrievable. (Using multimedia such as audio and video and making the material available on the Web are ideal ways to disseminate this information.)

Channel Partners

Alignment of channel partners with the external sales force is essential. If your channel partners provide a large part of your sales, then it will come as no surprise to you that there is no better way to grow bigger than to expand your alliances with value-added resellers and dealers. Depending on the arrangements that are in place, there are areas where small improvements assist greatly in empowering your channel partners to become as effective as possible.

Conflicts regarding market segmentation and territories, product pricing and margin allocations, rebates, preferred pricing, and product mix all need to be dealt with, and improvements in these areas will significantly increase your ability to grow. Training and marketing are the other operational areas that are often lacking, and more attention needs to be given to incorporating the alliances into the company ecosystem at a deeper level.

The measure of trust between channel partners is often determined by the amount of support they receive and the philosophy of "partnering" in general. There are, of course, some business models that rely entirely on channel partners, and these business models are ideal to emulate, as they set the expectations for others that are less able or willing to reach that level of association. Specific opportunities may present themselves in the following areas:

- *Adaptable business model.* Perform business reviews and customer account planning allowing for an adaptable compensation, commission, or margin model that produces a bias toward your company and its products and against your competitors.
- *Knowledge sharing.* This is done in varying degrees; however, an area often overlooked is the exchange of competitive information. This is a two-way communication where you can learn valuable on-the-ground insights regarding sales tactics.
- *Certification and training.* A regular checkup of partners' qualifications and certification criteria should be included in any agreements. You should approach this with the attitude that it is an opportunity for improvement rather than a process for elimination. In many cases, partners are found to be out of compliance with their entry certification mainly because of lack of training or because some other form of support was not properly or adequately provided.

- *Marketing alliances.* Partners need to be intimately involved in the development of strategic and tactical marketing plans. Some companies offer marketing kits for their marketing programs, allowing partners to replicate marketing-oriented events independently using the same content for branding and messaging. In some cases, partners are permitted to incorporate their own branding and company logos. The small task is to simply package a lot of what marketing has executed or is planning to execute and make it available to partners with guidelines and usage manuals. With this practice, it is common to provide incentives to partners, and a share of the cost of marketing activities is included in the agreement between the parties as business development funds or comarketing investments.
- *Product access and support.* In companies where the partner network is the sales organization, this item may not be as relevant as it is for those whose partners represent distributors or specialized market services. The issue is access to the latest products, and the ability to demonstrate them, potentially slowing the sales process and increasing the risk of not closing deals. The ideal is to allow partners the same access that the internal direct sales force has and to share resources and costs of maintenance if applicable.

Bring Down the Walls

One of the benefits that a matrix organizational structure provides is the ability to create teams across divisional lines so that resources can be shared in an effective way, especially when it comes to projects. The fact is, matrix, functional, or hierarchical structures all can create walls between departments, and this issue alone can be one of the biggest impediments to growth in a modern business. Although volumes have been written on the subject, and there are a myriad of solutions, rarely does anyone come up with simple remedies to improve communications and aid in cross-flow knowledge sharing.

Ironically, technology can both be responsible for building the walls and be equally useful in bringing them down. Traditionally, business systems were purchased one department at a time and often could not readily be integrated with other departmental systems. The reality is that different business systems from different software vendors were difficult to integrate with one another. They also looked and behaved differently and had their own unique forms of reports. If there was to be any integration between departments, it had to be done on an ad hoc, need-only, manual basis. The idea of attempting knowledge sharing was inconceivable because of the extra work it would involve.

Thankfully, while technology can break down the barriers, it can also be used as the central portal for knowledge sharing, not only across divisions within a company but also across global boundaries. Here are two related elements that can be used as independent objectives when it comes to increasing the flow of information:

1. *Self-integrated business systems.* There is no other single item that can be as effective in reducing costs in the IT department, in increasing transaction flow across departments, and in disseminating information throughout a company than a self-integrated business system. The operative word is *self-integrated.* In other words, the software solutions vendor has designed and developed the application so that it is already integrated—out of the box, as it were. A business system that covers all areas of the business, including customer relationship management, supply chain management, manufacturing, financials, human capital management, and business intelligence, is ideal. The most expensive part of operating a computer department is the maintenance costs associated with keeping all the applications running together and providing management with statutory reports. Freedom from that burden and cost will provide savings and reduce the internal fragmentation that often blocks growth; it will

also allow scalability, not to mention better management information and visibility for the business.

For most businesses, the reality is that a wholesale replacement of all their business applications at once is not feasible; therefore, the recommendation is to select a system that comes fully integrated but that can be implemented in modules. This allows small and incremental advances toward the end goal. The key is that all the parts of the system are fully integrated, including the reporting and business intelligence functions, *and* that once any part of the system is implemented, there are no further installation requirements. Furthermore, the use of additional modules should be achieved simply by turning them on, with some implementation setup only. Systems of this nature are available on the market today, and while they were once in the price brackets of only larger corporations, they are now affordable for most size businesses.

One of the most significant ways for any business to remove barriers to growth is to have systems in place that are fully integrated and that can scale as the business grows without the need to replace applications software.

2. *Knowledge sharing.* Implementing a searchable knowledge system can take years, even decades. However, this is such an important factor for growth that any capability is better than none as you take the first steps toward developing a culture where information, experience, and ideas can be shared across the organization. The integrated business systems will provide a great deal of valuable information and insight based on the transactional aspects of the company, and this is useful for visibility and forecasting. In many companies, though, this form of companywide information based on documenting people's experience and ideas is rarely created.

Intellectual and proprietary property is the currency of value for many companies, and it is built up within organizations by employees who combine experience and talent; it is lost when these employees leave. The void that a departing employee creates is not easily filled, and there is a price to pay. It is therefore essential for a growing company to keep the innovative momentum and to capture knowledge in a form such that it can be easily dispersed, accessed, and used.

To address this issue by doing anything small is a challenge, but there are definite first steps that any business can take to begin the journey toward having more comprehensive systems. Knowledge databases are a start, but there need to be two additional functions to make them useful. The first is the ability to associate information and distribute it across the organizational boundaries, and the second is the ability to use this exchange as a means of executing corporate or companywide initiatives fast. In essence, what this means is that when knowledge and content are coupled and transmitted with instructions on how to effectively plan projects, with open lines of communication to all relevant points in the company, execution is rapid and quality is assured.

Small Is to Fast as Big Is to Slow

In our economic era, time to market remains an essential criterion for competitive advantage and overall success, but time from *prediction to market* is just as important as speed to market. With technology playing a real role in accelerating and assisting in productivity, the process of whiteboard to billboard is becoming increasingly faster. When this is supported further with manufacturing efficiencies through "lean manufacturing," real savings are being realized and adopted. The bottlenecks, however, are not in the technology or in the manufacturing processes, the way they used to be. A common problem is attempting to handle too many big things at once. The net effect can be to slow things down.

When an organization instills in its employees a culture of continuous improvement, doing many small things can be better than doing a handful of big things. The logic is simple: doing more means greater opportunities for doing things better next time. The proposition of becoming a bigger or better company by small incremental improvements is based on this notion that the more you do, the more you improve—provided what you do is within your reach.

In the 1980s, when I was overseeing several technology projects around the world for Coca-Cola, an interesting trend was emerging. The projects were basically the same in scope, with the objective being to implement a new route settlement and distribution system. The projects were all for Coca-Cola bottlers, and what this meant was that since the bottlers were under franchise agreements, they were mostly running their current systems in a very similar way. The only exceptions were for local geographic requirements, and they mainly had to do with terrain rather than with internal systems. Some bottlers wanted the "big bang" approach, where all systems would be implemented at the same time with one go-live date. Others decided to take a more conservative approach, introducing modules of the overall application in stages based on the skill level of the staff. Once the users understood the system and demonstrated competence with it, management would introduce the next set of modules, then the next, until the entire system was finally up and running.

A pattern became obvious: for those bottlers who decided to implement all at once, there were long lists of "post-live" issues that needed to be resolved before the system could be signed off on by management. The lists had a combination of technical and people-related issues. The definite pattern that emerged here was that in the post-live issues lists, similar requirements appeared each time, only being contextually different based on the specific data issues, adequate training, user acceptance, and so on. The fact was that despite the preparations, only a small handful of issues were new from one large implementation to another.

In contrast, for those bottlers who decided to take the modular approach, when they came to implement the next set of modules, it took less time. In fact, it took exponentially less time. It got to the point with some bottlers that their users were saying that they felt confident enough to implement the last remaining modules by themselves. It was clear that there was a leveraged learning experience each time new modules were added. The other extraordinary outcome, almost without exception, was that the incremental approach took no more time than the big bang; in fact, in about half the cases, it took less.

There were no significant variations in skill levels, with one bottler having more than another. Each started with the same level of knowledge, and all were given the standard training that came with the package. Those using the phased approach were more successful for a specific reason: they were better prepared each time another part of the system was installed. What this really meant was that the prior experience of using the system alleviated fears and helped to make the new system work. This approach provided the opportunity for a continuous and incremental learning process, so that by the end of the project, the users were so prepared that they felt they no longer needed outside assistance. Further, this approach involved every user, manager, and executive staff member every step of the way.

What is important to note is that each module that was implemented affected a different part of the company, so not all the people were involved all the time. There was a core project team, but the users were different each time. However, each of the modules did touch other parts of the organization each time. The behavior of other departments enabled the users to prepare and respond according to whatever it was that affected their unit.

People Plus Process

Thinking small or the small way is about incremental improvement behavior directed by a common purpose or goal. Becoming big the small way means that there are a number of functions in place:

- There is an acceptance of the idea that doing many small things as incremental steps toward a bigger goal is a valid strategy.
- People feel empowered to make incremental improvements in their jobs.

- Everyone in the company understands the overall goals of the company, and line managers know how to interpret those goals that are in their domain of responsibility and to encourage their teams to act where required.
- Knowledge and content, including experiences, are shared freely.
- Everyone instinctively knows what to do when an instruction comes from the top, or from anywhere else in the corporate structure.
- Systems are integrated not just in the IT area but in the business processes that link one adjacent department to another.
- People have clear, motivating compensation incentives that are both monetary and nonmonetary in nature.
- Teams are rewarded and individuals are acknowledged for accomplishments.
- The attitude of "good and can be better" is cultural.

Building a culture for success is not an easy task. The issues are not so much about accepting the challenge of success and the idea that it is a good thing as they are about how employees respond when they are asked if they feel that they had a recognizable role in achieving that success.

Starts at the Top

It is possible to get bigger and better using small incremental advances, and we have seen examples of tactical ideas and ways to promote and support growth. Management's role is that of an enabler. The main area of focus for management is communicating the goals.

Listening to countless management presentations regarding strategic direction, goals for the company, and vision statements, I have found that most employees are unable to intuitively translate big-picture objectives into their daily jobs. As soon as everyone leaves the presentation and falls back into his or her day-to-day routine, there is a disconnect concerning what that big picture really means. I have spoken with a number of teams after such presentations from companies I have worked at and there are astounding similarities. While there is usually a genuine sense of enthusiasm, there remains a void in employees' minds that leads to confusion. In any companywide agenda, in order for all employees to understand how they are to contribute, the following questions need to be answered:

- What needs to change in order to accomplish these goals and objectives?
- What new behaviors will be needed?
- If I keep doing what I have been doing, will it be enough?
- Will it help in my professional development if we achieve these goals, or will I become redundant?
- Is there a bigger picture or purpose for these goals?
- What is expected from my boss?
- Does my boss know what this means to us as a team?
- How will I be personally responsible?

The list above may be a good checklist for any senior executive who intends to make a speech to employees regarding vision and objectives. It is equally important that line managers take this all the way to the shop floor, for it is a key factor in implementing a think small, act now culture.

Works from the Bottom

If we were to say that thinking and behaving small is an art with a structure much like that of any other art, where the physical representation defines the parameters of the art but not the art itself, then all the creative ideas and immediate repairs work from the line-employee level all the way to the executive suite. Everyone is involved, and everyone has a place.

Employees need to feel that they will be heard and that they are truly empowered, supported not only by their immediate managers, but also by upper management. They have the right and the authority to use their intuition and creative ability to make something work better. This is a mantra that needs constant chanting so that it enters the hearts and minds of longtime employees and is immediately recognized by new ones.

Management needs to encourage and support a culture where small improvements occur every day, not just on an as-needed basis. Why do employees ignore the fact that something is not working and just keep on doing it? It's rather like leaving garbage on the street, hoping that some day someone will pick it up, or the famous "not my job" syndrome. The fact is that most employees are afraid to make changes unless they know that doing so is OK. Most employees will not make changes for the sake of change, but will do so to make their lives easier. If those changes are pointing in the same direction as the corporate goals (as they were communicated so well by management), then we are getting ready to advance to any level of growth.

Calculating the Risks

Thinking in terms of small incremental improvements has the added benefit of being low risk. Line managers have the responsibility for ensuring that the changes made within their areas of responsibility are within the scope of the flexibility that employees have to act on these changes. The emphasis is on *improvement* and on alignment with well-defined objectives. Once this is understood, behaviors are not radical. The fact that employees feel unrestricted in their ability to make their jobs easier and feel comfortable bringing issues to the table for resolution does not translate into wanting to change things just for the sake of change.

The way to administer this authorization for change is by assessing the outcomes. In other words, making changes can continue only if the changes are enabling employees to carry out their duties more easily. If there are deviations that require large-scale changes, these items need to be brought back for approval and put on the agenda at team meetings. No matter how big the initial problems may be, managers must encourage their teams to find tangible improvements that are within their means. In cases where the only solution requires outright replacement, managers should escalate the recommendations with the full knowledge and confidence that they have exhausted the small change options.

Visibility of Changes

Whenever changes are made that bring about a significant improvement in any one area, they usually add value elsewhere. I call this the ripple effect of small improvement behavior. For example, processing payments faster in accounts receivable has an effect on cash flow, allowing the allocation of more funds to other parts of the business. A way to increase the momentum of the ripple effect is to share the changes made and the results they produced. Naturally, not all changes need to be communicated, but those that had a bigger than expected impact are bound to be useful elsewhere in the company. It is surprising to see how many departments that have worked hard to become more efficient (and have been recognized by the rest of the organization for doing so) hoard information, treating what they did as intellectual property that has to be kept confidential from the rest of the organization for fear that someone will steal their ideas for his or her own benefit.

There is no harm in intracompany competition provided it is done for the right reason and in the spirit of dedication to the common goal. Competition begins to become destructive when teams and individuals feel threatened, believing that their good work will be used against them or that someone else will receive recognition for their ideas. This is why it is important to reward at the team level. Attitudes can be changed as long as there is a proper reward system in place that encourages the distribution of knowledge. Managers and senior management need to be mindful of this. Recognition of individuals should therefore include not only their contribution to their immediate line of work, but how they affected other parts of the company, and to what extent they went out of their way to do so.

When sharing is encouraged, it soon catches on. Others follow when they see that accolades are given to those who, in the line of duty, were able to improve things outside their sphere of work.

To set this ball rolling, managers need to actively convey their team members' work to other parts of the company. Part of the readiness program to stimulate small improvement behavior is for managers to have this as part of their agenda. I would go so far as to make the companywide distribution of small improvements a key performance indicator for managers.

Mentors Wanted

There will be people who are skeptical about the system, especially those who have been with the company for a long time or those who feel that they have heard all this before. Others still will not feel that making improvements is their job; to them, it is always someone else's job. To coin a modern management phrase, those who "won't get on the bus" need to be scrutinized, but the issue is rarely competence—it has more to do with willingness. This stems from a "what's in it for me?" attitude.

On the other hand, there are those who see real opportunity to flex their creative muscles and apply changes that they have been bursting to make for some time. Once the recognition system is in place, these more enthusiastic and motivated individuals should not be seen as threats to others. They should be encouraged (and recognized) as mentors to their peers. Peer-to-peer mentors often have more influence than managers.

Expect Big Things from Small Contributions

Part of the process for encouraging employees to think about and perform small improvements is to set goals and targets at the business unit level. It is the basic step in alignment with the overall company objectives. This creates an atmosphere in which staff members will want to seek out those improvements that will bring the biggest bang for the smallest buck. I am amazed at the number of ideas that were once bottled up inside staff, which, once released, made vast improvements in productivity and output of work—ideas that, working alone, I most likely would never have thought of myself.

CHAPTER 8

SMALL TACTICS WORKSHOP

In this chapter, we will bring together a lot of the ideas and small changes that we discussed in earlier chapters and organize them in order to produce an action plan. The workshop and the accompanying reference notes can become the centerpiece for communicating this new culture of enabling and empowering employees. In order to do this in the most efficient manner, the workbook-style approach is intended to be completed in real time. There are eight parts to the overall plan, and templates in tabular formats are available for each of the sections.

The objectives of the plan include complementing any existing plans and strategies that you have in place. Rather than being an attempt to restart any activities that are already in place, the intention is to provide areas where insertions that will lead to improvements can be made. The criteria are to make small changes with potentially large positive outcomes in order to start a process in which small incremental changes become a normal part of people's everyday style of work. Therefore, the plan that will come out of this process is the starting point and requires reinforcement over time. As results are seen from the actions coming from this plan, the ongoing activity is to renew the plan with a new set of ideas and criteria.

The plan is developed by conducting a series of workshops. There are eight workshops with an activity at the end of each one. Each of the activities creates output that can be added to the plan.

It is recommended that the activities be done in the order provided. The information needed for some sections may not be immediately available during the workshop meeting; if it isn't, the necessary information must be found and the plan updated later. The purpose of the plan is to identify areas where small incremental changes will provide the greatest return. So far, we have looked at a number of ideas, methods, and processes where small changes will assist and create growth, but we now need to tailor these specifically for your business so that you can identify and select the things to do first. The specific areas we will focus on are these:

1. Market assessment and opportunity analysis
2. Building a marketing strategy and plan
3. Identifying the competition
4. Increasing sales pipelines
5. Developing the channel partner networks

The plan is a starting point that sets in motion a process for involving every employee in the company in a path of continuous improvement under the structure that is being outlined here. Line managers can take portions of this plan, broaden the scope, and reach out to find other things over time as part of the improvement process. Therefore, the execution of this plan as it stands will bring out the biggest benefits for the smallest efforts, but it is also the start toward a continuous improvement process.

Workshop Format and Facilitation

The workshop may be done as an individual assignment where you go through the activities and call upon relevant members of the organization for the information, or it may be done in a meeting, with participants representing a cross section of key parts of the company. If a meeting format is to be used, at a minimum there should be representation from operations, sales, marketing, partnerships, production, and R&D. Managers and delegates that they nominate are preferred, as this will enable feedback and input from both the management level and the operations level. The facilitation of the proceedings is straightforward, and the only preparation required is a review of the questions from the workshop activities to become familiar with the subject matter and the data. Where there is a need for more information, this can be found offline, as the plan will come out of this process in draft form.

Each of the activities has a formatted that can be used to input the required values and information. The implementation and prioritization of the plan are developed in the next chapter. The SMALL Tactics workshop flows into a process where the activities are to collect the data, make fundamental decisions, and apply some creative ideas that will not require major changes to existing operations or business functions and will promote and increase growth.

Socialize the Plan

The completed activities become the plan, and the resulting document will become the central document to which any amendments and refinements are made before it is distributed within the organization. An abridged format can be used for saliency. Everyone in the company should be given an opportunity to provide feedback to management, and this should be communicated to the core team to permit further adjustments. This does two things: it allows buy-in from everyone, and it begins to communicate that management is serious about having everyone involved in the process of change for bigger success. Often plans are handed down as instructions isolated from the bigger-picture objectives. There should also be an open forum for staff to send their questions, and nominated persons from the core team can be made available to answer these questions in a timely manner.

The communication of this document is also the basis for the transition to becoming a company that embraces intuitive action by employees to carry out small steps within their respective departments. It is important that all employees understand their role and how they are connected to the bigger cause. This document provides a reference for creating an internal presentation that can be used in meetings and also disseminated across business units and channel partners.

Therefore, the format requires looking into eight different areas of the business and probing for specific details by asking a series of questions that will be used for three purposes:

1. Identify the areas that need the most attention with regard to becoming bigger and better and promoting growth.
2. Set priorities for attention within those areas.
3. Apply metrics to measure progress and allocate tasks to owners.

The areas that will be covered relate to key parts of any organization that have a direct impact on growth and efficiency. There are other areas of the business that may need to be addressed that are not covered here; for example, human resource management is not included. Since there can be an impact on growth if human capital is not in place, this area may be added using the same methodology used for other sections at a later time.

Goals and Objectives—Market Assessment

In any planning process, there is a need to ensure that you understand the market you are in and what markets you wish to grow into. Often market assessments are done by looking at the predicted size of markets given by market research, taking those predictions at face value, and making assumptions based on them. Take, for example, the small and midsize enterprise market, which is estimated to be over $43 billion. You need to look at that number with filters to determine what percentage of it is actually *addressable* by you.

Often segmentation does not go far enough in determining who and where the most likely customers are. What is generally the norm is to find an approximate market as a "catch-all." In other words, you want to make the market segment as broad as possible to make sure you do not miss out on some area. The downside of marketing too broadly is cost. Think of the last direct-mail or e-mail campaign that went out to the "likely" market target list. It is far better to narrow the target and be relevant to a smaller group than to open the field in the hope of playing the numbers game of greater returns.

Experience shows that it is better to market specific products and services to several niche markets than to go for mass. The development of goals and objectives should show the possibility of expanding into adjacent or niche markets. The small but significant addition is to be able to delineate markets according to the usual segmentation rules, but to add buyer behavior and spending. While the SMB market is a huge market in terms of monetary value, the fact is that within that one market there are several segments defined by size of company, geographic locations, and other such criteria.

Adding further demographic criteria produces enough distinctness for the identified segments that need to be marketed to differently. For example, SMBs in a certain size range prefer to buy from local trusted advisors rather than large corporate vendors, even though they want to buy the same type of products and services. Others with smaller revenues want to buy packages, with products and services bundled in. The impacts of both these nuances are significant when it comes to your message, your product presentation, and your selling approach.

Therefore when you are looking to revise your goals and objectives by taking market opportunity into account, listing the industries and subindustries you sell into today and comparing them with the size of the markets you are considering provides valuable input for allocating budgets and revenue targets. You may find that once you look at the opportunities and the addressable markets you can actually move into, your initial estimated growth percentage may be low.

ACTIVITY 1
Market Assessment and Opportunity Analysis

The purpose of this activity is to produce an analysis of where you are selling today in terms of industry profiles. By looking at the size of the market and where your business is coming from, you will gain valuable insight for establishing where your investments have been going and for comparing this with overall market opportunities. Other parameters will provide indicative signposts regarding potential niche markets. Bringing these data points together in one place provides useful input for setting or reviewing annual budgets and revenue targets. It is recommended that Figure 8-1 be included with any other form of market assessment and opportunity analysis that you have in place today. The purpose of this is to add those finer points that will further validate the direction of the company in terms of finding where the growth opportunities are. It is important that the data provided are as accurate as possible.

Sources of data for overall market size may be obtained from various sources, including industry analysts such as Gartner, IDC, AMR, Forrester, Hoovers, OneSource, and a myriad of others. Some are available on the Internet at no cost; for example, www.buyusa.gov offers data on a broad spectrum of industries that are closely aligned with SIC codes, and also provides international data. Other sources charge a nominal fee for the research materials.

Fill out Figure 8-1 in the following order:

1. List all of the industries and subindustries that you are selling into today, with the number of customers alongside each of the classifications. In Chapter 3 we referred to SIC classifications, and these will be useful here. Write the actual number of customers and the percentage of your total customers for each of the classifications.
2. Alongside each of the industries, add the product or service that you provide.

Priority Rank	Adjacent Niche	Product/ Service	Industry/ Subindustry	Number of Customers	Percent of Total	Overall Market Size	Direct/ Indirect
	1. 2. 3.						
	1. 2. 3.						
	1. 2. 3.						
	1. 2. 3.						
	1. 2. 3.						

Figure 8-1 Goals and Objectives—Market Assessment

3. Using the SIC or similar classifications, list those niches that you could easily address based on where your strengths are today. You may assume that some modifications to your product or service may be needed. At this stage of the planning, you do not need to know the sizes of these niches, as you will approach the niche markets with a view to entering and expanding as you go. Most niches will be small. The point is not to look for the biggest niches, but rather to determine what niches you can potentially enter and expand from there. List up to three niches for each industry you are currently servicing.

4. Determine the best sales model for entering each market based on access, customer buying preference, behavior, and product skills required. For example, should you use direct sales or an indirect method involving channel partners? List the way you sell to these segments today. If you already sell both directly and indirectly, write down the percentage of overall sales that comes from each—for example, 60 percent direct, 40 percent indirect.

5. Using independent market research, determine the total number of customers in each of the industries you have listed.

6. When you have all the data listed, prioritize the markets according to the highest opportunity for growth. It will become apparent where the opportunities to (a) continue to grow and (b) grow into are.

Once your priorities are set, you can then decide whether to go after all the opportunities in order or to select from the top of the list those that you feel you can realistically tackle given your available budgets and resources. The importance of having this information in one place is to provide a view of where the company has been performing and where the next best opportunities are for growth.

Building a Marketing Strategy and Plan

Developing a marketing strategy and plan can be a long and time-consuming process. The elements that are being addressed here are intended as complementary input to your existing marketing plan. The purpose is not to build an entirely new plan, but to address those specific areas where closer attention will make a positive difference to any plans you may already have in place today. If you are in the process of developing a new plan or are thinking of creating new campaigns to increase revenues and expand into new markets, the activities listed here will be beneficial additions.

The main focus will be on determining the specific customer needs that your products and services are addressing today and how you can modify those products and services, change their positioning, or repackage them to enter new markets and grow the business without big investments or disruption. The aim is to look for the smallest changes with the highest returns. In order to do this, you will use the priorities from Activity 1, with a focus on the products and pricing strategy. You will also compare that information with the competition to arrive at areas where you feel you can differentiate yourself as having unique value.

Contrary to popular belief, price can be part of the value that you provide to your customers. The finer point, however, is that providing value is not about being cheap or offering heavy discounts; it is about the way you price and bill. For example, customers may see value in being charged based on milestones or by payment schedules. Therefore, while the argument that price alone is not the value is true, price can be the difference between making and not making the sale. This is why customers' buying behavior is so important when it comes to segmentation and market analysis.

The specific areas that we will be addressing are the following:

- *Benefits analysis.* Determine the specific pain points and issues within the industries you service and match them with a value proposition from the products and services you currently provide.

- *Pricing strategy.* Determine some of the ways in which you can increase your value by differentiating in terms of the way you price to customers rather than by offering discounts.
- *Integrated marketing.* Develop an integrated marketing approach to leverage existing and new marketing activities with one another for optimal demand generation.
- *Barriers to entry.* Identify barriers to entry, such as legal, compliance, geographic, and government requirements, for any proposed new markets.
- *Marketing communications.* Establish a communication and information-sharing process to ensure that sales and marketing are synchronized at all times.

Benefits Analysis

The more closely you associate benefits with issues, the better the response from your customers and prospects will be. The identification of industry pain points requires finding the common and major issues that a particular industry is facing. There are various sources for this type of information, such as industry journals and research, but a great deal of the information you need can come from internal sources, especially from sales. In each of the industries that you currently service, there are specific economic, competitive, compliance, or regulatory pressures facing that industry. Listing these is the starting point for matching those issues with your solutions. This also becomes the setting for the message and the description of the value proposition for each of the products and services you provide.

Once you have determined at least three major business issues for each of the industry categories you currently sell into, break down those issues further by determining who in your customer's organization would be most likely to be feeling the pain or would be responsible for finding a solution. It is possible that the same pain point is owned and shared by a number of different people in the same company. That is perfectly valid; however, the way you solve the problem and the way you present the benefits will differ depending on the audience you are addressing. We cover this in more detail later in the workshop.

Activity 2
Industry Pain Points

The purpose behind this activity is to produce an analysis of where you are selling today in terms of industry profiles. Comparing the size of the market with where your business is coming from will provide valuable insight to establishing where your investments have been going compared with overall market opportunities. Using the format of Figure 8-2, fill in the following information:

1. List the industries or subindustries that you selected in Activity 1. You may have decided to select either a subset of the industries that you are servicing or the complete list.
2. Itemize the pain points experienced by customers in those industries. This will be a cross section of issues driven by external and internal pressures.
3. List the product or service that you offer that addresses those specific pain points. Use your official company product names where possible.
4. List the unique benefits and value that those products or services provide to relieve those pain points. In some cases, a one-to-one correlation can be made between a pain point and a unique benefit that you provide. It is also possible that one benefit can relieve more than one pain point. What is important in this process is to match uniqueness with customer issues.
5. The last step is to decide who within your prospects' and customers' organizations would be most affected by the pain points you have identified. This provides two valuable pieces of information: (a) it makes specific where in the organization this problem has the biggest effect, and (b) it identifies the

Industry/ Subindustry	Pain Points	Addressed by Product/Service	Unique Value and Benefits	Affects Customer Title
	1. 2. 3.			
	1. 2. 3.			
	1. 2. 3.			
	1. 2. 3.			

Figure 8-2 Industry Pain Points

owner or the person who would be most accountable for finding a solution.

Pricing Strategy

The pricing of your products and services can become a contentious issue when there is a tension between value and selling price. There are a number of criteria that need to be considered, including maintaining an acceptable margin, competitors' pricing, and overall market entry pricing. The purpose of this exercise is not so much to change the price of your products and services, but rather to look at creative ways to increase value through pricing that may make your offering more appealing regardless of the price.

If you have a basic price list where the prices of goods and services are given as lump-sum amounts payable on invoice, there may be other alternatives that more closely align with your customers' cash flow and business budget cycles. Therefore, a small incremental addition that may make your pricing competitive is not about the price itself but about the payment options that you are able to provide to the customer.

There are various forms of pricing strategies, and some of them are more adaptable than others to alternative pricing options.

Market-Based Pricing

Pricing is determined by a process of analysis conducted with industry analysts or marketing consulting organizations, where sample customers are polled and a consensus is arrived at based on a balance between what customers are willing to pay and what competitors are likely to do. This approach is commonly taken when new products are introduced and a much lower than normal price is offered for a limited period of time to attract buyers.

- *Competitor-based pricing.* This is a direct-match model in which prices are matched. This model is used in the retail industry, where competitors will match one another's prices on products that are the same.

- *Cost-based pricing.* A cost-based price is determined by calculating the overall estimated costs to produce, market, and sell the product or service, then applying a profit margin on top of the basic costs. This model is most often used where there are specific, tailored build-to-order requirements, generally for large or one-off types of products and services.

There are other pricing models that are often used in conjunction with overall pricing strategies, such as loss leaders, limited-time pricing, and rebates. All of these have their place and can be useful as part of promotions and incentives. The optimal pricing strategy is to use a combination of pricing alternatives so that you offer (a) more consumption-based options than your competitors to enable customers to buy based on their size and usage, and (b) financial choices for customers to work within their budgets, allowing them to buy sooner rather than later.

In each of these pricing models, the pricing alternatives that follow can be incorporated:

- *Subscription-based pricing.* This pricing model is based on a service orientation where a fee is paid on a regular basis for a contracted period of time. The renewal period can be determined based on the type of product and/or service that you deliver. The fee can be paid in equal installments, or it can vary depending on the level of service or the number of services that are being requested at any one time. The attractiveness of this arrangement to customers is that it often converts the purchase from a capital expense to an operating expense. It is also predictable, so the customer is able to budget more accurately, knowing the fixed and variable costs over the period of the agreement. This type of pricing is popular in technology services, especially where hosting or outsourcing services are being provided. It is well suited for a services-oriented business where standard services are being offered, with customers being able to add services over time.

– *Transaction-based pricing*. This is similar to a usage model. The unit of measure is at a "transaction" level, representing a consumption rate. The best examples come from telecommunications and utility providers, which bill based on consumption. This model can be applied to a host of other products and services where a lowest common denominator that fairly represents an amount being used can be established. Customers are particularly attracted to this type of pricing if their business has peaks and troughs that affect their usage rates of the product or service you provide. Seasonal businesses will find this very cost-effective, as carrying the same costs for products and services when their plants and offices may be shut down or running with skeleton staffs is often burdensome. One of the considerations for this type of pricing is to ensure that there is a mechanism available that will enable you to account for and bill according to the units of usage. The units need not be at a transaction level, as telecommunications are; they can be on a module or maintenance agreement level as well.

– *On-demand-based pricing*. This is similar to the subscription model in that there is generally a set fee over the period of a contract term, but the subtle difference is that with on-demand pricing, the user is able to turn any of the services that are being provided on or off and be charged accordingly. Your products and/or services need to have characteristics that allow services and/or usage of a product to be disabled or increased by the customer and a corresponding billing system that is able to keep track. This is an alternative pricing and billing option that customers feel they have control over.

– *Finance-based pricing*. This is one of the easiest models to administer and attain. It involves simply taking the total price of your products and services and offering a financing option that you arrange with a suitable finance company (or your own), making the relationship as seamless to the customer as possible. This is a win-win for both you and the customer. It relieves the customer of the one-purchase-price burden, freeing cash and often allowing the cost to be expensed, and it offers you a financial incentive to make this type of deal on your customers' behalf.

This model is used widely where financing and leasing options are being offered for a multitude of products; however, the finer distinction here is to offer financing for both the product component and the service or maintenance component. This may include installation and implementation costs. If you can add all of the costs associated with delivery and provide financing or leasing as one amount, this can be a differentiator, especially for small and midsize companies. The barrier is often that the implementation, installation, or ongoing warranty service is done by a third party. The challenge is to get all parties on board and come up with a way to develop a one-stop shopping capability where the customer pays one monthly installment and everyone is paid behind the scenes.

- *Milestone-based pricing.* In this model, there is a delivery aspect to the products or services. This model is often used with professional services, particularly with IT services, where there are specific achievements and objectives that need to be met in order for the step in the billing cycle to be approved for payment by the customer. Milestones need to be agreed upon up front, before any settlement is formally made, and the amounts payable should include a percentage based on milestones and another based on time and resources consumed. In other words, the payments cannot be based solely on milestones. This is a one-way risk scenario. To prevent this situation and to avoid being left short if there are any unforeseen delays, milestone-driven pricing and billing should represent a fair percentage of the overall contract amount. Milestone-style agreements that have worked successfully have consisted of:

- A 20 percent up-front fee
- 20 percent of the usual time and materials fee
- 60 percent based on milestones (provided they are not more than 90 days apart)

Each of the additional pricing models offers alternatives that may increase your chances of winning more business, especially where cost is a concern of customers. The more options you have available, the more reasons there are for a customer to buy from you, all other things being equal.

ACTIVITY 3
Pricing Alternatives

In this activity, you will look at each of the products and services that you are providing and make an assessment of whether you can add more pricing alternatives that will make you more competitive and also remove any cost objections from customers and prospects. Using Figure 8-3:

1. List the products and services that you provide by their price list names.
2. Identify the unit of measure that you are pricing on today; in other words, is it by product unit plus service and maintenance, license and implementation, or monthly or annual fees?
3. Identify whether, with minor alterations, other pricing alternatives could be offered, using the codes provided.
4. Describe any prerequisite actions that need to take place before the new pricing options can be offered. This may mean involving other parties, such as finance companies, your channel partners, or other business associates to which you outsource part of your products and services.

The actions that follow from this are these:

1. Decide to add at least one additional pricing alternative for each of the product lines that you have.

Product or Service Name	How We Price to Today (Unit of Measure)	Possible Pricing Alternatives S, Subscription, T, Transaction, OD, On Demand, F, Finance, M, Milestone	Prerequisite Actions

Figure 8-3 Pricing Alternatives

2. Create an action plan to find the relevant partners and resources to make the new pricing arrangements available. If you are able to add one additional pricing alternative each year, you will be able to have a stronger competitive position without always needing to resort to discounting and rebates.
3. Publish the new price list.

Integrated Marketing

Integrated marketing can take many forms; therefore, rather than try to define it, we will describe its purpose, which is to ensure that you get the maximum output from any investment you make in any marketing activity—period. Leveraging marketing activities with both internally initiated and third-party actions will elevate sales productivity, increase demand generation and prospects in the pipeline, and raise awareness of your brand. There are a lot of areas in the marketing function, and you should select those that have the most direct impact on generating business.

A good example of a company using integrated marketing is Nike. Its marketing approach is based on having consistency across all its collateral. It integrates its communications, branding, advertising, sponsorship, online marketing, and store point of sale, engaging its customers in a uniquely identifiable experience. What makes this work for Nike is that the messages have a common theme at every customer touch point.

HP ran a campaign along similar lines when it realized that a lot of the functionality in the area of multimedia capabilities that Apple was exploiting was also available on its PCs: "The Computer Is Personal Again" program. Consistency was also a key discipline here, but HP went one step further and finessed its message based on the marketing media being used. In other words, it kept the essential elements, the look and feel, consistent, but clever nuances were used, with its television ads more "personal" than its print ads, which were more awareness and interest driven.

Whether you have an in-house marketing function or outsource parts of your marketing, no doubt you have planned some marketing activities. The purpose of this exercise is to list those marketing activities and connect them in order to fully exploit them. In some cases you may want to add activities that may be useful as interim communication events to support the ones you have.

When it comes to determining the return on investment (ROI) for marketing, you first need to aggregate the activities in such a way as to be able to measure their effectiveness, manage them and make decisions as to whether they are working, and decide to take different actions or stop them altogether. Conventional marketing techniques assume that if something is not working, the solution is to do more of it. For example, if an e-mail campaign is not attracting the level of responses expected, then the tendency is to increase the mailing list size and do more e-mails. This is particularly true when it comes to advertising campaigns, where the response to a failure to achieve the desired awareness levels is bigger and broader ads.

The fact is, most marketing campaigns are managed as a long list of activities, without any integration between the activities and the constituents that are affected. There are three areas where ROI can be increased:

1. Leveraging a set of activities for a common goal or objective
2. Communicating and aligning with sales
3. Managing effectiveness

If you follow a basic model of marketing known as *AIDA*, this will help you determine where the linkages and leverage points of the list of activities need to intersect. AIDA is one of the best models to use, as it is simple and follows a natural behavior in any sales and marketing process. You will easily see how to link your list of activities once you get even a basic understanding of the AIDA model for marketing.

What Is AIDA?

- *A = Awareness.* In any buying process, it is only natural that before anyone can buy anything from you, that customer needs to be aware that your product exists. In highly competitive industries, marketers attempt to heighten this awareness, trying to create as big an impact as possible in order to move the buyer to the next phase. Depending on the complexity of the sales cycle and the product or service, the period from awareness to purchase can be very short or can be several months. Regardless of the time frame, you cannot get to a purchase without making yourself known. While the concept is simple, when you look at the number of "exposures" to advertising, amounting to over 600 each day[1] (whether you notice them or not), awareness is an increasingly important consideration when developing any marketing program.
- *I = Interest.* In this context, interest is defined as taking the next step after being aware. The two are sometimes confused because they are tightly linked; however, taking an interest comes from a combination of awareness and curiosity.
- *D = Decision.* Interest leads to a process of further investigation and finding out more. When prospective buyers feel sat-

isfied that they know everything they need (or want) to know in the course of being interested, they make a decision as to what to do next. At this stage, this may not necessarily be a decision to buy, but rather may be a decision to proceed with finding out more.

• *A = Action*. In this phase, taking action is moving into a buying cycle. You cannot presume that this will result in a purchase, but it is here that the behavior starts to have inclinations in this direction. The prospect has moved to a level where one can categorize it as being a "lead" for a sale. It is at this stage that the sales process can effectively begin.

Since these basic steps are present in any purchase, when you are designing a marketing campaign, the AIDA process provides the basis for understanding that marketing activities need to be a series of interrelated steps rather than a list of tactical things to do. In each calendar year, most companies engage in a number of marketing-related activities. All of them, whether they are internally or externally driven, should be looked at as focusing on one of the steps of the AIDA behavior flow. For example, advertising is basically about awareness. While in the domestic consumer markets, it is influential as part of a delayed buying process, it is rare for business buyers to go directly from ad to purchase; while this does occur in limited circumstances, it should not be relied upon as a sustainable strategy to generate income.

Conferences and events have a value in that they are able to take the prospect through awareness and into interest during the same experience, which takes place in a single location and within a relatively short period of time. Any type of seminar also has similar effects. In general, any activity that is initiated by invitation and where attendance is required (including online events) will go as far as producing interest. The follow-up that occurs afterward is where the decisions and actions take place. These follow-up activities engage the prospect at a more specific level of detail (now that you know what the prospect is interested in). The follow-up call after attending an event is intended to serve this purpose. It is assumed that the attendee is ready to make decisions after having taken the time to come to your event. The reality is that postconference calling has the same effect as cold calling. The reason is that the knowledge about your company is usually insufficient to satisfy the interest and enable the prospect to make a decision either way.

The lesson from this is to provide as many specific opportunities for interaction as possible after a conference or event. The level of responsiveness will determine whether to qualify prospects as "sales leads." Whether you are measuring marketing's performance using ROI, key performance indicators (KPIs), or management by objectives (MBOs), one of the items needs to include making *sales more efficient and effective.*

How can you make some small changes to what is in progress and planned in order to achieve an integrated marketing plan?

The first step is to do some initial preparation. What you need to begin with is a list of all of your planned marketing activities, irrespective of their nature or purpose, for the next 6 or 12 months. The reason you need to do this is so that you can categorize the activities and identify their location on the AIDA process flow. Once you have done that, you can then determine how to connect the activities to ensure that you get the most leverage, and then you can look at possible holes where you may want to add activities or customer contact points. Figure 8-4 shows the location of different activities on an integrated marketing flow diagram, using a format that brings together the current elements of existing campaigns and programs. This format may be modified to suit specific needs, but the main purpose of describing the marketing calendar in this way is to highlight what may be missing and where opportunities to ensure consistency of brand, message, and content can be applied.

The integrated marketing flow diagram is a good way to represent where activities may be linked and where the message and content need to be consistent. The most effective use of the integrated marketing flow diagram can be achieved if all of the marketing campaigns are assembled and consolidated, showing the overall picture of all activities. The benefit of doing this is that it not only allows you to establish links among activities, but also

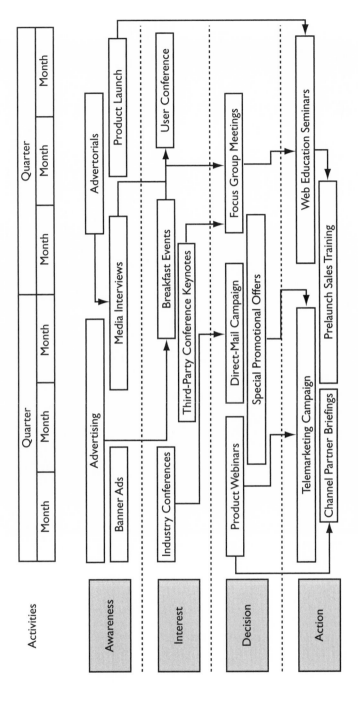

Figure 8-4 Integrated Marketing Diagram

highlights areas where messages and consistency can be maintained, especially when it comes to building out content.

ACTIVITY 4
Building the Integrated Marketing Flow Diagram

Using the format of Figure 8-5:

1. Following the model in Figure 8-4, place the currently planned activities in the diagram. Their start and end dates should be represented along the activities timeline. Where a series of activities is being repeated, add a separate box for each repetition.
2. Link activities according to the AIDA process, taking note of where there may be gaps. Consider a prospect that has just become aware of your company and its products and is interested in developing a relationship with you. What would provide a valuable experience that, if followed, would satisfy your criteria that this is a qualified lead on which sales should expend resources?
3. Overlay the content and messages that apply to each of the interrelated activities. For example, does the advertisement have any relevance to the conference, or to the Web seminar or direct mail? Is the information that is being provided at the company level and at the products and services levels aligned with the overall messaging and positioning for this year?

Where this is most useful is in showing gaps in activities that may not adequately provide the opportunity for prospects to build a relationship with you. When a simple list of marketing tasks is laid out in this format, it is often easy to determine whether too many items are being done in isolation and have disparate and incongruent messages. I have seen marketing plans that went straight from an advertising campaign to telemarketing as lead generation without anything in between and were expected to produce results. The results, not surprisingly, were low.

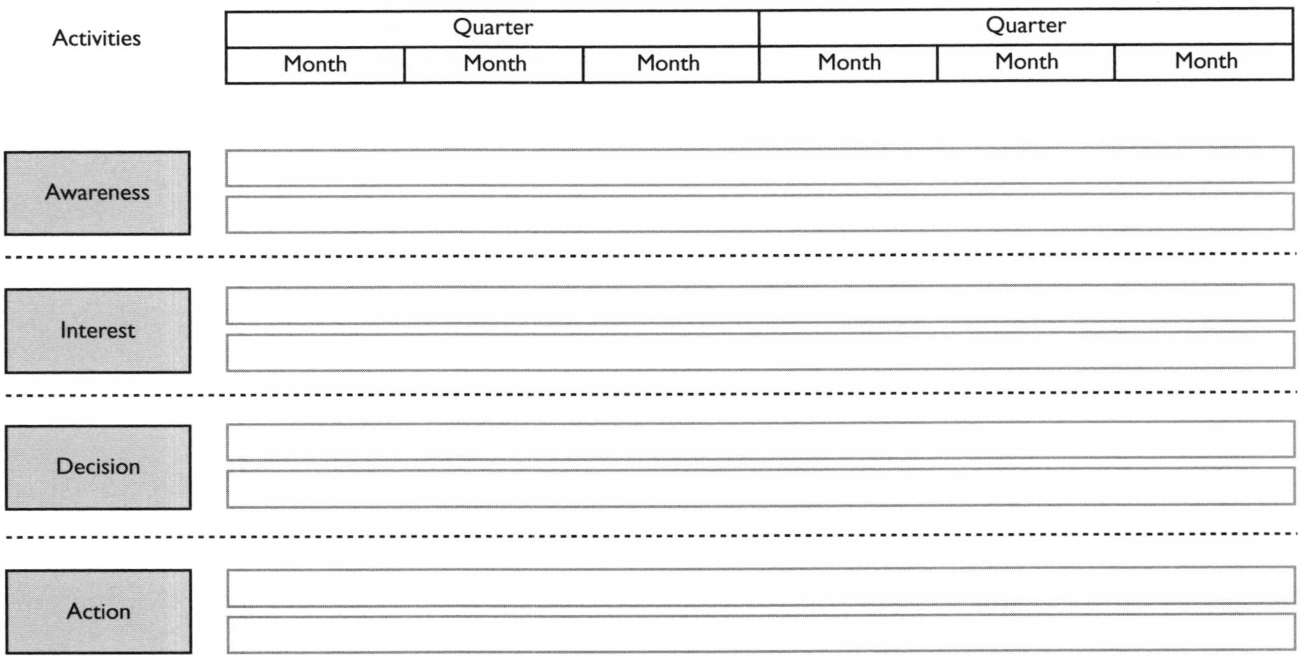

Figure 8-5 Integrated Marketing Template

It is important to note that tasks should not be inserted for the sake of completeness; instead, they should progress and provide the opportunity for customers and prospects to engage with you at deeper levels. For example, after prospects have attended a conference that created an awareness of your company and its products, sending a direct-mail message inviting them to a topical Web seminar or focused breakfast event would move them from the awareness stage to interest. Tracking their attendance at both is valuable information, suggesting that their level of interest is moving toward the decision and action phases.

The interim activities need not be complex in nature, and by applying some creativity, they can be accomplished at relatively low cost. There are small inclusions at the end of each activity that are often overlooked but are necessary to maximize the output of leads at the other end. One of them is ensuring that there is a selection of actions that the attending prospect or customer can choose from at every interaction or touch point with you. This means that there should be such a selection of actions at the end of every presentation, advertisement, banner ad, e-mail, voice mail, white paper, brochure, product sheet, CD, DVD, or promotional item (yes, promotional item).

Give the customer or prospect a choice of follow-up activities; these can include Web site demonstrations, focus groups, reading an upcoming article, a Web seminar, a free training session, an online product demonstration, and so on. Once the diagram is complete, it can be distributed internally and is an excellent communication tool from marketing to sales.

The next layer of information required on top of the integrated marketing flow diagram is the proposed content and messages. When you look at the Message Tree discussed in earlier chapters, you can now see how it fits into this process. In each of the activities, the high-level message needs to be inserted and used on every occasion. Even if there are products that are widely different in nature, the level-one message should apply. When you look at the marketing program in this way, the task of the marketing department is to ensure that supportive collateral is available. This brings us to the area of the marketing bills of materials (MarBoms) and marketing communications (MarComms).

Marketing Bill of Materials

In earlier chapters, we discussed the need to maintain an inventory of the collateral and support materials that are in circulation. Without knowledge of what materials exist and are used to communicate with customers, any work that is done to increase awareness and become more competitive is diluted. While determining what exists may seem to be a simple task, you will find that uncovering and recovering those old brochures and product pamphlets that are being handed out on a daily basis may take some time. If necessary, broadcast to the company, asking people to name the materials they are using. What you will find is that every corner of the organization will have a stash of marketing materials that are out of date, inconsistent, or simply inaccurate. Marketing, with management's support, should broadcast an amnesty and ask people who have these materials to exchange them for revised and fresh versions.

There are efficiency gains from having an up-to-date library of all content. When new products are launched or revisions are released, such a library makes it much easier to revise the content and materials and to change and manage the outgoing distribution. There are three broad categories of materials that should be kept:

1. Marketing
2. Online
3. Sales

By categorizing materials into these three areas, it is easier to determine the content usage with respect to the integrated marketing flow, making it easier to determine what content is needed and where. In each of the categories, classify each individual piece of content, using the AIDA codes. For example a brochure falls under marketing and has a classification of awareness.

The list in Figure 8-6 provides examples of the way marketing assets may be classified that you can use and add to as required. Other columns may include Revision Number, Industry Name, Content Owner, Partner Specific, and so on. In some cases, materials may be used for multiple purposes, such as marketing events and sales presentations. Codify them accordingly, as the aim here is to have one central repository for all materials.

Marketing Communications

Just as the marketing activities need to be as integrated as possible, the same applies to the external and internal communications. The idea of keeping "on message" is a powerful objective and should be maintained at all times. One of the easiest and most effective ways to have consistency of message is to decide where the clearinghouse for all outbound communications is. In most cases this is the press relations (PR) department, but a discipline needs to be invoked to prevent leaking of information or maverick communications by unauthorized staff.

The communications clearinghouse need not have an approval authority; its role and responsibility is to ensure that the distribution of information is aligned with the company's agreed-upon messages and value statements. It is also able to make judgments about the timing of the dissemination of information. It is therefore important that a representative of this function has knowledge of key company objective and issues. This clearinghouse function will be used for managing the transmission of both good and not-so-good news to the media and the public.

A small step that has proved to be successful is to select and nominate qualified staff to be the company's "official" spokespersons. The rule is that any press or other related activities or requests directed toward anyone other than the official company speakers must be passed on to one of them or to the PR department. The names of the spokespersons need to be clearly communicated to all employees, and strict adherence to this policy must be enforced. A media training program for all of the official

Marketing Online Sales	Content Name	Brief Description	AIDA Classification (A, Awareness, I, Interest, D, Decision, A, Action)	Internal/ External Use
Marketing	Brochure	Company-level brochure	Awareness	External
Marketing	Advertisements	New product launch	Awareness	External
Marketing	Data sheets	Product A	Interest	External
Marketing	GTM strategy	Strategy for fiscal—includes budgets	Awareness	Internal
Marketing	Elevator pitch	Company and products presentation—generic	Awareness	External
Sales	Profiles	Customer profiles and testimonial sheets	Interest	External
Sales	Call guide	Telemarketing call guide for Product A	Decision	External
Sales	Product sheets	Product technical sheets with competitive data	Decision	Internal
Sales	Product family	Product information kits—multimedia	Action	External
Sales	Marketing calendar	Schedule of upcoming marketing events	Interest	Internal
Online	White papers	Technical white papers—by product and service	Interest	External
Online	Online demo	Downloadable demonstration—Product A	Interest	External
Online	Customer profile	Customer profiles with interactive video	Awareness	External
Online	Analyst report	Analyst report and industry commentary	Interest	External
Online	Press releases	Current product and company releases	Interest	External

Figure 8-4 Marketing Bill of Materials (Mar Bom)

231

spokespersons that will include the company's message and positioning statements and themes can then be put in place.

What this ensures is that regardless of the press event, the answers and statements that are made will support the overall messages and values that the company has decided on. This type of solidarity is powerfully competitive and shows customers a real strength: the company is speaking with "one voice" and everyone is saying the same thing. Holes in communications are the fodder that competitors' salespeople live on.

Obtaining a discipline of keeping on message will take time, but there are small improvement disciplines that can steer communications toward being aligned.

ACTIVITY 5
Centralize Marketing Communications

1. Decide where in the organization and who should be responsible for being the communications clearinghouse. The most logical area for this function is, of course, the PR department. In situations where this is outsourced or done by an external agent, a formal process should be instituted and made part of that agent's responsibilities. A representative of this department or area will need access to senior management meetings and to privileged information. Therefore, in cases where the PR function is external, an internal representative needs to be assigned.

2. Select a group of key employees who represent the major facets of the organization who can be media trained and delegated as the official spokespersons for the company for their areas. Decisions on press interviews, analysts' briefings, or any other formal eternal communications need to be made by the relevant authorized person in the PR department. PR is all about relationships with key media and industry people; therefore, the monitoring of proceedings and relationships needs to be correlated with the organization and briefings.

3. Engage an external media company to conduct media training for the designated employees. Ensure that the training program is tailored for your company-specific needs with regard to the type of media that will be involved and, most importantly, how to respond and manage speaking engagements to keep the company message intact. This training needs to be given at least once a year or whenever the company's key messages are changed.

Describing Your Competitors

In Chapter 6 we looked at the importance of differentiating by being uniquely identified as a key to competing. What we are dealing with in this portion of the workshop is making sure that you know what you know and find out what you do not know. Understanding your competitors is something like detective work. It must be done legally, the information needs to be made available by proper and transparent means, and the picture needs to be pieced together. Often competitive data from various financial and company resource libraries are thrown together, and that is it. What you need to be able to do is to map the strategy that your competitors are executing at the company and product level.

Therefore, while financial and product-related data about your competitors are valid, what is more important to understand is, what are they up to? Therefore, what you want to do is take notice of changes. Where and what are your competitors altering or doing that is fundamentally different from last time or what you know to be their usual business practices? Some of the changes that need to be noted are these:

- Has there been a sudden change in price or pricing methods?
- Are they discounting more than usual?
- Are you seeing them in competitive sales campaigns as much?
- Are you seeing them in industries where you never saw them previously?
- Has their direct sales force increased or decreased?

- Where are they opening offices?
- How many big deals have they won in the last year?
- How many small deals have they won in the last six months?
- Has there been a change in the ranks of senior management? If yes, where did the new people come from?
- Have they started an acquisition strategy? If yes, where?

This type of information needs to be part of the overall competitive intelligence that is being collected and distributed to the sales organization in a confidential and efficient manner. Understanding your competitors' movements will provide indicators to the ways in which they are planning to go against you. The main goal is to avoid surprises and having to confront any of your competitors' actions directly.

Observations based on the activities of and data about your competitors will begin to provide trends and patterns, especially concerning the way your competitors go to market. It is unusual for a company to launch products or services very differently from the way it did it the previous time. This information about your competitors becomes valuable when you piece together the seemingly minor details that come from press releases, earnings, and other public communications. Knowing your competitors at this level allows you to counter them, be proactive, or take cautionary measures. To do this, you need to allocate resources to keeping a vigil and reporting any movements by your primary competitors on a regular basis. A standard report format is advised for brevity for those on a need-to-know basis.

Any patterns and trends should be viewed with the goal of identifying your competitors' weaknesses and strengths. In other words, if a competitor is customarily late at launching products after it announces them, then this is a weakness that can be easily exploited. I once worked with a salesperson who kept a log of the number of times that his prime competitor was late on product delivery and produced a PowerPoint slide showing the dates products were promised against actual delivery dates and, more important, showing the impact that this had on customers.

This knowledge, coupled with your consistent communications regarding your unique capabilities, will increase the chances of your being in a leadership position. Sustainable competitive advantage may sound like a cliché, but it is the most effective way to navigate and mitigate competitive pressures. Picking your battles is just as important, and when it comes to differentiation, those that know their customers the best and can play to those customers' needs will win more often and create a greater sustainable advantage.

ACTIVITY 6
Keep Track of Competitors' Movements

Figure 8-7 provides a simple reporting template that can be easily updated on a weekly basis with information that allows you to monitor competitors' movements. Keeping the form short and updating it on a weekly basis allows for easy reference and makes it likely to be read when it is distributed.

Competitor Name	Company Profile (Revenues, Employees, Locations)	Product Profile (Prime Products/ Services)	This Week's Activity Scorecard (Press Releases, Hires, Customer Wins, Acquisitions, Product Launches, Partner Alliances, Announcements)

Figure 8-7 Weekly Competitive Monitor

1. Using the format in Figure 8-7, allocate resources to soliciting both information from within the company (mainly from the sales force's experiences out in the field) and publicly available external information related to what your competitors are doing. Initial sources can be industry analysts, press, and other industry watchers. There will be weeks where there is little information and others where a lot will happen.
2. Make the competitive monitor available to all salespeople on a regular basis, and get their feedback and other input from them whenever possible.
3. On a monthly or quarterly basis, review your competitors' major milestones and compare them with what you have done in the same time period. Identify any weaknesses, such as broken promises, issues with customers, and so on.

Increasing Sales Pipelines

An issue that faces marketing departments is their ability to determine exactly how much investment will be required in order to support the specified revenue targets. Most companies struggle with making any direct correlation between the marketing investment and resources expended and the revenue numbers. The answer depends on how and from what side you are looking at the question. Marketers will argue that "without marketing there would be no revenue"; then again, if you ask the salespeople, they will probably counter with "marketing does nothing for us." While these are extreme views, I have yet to come across a company, large or small, in which sales and marketing are so intimately connected that either party would ever admit that without the other, not a penny would ever be made.

Therefore, a small, simple, and easily administered process is to perform some basic calculations that will help both marketing and sales appreciate each other's efforts to arrive at the same goal. Commonly referred to as the "sales funnel," it is a way to determine the amount of effort on the part of marketing that is required in order to produce the desired number of qualified leads

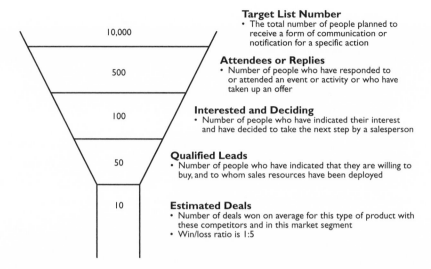

Target List Number
• The total number of people planned to receive a form of communication or notification for a specific action

Attendees or Replies
• Number of people who have responded to or attended an event or activity or who have taken up an offer

Interested and Deciding
• Number of people who have indicated their interest and have decided to take the next step by a salesperson

Qualified Leads
• Number of people who have indicated that they are willing to buy, and to whom sales resources have been deployed

Estimated Deals
• Number of deals won on average for this type of product with these competitors and in this market segment
• Win/loss ratio is 1:5

Figure 8-8 Leads to Sales Funnel

so that sales can make its numbers (see Figure 8-8). Where the concept of the sales funnel has been adopted, its credibility has been questioned when it is used for a large number of campaigns across different industries, product groups, and market segments. The concept of the sales funnel is actually sound as long as the data used are specific.

If we look statistically at a real-life example of what happened in a marketing campaign designed to create demand, we can see how the percentages correlate with the figure above and how large amounts of resources and investment can quickly diminish to small results. In this example, 1,000 prospects were targeted with a mail and telemarketing campaign. Of this total, only 6, or 0.6 percent, were qualified as leads for sales. The numbers ran as follows:

Number of contacts removed after the first call:	403
Number of prospects requiring more than one call:	279
Number of prospects where calls created an "interest"	202
Number of prospects still active after 30 days	73
Number of prospects removed after three calls	37
Number of total opportunities passed to sales	6

While these numbers may seem low, several companies in different industries report similar results, with the highest being a manufacturing company that reported a 3 percent return. Depending on the amount of revenue that each opportunity represents, these numbers may be fine. However this is not the end of the cycle, and it is here that discrepancies can be found between sales and marketing reports.

Marketing will report that six leads were passed to sales. Sales will tell you that it sold two. The reason is obvious: sales has to deal with competitors. Therefore, the metric that needs to be included is the win/loss ratio. This ratio is the average number of times a deal is completed compared to the number of competitive deals anyone is engaged in at any one time. In this case, the win/loss ratio is 1:3. On average, of every three competitions engaged in, one is won. Once we introduce this factor, the sales funnel becomes more meaningful, and marketing can adjust its estimates in accordance with what is actually going to produce revenues.

To assess the amount of effort required to meet an objective, the planning process flips the sales funnel upside down and starts with the end in mind. In other words, if the objective is to make 10 deals, then by working backward, marketing can determine the number of prospects it needs to attract in order to achieve that goal. While this example is linear to illustrate the point, the funnel can be added to by different activities ranging from mail campaigns to live events. The key is to make sure that the number of targets is within the range so that once the targets flow through the process, the desired numbers can be met. This simple formula is also valid if sales are expressed in terms of revenues. Simply divide the total revenue by the average deal size for that product and segment, giving you the number of deals required. For example, if the desired revenue target is $100,000 and the average deal size is $10,000, the total number of deals required will be 10, and you can work back from there.

Activity 7
Marketing Sales Planner

The marketing sales planner is basically the sales funnel in reverse; therefore, you are required to start with the total in mind. An alignment between the budgeting process and how these numbers are obtained is important. Often sales budgets are allocated based on sales territories for a specific set of products or all products. Consideration of running campaigns at a territory level will be helpful. If this is not feasible and all campaigns are run nationally or globally, then the totals will need to be aggregated. Using the format of Figure 8-9:

1. Take the revenue budget number and divide this by the average deal size. This may vary by region; and if this is the case, then take the variations into consideration when aggregating the figures. In the Conversion Factor column, fill in the factors you used, and in the Number column, give the calculated number of deals (rounded up).

2. In the Prospects row, you will need to determine directly from sales the number of deals that are won given the number of sales campaigns typically done for this territory or product area. This factor changes periodically, but taking the total number of sales campaigns for the last six months will be sufficient. To determine the number of prospects to determine the conversion factor, therefore, multiply the number of deals by the win/loss ratio. For example, if the win/loss ratio is 1:3 (won one of every three sales campaigns), then multiply the number of deals by 3 to give you an idea of the number of prospects required. Fill out the win/loss ratio used and the total number of prospects required.

3. Based on recent and past campaigns, determine an average percentage of those that were classified as leads that became prospects. Remember, these are people who have gone from awareness to decision and action. They have agreed to have someone call them and initiate a sales process. Divide the

Activity	Conversion Factor	Number	Supporting Marketing Activities
Deals			
Prospects			
Leads			
Attendees			
Events			

Conversion Factors Legend
Deals—Total revenue/average deal size
Prospects—Win/loss ratio expressed as W:L 1:3 (1 in 3 is won)
Leads—Average % respondents/attendees who invite sales
Attendees—Average % respondents to this type of activity

Figure 8-9 Marketing Sales Planner

number of prospects by the percentage amount. For example, if 2 percent of leads become prospects, the conversion factor is 2 percent; multiply the number of prospects by 100 and divide by 2. Insert that number in Leads with the percentage used.

4. Using much the same procedure as for item 3, determine the average percentage of replies that come from invitations for action that you send. These include direct mail, e-mail campaigns, Web seminar events, and any physical events. Once you have arrived at the percentage of respondents, calculate the number of attendees you will need in order to supply the required number of leads. Multiply the number of leads by 100 and divide by that percentage. For example, if the total number of leads you determined was 200, and the average response rate is 0.5 percent, then you will require 40,000 attendees (200 × 100/0.5).

5. In the Events section, determine how many events will be required to attract the attendee population. For example, a conference may attract 5,000 attendees, 5 direct-mail campaigns may bring 2,000 each, and an e-mail blast may bring 25,000 replies, making a total of 40,000. If other marketing activities are being used, such as banner ads or

advertising that is specific to this program, these should be looked on as awareness activities; if leads are generated by these activities, consider them bonuses. You are dealing with activities that are specific to creating demand, and therefore they invite and present the receiver with an opportunity to take an action to move closer toward your products and services. Itemize and list the nature and approximate number of targets for each of the events proposed.

This figure also provides a good indicator of the investment required to meet the objectives, in terms of both budget and resources for activities. After the final calculations, the number of contacts that need to be made in order to reach sales goals is often surprising. Partner and channel-related sales may be taken into consideration and the numbers adjusted accordingly. The other adjustment that may be made is for a new product launch where an increase in sales is expected. The metrics and conversion factors can be altered to allow for these if necessary.

Develop Channel Partner Networks

In any business, using partners as an extended indirect sales force that can sell and promote your products and services is becoming more essential for producing rapid growth and increasing profitability. The development of partner channels or distribution networks, sometimes known as "marketing channels" or "channel resellers," can increase market *coverage* and *leverage*. The focus within this module will be on recruitment of partners to maximize both coverage in market segments and leverage in terms of finding partners with ready-for-market resources who have the necessary skills to take your products and services to market as rapidly as possible. Campaigning for and selecting partners has become as competitive as competing for customers.

The challenge of finding and signing partnership agreements is compounded when you are looking to grow into new market segments and niches, where achieving the fastest time to market often means using existing outlets and leveraging your available expertise and knowledge for those proposed target sectors. If you do not have an effective network of partners and distribution capabilities, you may miss windows of opportunity in developing in niche markets.

Given competitive pressures, the emphasis in recruiting partners is placed on selecting those that have the biggest coverage and signing them up as quickly as possible in order to get the upper hand over any other potential competitors, sacrificing an in-depth assessment of partners' readiness and ability to allocate resources to your specific products and services and to become active in that market. Another challenge is resolving priority and loyalty issues, as your partner may be selling and marketing your competitors' products as well, and its distribution of your product to your desired markets must be supported by a business model that justifies your being added to the price list alongside the others. The latter is potentially a short-term issue that can be resolved by increased incentive and marketing efforts; however, the main impediment to growth is a gross underestimation of the effort required to bring the partner to market.

Our focus in this module is on recruiting, motivating, coordination, and management of partners. In particular, in the selection process, an approach that balances the opportunities that potential partners can provide because of their market coverage and presence, their ability to go to market with you quickly, and the ongoing management and support required to sustain them needs to be taken. Given the diversity of markets and the wide spectrum of partner networks, this can seem to be a complex task, and a dedicated function within your company to manage partner relationships and channel performance is often needed. This role is becoming increasing important, as gains from cost savings are being recognized, especially where there is a high cost of sales. It is possible to simplify this complexity in a way that will concentrate more of your effort on recruiting and development rather than purely on adding as many partnerships as possible to the company Web site.

Determining the optimal distribution flow for your products and services is a good start toward simplifying where you need to focus your resources. What generally happens to companies that experience spurts of growth over time is that they end up with a multitude of combinations of different types of channel structures, largely inherited as a result of signing up individual partners that belonged to supply chains with multiple layers of distribution networks. Decisions about *exclusivity* are also important and can affect a partner's motivation. Providing exclusivity to some channels and not others may soon lead to conflicts that will affect loyalty and long-term relationships. Therefore, having a clear understanding of whether or not you will provide any exclusivity arrangements should be made clear in the initial discussions and made company policy.

This takes us back to the importance of recruiting and selection. Determining and defining the ideal partner goes a long way toward solving a lot of management and maintenance problems further down the road. If there is one word that can sum up the majority of relationship issues between manufacturers and channel partners, it is *assumptions*—assumptions made by either party regarding the other party's roles, support, attention, training, marketing development funds (MDF), sales, margin, products, services, Web site links, conferences, dollar amounts, period, exclusivity, and the list goes on. These are areas specifically covered in the partnership agreement, but the assumptions stem from the fact that the company does not know enough about the culture of the selected partner and the way it is accustomed to doing business, and therefore its expectations.

Having a clear definition of the ideal partner overcomes a number of challenges later in the relationship, among them the support and resources required to go to market. Having said that, what also needs to be built into the specification are tolerance factors as guidelines for any acceptable exceptions. These accommodate reality but keep focus. There may be areas where there will be zero tolerance, for example, the partner's credit rating for financial stability. A simple list that outlines the criteria required is ideal in forming a template during the process of recruiting and prospecting for partners.

Often these criteria start with defining the type of partner. For example, will the partner be a distributor, wholesaler, value-added dealer (VAD), value-added reseller (VAR), integration service vendor (ISV), original equipment manufacturer (OEM), or agent? Each has its own criteria and requirements. Depending on the type of products and services that you offer, combinations may be appropriate, and these need to be looked at with respect to their relationships in the markets they service to avoid market conflict and overlap. For example, a distributor may be selling into a territory where you have also signed an OEM, so they are potentially competing with each other. Equally, in the technology and telecommunications industry, ISVs and VARs may become competitors if ISVs have their own network of VARs.

ACTIVITY 8
Channel Partner Criteria

Having fundamental criteria to determine the best fit channel partners and maintaining consistency in these criteria will provide the optimum channel partner network. The result will be congruence across the partnerships and a level of quality and customer satisfaction with the way your products and services are delivered.

1. Determine the market segments you are in. Make a list of the segments and niches that you have determined will represent solid growth opportunities.
2. Determine what types of partners will be most suitable for those market segments. Consider whether the best model would be a pure reseller, distributor, or agent model, or whether your products and services can be embedded into the partner's existing products and services.
3. For each of the partner types, develop a partner profile that clearly defines the partner criteria and characteristics required. Consider the criteria in Figure 8-10 as a scorecard to be

Partner Attribute	Criteria Requirement	Measured by	Importance 1–Low to 5–High	Tolerance Factor
Credit history	Credit rating	Meets specific rating		± %
Financial stability	Revenues/financial backing/working capital	Minimum entry		± %
Sales growth	Demonstrated consistent growth within the segment	% growth previous years		± %
Dedicated sales	Able to allocate dedicated sales personnel	Number of persons		± number
Customer service	Evidence of customer satisfaction and references	Number of customers		± %
Market presence	Evidence of market share in the market	Total customers		Min. number
Industry coverage	Number of industries or niches currently servicing	Total Industries/niche		Min. number
Delivery resources	Ability to deliver/maintain or support customers	Resources allocated		Min. number
Skill levels	Resources available for training	Resources available		Min. number
Prerequisite skills	Prerequisite skills required	Certifications/levels		Min. number
Marketing capabilities	Able to conduct marketing activities independently	Resources available		Min. number
Marketing budgets	Marketing funds allocated and budgeted	Amounts/quarter		Min. values
Relationship status	Partner will have direct relationship	Required Yes/No		None
Cultural alignment	Management values and relationships aligned	Key business ethics		
Investment	Partner will invest for long-term business relationship	Investment plans		Min. term
Business planning	Fiscal year compatible/budgeting cycles compatible	Same cycles exist		
Product integration	Able to embed/integrate product easily with current offerings	Development effort		Est. vost
Existing relationships	Competitive relationships exist	Assessed risk		Min. number

Figure 8-10 Partner Profile Attributes

included in the partner profile when selecting and ranking partners.

Executing the Plan

Each of the eight activities involves specific tasks that can be carried out and managed across the organization by the relevant business owners and leaders. It is important that the changes and what they represent in terms of starting a process in which employees feel that these changes represent an ongoing ability to improve are communicated to the rest of the organization. In the next chapter, we will look at how to roll out the changes from the activities in this chapter based on what will provide the biggest benefits first with the smallest of changes and disruptions.

CHAPTER 9

PUT SMALL THINGS FIRST

The main thing is to keep the main thing the main thing.

—Stephen R. Covey

Now that we have spent all this time developing the plan, it is time to prioritize and determine what are the activities that we want to start with that will make the biggest difference. The way we do this will be to ascertain whether the biggest impact will come from the front or the back office. In other words, will we get the biggest initial payoff from activities that relate to the way we interact with our customers and suppliers, or will we get it from our internal processes and the way we function internally? Both are important and both should be addressed; the question is, which one first?

Communicate First

Business is about people, process, products, and services that together create a perceived value that customers are willing to buy because they see the price they pay as being less than the value they receive from your product or service. Often companies communicate a change only when their plans are definite and everything is in place. This is not beneficial, as it usually leaves people with open questions and uncertainty about their roles and involvement. Small continuous improvement behavior may be implemented in two ways. One is to mandate it, in which case most people will find ways to comply only enough to keep their jobs, and the other is to use motivation, where people engage because, first, there is a clear personal value in it for them if they do it, and second, they can appreciate that it makes the company bigger, stronger, better, and so on.

In introducing this new incremental improvement behavior culture, using the latter strategy of motivation will require that you include signs of the progress that the company has already achieved. This communicates that improvements can be made, demonstrates strength, reinforces current competencies, and immediately involves everyone on a positive note. Communicating the intentions behind the planning also provides an opportunity for feedback and questions that can actually be beneficial in finalizing the plans by improving the execution process.

Apart from the uncertainty and potential for resistance, employees will be reluctant to improve their jobs to such an extent that their unit becomes so efficient that they are unnecessary. A way of preventing this is to keep the company's employees well informed about its success. This means being specific about how success is being achieved, whether it is through new markets, product innovations, new alliances, prestige customers, or a combination of these. Employees need to be constantly fed with the company's achievements and how those have been attributed to team efforts and the contributions of everyone.

Therefore, one of the first items on the agenda is to develop an internal communications plan for announcing small incremental improvement behavior and following this up with regular communications regarding success. In Chapter 6, we spoke about letting everyone know about wins in the company. This is part of the communication, but the communication as a whole needs to be broader, with line managers detailing their business units' successes and the relationship of those successes to the bigger accomplishments of the company. Employees need to hear these things both from the top and from their immediate managers.

Knowing What Is Important to Say

In any communication, the first thing to focus on is the core values of the company; the findings from Chapter 4 are invaluable as a starting point. What you were able to uncover there was the customer's perception of the value received from your company. Customer opinion is a solid, credible platform on which to integrate any other desired values you are striving for with objectives and goals. Core values need to be believed by employees. They should be included in chatter at the water cooler, where questions are being constantly raised to clarify them. I have seen management consider employees who have a genuine intent and who raise pressing questions to be negative and uncooperative.

Core values represent a belief system that is manifested in actions. For example, if a core value is customer service, then the activity surrounding any interaction with customers is to result in complete satisfaction. The problem with core values is that no one knows what they really mean to him or her as an individual worker. The term often comes across as abstract; most employees appreciate what it is, but they rarely understand what it represents for them. It is something like looking at a complex algebraic formula. People may recognize what it is and understand what problem it is intended to solve, but knowing how to solve it is another matter.

The importance of starting with core values is that they are personal. There are key ingredients when communicating core values:

- These values must be communicated face to face by business unit leaders and line managers.
- The values need to be circulated to all employees for their input and feedback in an open way, with no one feeling threatened by employees' comments and opinions.
- The values need to be supported by management and by the actions of the employees themselves.

- They need to take the personal needs of employees into account to the extent that the company is seen to accommodate its employees in order for them to uphold the core values.
- They need to stand for what is right and to contribute to the wider community, not just the business community.
- They must be separate from profit and loss statements or desires for grandeur.
- They must not be self-serving statements.
- They need to define the essence and spirit of work, service, and loyalty, and what dedication represents at your company.
- They must be motivational and acceptable.

It is imperative that management "walk the talk" when it comes to core values. There have been many examples in recent times where the declarations of a company's core values did not match the behavior and ethics of senior management. The biggest challenge in implementing a culture of small improvement behavior is to get employees motivated enough to carry out these improvements.

One way to accomplish this is to brief managers regarding the way they will communicate to their teams, having them ask employees what else is important for them to know. This is useful for opening dialogue and promoting the sharing of thoughts on different aspects of strategy and future plans. Management and staff members can comment on the direction that is being proposed, and splinter groups can also be created across the organization to discuss the impact of the proposed change of habits and how they feel they need to contribute and connect to it.

There should be house rules for this type of dialogue, especially when the feedback is made available to others through intracompany bulletin boards. Published comments should be simple to understand; they need to be constructive, and any improvements or concerns should be encouraged. What is not allowed is forceful negativity or radical ideas that have ulterior motives other than the welfare of fellow employees and the company.

Leadership from the Middle

Becoming a bigger or better company through small incremental steps implies that a lot of what is to be done is at the tactical level. Even though you are able to make small incremental improvements during the formulation of strategies and plans, affecting a company's behavior in a way that has everyone involved generally means improving or changing something at an operations or unit of work level. The leadership of this connected work comes from middle management. The fundamental difference between making big changes and making small ones is that small changes come from the ground up and need to be managed from the middle. Big changes are usually managed and owned by senior management, largely because there is such a large investment and so much risk involved that only senior management has the authority to make the changes and is assumed to be the most qualified and responsible.

The management of small incremental change behavior is delegated to business unit managers, line managers, supervisors, and so on by the senior management. The reason this needs to be the case is that you are dealing with small incremental improvements that in the aggregate make a big difference. It is to some extent inverting a large-scale project; in such a project, you know the big objectives, and each employee needs to figure out what he or she needs to do in a little corner of the company to make the big project work.

If you are executing a project of any kind (large or small), you need to make all employees aware of their specific tasks (nothing new so far). What is different with small thinking is that managers are given specific permission to allow their teams to make improvements within their area of work that not only advance the project, but make it better. That is one application of small thinking; another is in everyday work life. Therefore, the change management process involves the middle managers as much as it does the employees who work for them. The leadership required is to encourage teams not just to make the numbers, or make the goals, or achieve the budgeted savings; instead, managers should focus on how much better their teams are at performing their role in the company and how this improvement smoothes the path for growth.

This does not mean attempting to mandate an assigned number of small incremental changes per month or per quarter for each department. It means that all employees can make their jobs easier, their customers happier, and their internal constituents more efficient by knowing that they can make changes. The scope of the allowable changes is left up to the managers. Maverick changes and radical alterations have never arisen from this process. In fact, the opposite it true; people are at first too cautious to make any change that may seem too extreme without telling the boss first. After a period of time, people feel comfortable with their scope of reality; they know what small means for them and what they need to bring to their manager. The most important aspect is that people are now being encouraged and made to feel free to do this—that there is a focus on this—that management wants this to happen.

Influence, Not Authority and Control

Attempting to impose control and authority over small incremental changes as they occur during the course of a project or daily work can be counterproductive, as it signals that this is just another item for the things-to-do list. The most effective way to implement small incremental change behavior is by influence. First, business unit leaders, plant store managers, department managers, and supervisors need to lead by example, actively seeking out and making small incremental changes and bringing these changes to meetings and to the attention of their staff. In the first few weeks and months, this demonstration will provide an excellent form of mentoring and education, giving front-line employees a sense of the scope and an association with the type of changes that everyone is referring to.

Using influence is also the most effective way to counter any controversy or resistance by individuals who may develop negative views of what is expected from them or who fear that this may adversely affect them. The way that managing through influence and not control is best demonstrated is by not using a tally of who makes what changes, but rather using recognition. In earlier chapters, we covered how the reward system plays a role in invoking the culture. Staff meetings present the perfect opportunity to influence. Those who have made changes, no matter how small, are recognized for these changes *and* the positive result that these changes had on the department, fellow workers, and the company. It is important to make the connections. This is not just about making an individual's work better; the benefits are cast far and wide, even though the change is small. Remember also that we are talking about *incremental* changes. Therefore, in exposing good work, it should also be noted that this will lead to the next improvement and the next and so on.

Rewards and recognition are always delicate matters in any company and at any level. The important thing to take into consideration is that rewards should be at a team or department level (even if people who were not directly involved were rewarded, this sends a strong message to them to step up and not feed off colleagues, as this will be noticed by others). Individuals can be singled out and recognized for their contributions to the team.

If you reward and recognize people often enough, and it is a good idea to make this part of the agenda for the regular weekly or monthly staff meetings, it activates people's thinking when they go back to their work posts. I have heard skeptics say that people will not actively make improvement changes, as they see this not as part of their job, but as part of their manager's or someone else's job. The fact is that where I have introduced this method of influencing people to make small improvements knowing that there are incentives and rewards (not necessarily monetary ones), people are more than willing to step up.

There will be two kinds of attitudes and two types of changers. The first attitude is one of embracing the ability to make small changes and then actually implementing them. The second attitude is one that, while also recognizing the ability to effect changes, then finds excuses for why they can't be made. The two types of changers are those who will have a different idea of small and propose large-scale changes (as the only way to improve) and those who will feel that taking five minutes less coffee break is all that is needed to turn the company around. Influence and communicating by example are the way to level these out. Also, it is perfectly valid to bring in examples from other departments and business units. As the manager, you may be more exposed to and aware of what is happening in other parts of the company than your staff is.

The Freedom of Small

Employees who know that they now have the freedom to make small improvements that will be beneficial for the longer-term running of the department and customer service will, at some point, hit a wall. After making a series of small improvements, you may find that not much more can be done. When this happens, employees may once again feel disempowered, seeing themselves as being back at the status quo and even threatened. To avoid this, you need to move the application of small incremental changes from day-to-day processes and functions to specific projects that are in progress. Projects are always available in every organization, and when a manager recognizes that a staff member has an eye for making small improvements, offering that employee to other related projects as a resource represents recognition and expands the employee's horizons, not to mention boosting morale.

It is cross-sharing of skills and resources that builds strength, and where matrix structures exist, making people part of other projects and bringing in those who have the reputation for being able to spot small improvements and act on them starts a wave of excellence that when encouraged reinforces the culture. Selecting and nominating employees to work on other projects because of their track record of making their own jobs better relates directly with the desires of most companies as they attempt to implement performance and talent management initiatives.

The big value that comes from small incremental changes occurs when managers emphasize the incremental part. This is an ongoing process that can extend beyond the immediate department or business unit. The attitude that develops is that things can always be done better and there is always something to improve somewhere in the company. In earlier chapters, we spoke about the importance of sharing knowledge across the organization and showed that small improvements in one area will ripple to others. It is logical for performing employees to follow this route as well.

The benefit becomes obvious when employees from different parts of the company who are known for their ability to make small improvements come together to work on a project and immediately create a working environment in which all concerned insist on high-quality work. Volumes have been written about companies that attempt to instill innovation and creativity within their ranks, with most reporting that ideas generally come from a precious regular few. While the exact reasons for this are unknown, it is likely that most employees either do not know how creative they can be or do not understand where the creativity needs to be applied. Small improvement behavior unleashes creativity and ideas in a staggered approach that is highly manageable.

Putting small things first means that changes start at the business unit level and then may expand across other parts of the company. In fact, within the business unit, small changes are initially limited to specific units or processes within an employee's daily work. Interactions with customers and internal business transaction processing are good places to start. The scope of changes in the initial stages is isolated to individual tasks, making them easier or more efficient. A skill will develop. This skill will be recognized by line managers as the requests for small changes may open broader issues. This is a positive indicator that small is turning into big.

Growth Efficiencies

Efficiency is the obvious area in which small incremental improvements will be focused, although it is difficult to assess and is based on subjective benchmarks. If something that in the past took four hours to do now takes only two, is that considered to be the most efficient? Or was two hours the normal time the same activity used to take, and doing it in one is considered "more" efficient? There really is no answer unless someone first sets a baseline. Therefore, small incremental improvements in efficiency should be viewed not only in terms of empirical measures of time or throughput, but also in terms of the overall increase in benefits and quality of work.

Ultimately the gains will come from spending less time on the same amount of work, as areas where this can happen will be the first ones that employees will identify. Redundant non-value-added tasks will be the first to go. While these cuts should be commended, the measure of efficiency has to relate to supporting the overall company objectives. The reason for this is that in making the department more efficient by streamlining processes and cutting out unnecessary work, the danger is that the focus remains on the department. In other words, are you more efficient in terms of helping to grow the company as a result of these changes?

This focus is especially needed in the first stages of allowing small and incremental behavior to take place. The objective is to reduce the energy spent on just finding things to change, instead tuning in staff members to those areas that have a more direct connection to growth. In the early days of implementation, it is recommended that people get used to making small changes and feeling good about it; managers then need to steer the activities toward a steady refining of the ideas and areas for improvement that relate to an efficient way to transact more business.

Scalability—Technically Speaking

Scalability is related to efficiency; it differs only in that to be able to scale and handle any size volume for growth, some efficiency needs to be there. Efficiency involves streamlining; scalability is about throughput. Scalability works on the same principle as an accelerator pedal in a car. The same engine is capable of going slow or fast, but always relative to the amount of pressure applied. Therefore, scaling for growth is the ability to build an engine that under any growth pressure can move at the pace required without reaching a point where it slows down, stops, or creates more problems.

Scalability is created by looking at the support systems. There are two areas where scalability can hit a barrier. One is in the manual procedures required to process transactions, and the other is in the computer systems that support these procedures. In either case, changes need to be made to allow for growth. One of the top reasons that companies replace their computer applications is that the systems cannot handle their growth. In other words, the systems may have become too slow, have antiquated processes, be unable to exploit new technology, or require high maintenance and labor effort and cost.

Therefore, one of the first things that needs to be considered is the systems that are supporting the business. If you look at the way computer systems were purchased in the past, it is likely that they were selected based on the needs of each department or function in the organization. That is, the finance department selected the finance system that was the most suitable and that fit with the budget it had available at the time, the manufacturing plant did the same, the warehouse and logistics acquired their supply chain management system, sales did its own thing, and so on. Most likely these systems came from different vendors and are based on different technologies. Some will be more technically advanced than others.

In earlier chapters, we reflected on computer system replacements that oversolved what were initially simple problems. This is true for individual department issues; however, when we are dealing with the ability to scale the business and provide computer systems that can enable and sustain the growth curve, our purview is much broader. In keeping with the main tenets of small incremental changes, the business application selected should be one that is fully integrated, offering a complete range of departmental and business flow processes built on a single technology platform and database. The common terminology used for these types of applications is "business suites." While they were traditionally designed and built for larger corporations that insisted on integration as a key criterion, these business suites are now being made cost-effective for small and midsize companies. Their advantage is that while they are fully integrated, with one common database where the information is logically stored, they can be implemented in a modular fashion.

The importance of installing once and implementing as needed is that this follows the principle of small incremental improvement. Going back to our legacy systems problem, it is likely that some of the systems will scale, whereas others simply cannot. The problem with this is, unless all the systems scale in unison, a weakness is created, causing bottlenecks or, still worse, lost business. As we implement small incremental changes, thereby increasing the number of transactions, some areas of the business will experience a greater need for faster, more seamless processing technology than others. The obvious areas are sales and order processing, followed by accounting and purchasing, manufacturing, warehousing and logistics, then finally finance and human resources.

Selecting a system that permits implementation by modules for each of these functions and being able to turn the modules on as needed is key to scaling the business. Attempting to replace all or the majority of systems at the same time has a high failure rate. There are a variety of reasons why this is the case, chief among them being the inability to adapt to the extensive changes in the business that the replacement required. Therefore, an audit of the current systems needs to take place, with an assessment and report on where, in priority order, the likely issues would be if the business were to double the number of transactions it handled in the next quarter. Having done that, you can select a computer system that has out-of-the-box integration and that can be implemented by modules, with, just as important, the ability to implement the modules at any time in the future without having to reinstall or reimplement what you have already done.

Discipline before Adaptability

The business will grow quickly even though you are applying small incremental improvements and advancements. Typically, areas that were previously blocking progress will run more smoothly, allowing greater productivity; customer service will rise to a higher standard, creating positive reports momentum; and sales will increase. If you adopt the principles of small thinking, you will move into adjacent niche markets, and therefore the repackaging of some of your products and services will spawn other new products and services. You will attract a new set of clients with different expectations, demands, and cultures. All these new facets of your growth will require that you adapt quickly.

Adaptability therefore involves a wide range of aspects of the business. Ironically, to be able to be agile and flexible enough to accommodate changes, a business first needs to have well-structured and disciplined systems with the appropriate competencies in place. Companies fall into the trap of taking on business from brand new areas in the hope that their systems will be flexible enough to cater to the never-seen-before nuances, creating disorder in operations. The main reason for this disorder is that the processes that were in place had become too rigid. In the software engineering business, this is like having hard-coded data within the program's software code. Every time a change is needed, you have to change the hard-coded data and recompile the program or programs. The remedy is to have the data available as external files that can be accessed and changed by users, so that when the standard programs are run, they read the tables and pick up the correct values.

Adaptable business processes and systems need to follow the same philosophy. There should be standard operating procedures that are flexible enough to *allow changes*. This is a slightly different approach to being adaptive, in that it is not so much about not having systems that are too rigid as it is about having systems that cater to changes. Fragmented (but flexible) systems lead to chaos; streamlined and well-structured systems with built-in provisions for additions and changes mean smoother transitions and tighter integration.

Standardize for Quality

Standardization and quality have been written about extensively ever since Total Quality Management (TQM) and the International Organization for Standardization (ISO) and its standards 9000 and 1400 became household names. These and other methodologies derive quality from standardizing what I call the foundation processes. These are the fundamental functions that the business carries out in the natural course of manufacturing products, distributing them, and performing other related business functions. Often known as standard operating procedures (SOPs), they have a distinct place when it comes to becoming a bigger company.

You cannot scale or become efficient unless you standardize the fundamentals of the business. These are generally big company issues, and so you may be wondering why they are included in the context of small improvements. There are two reasons: first, there are some small changes that can help enormously when it comes to standardization, and second, without standards in place, all the other small incremental improvements will actually support and increase nonstandard practices and processes, potentially making things worse.

The good news is that SOPs are available. The first thing to do is to make sure that they are up to date and ensure that everyone knows that they exist. SOPs are excellent starting points for developing small incremental behavior in any department or team. What will happen is that by applying small improvement behavior, staff members will intuitively be on the lookout to keep the standardizations in check. Employees will notice discrepancies from standardized processes and, with their newly empowered ability to effect change, will make the small incremental adjustments needed to comply. A self-cleaning operation will result.

Going back to the earlier point regarding the areas where *small changes* can bring you closer to having standardization, the following are some areas that may be useful:

- *Naming conventions*. This covers the names of products, services, definitions, documents, processes, policies, and anything else that is commonly used within the company.
- *Forms*. Gather all internal forms in one place, preferably on an internal Web site behind the firewall, categorized and filed for everyone to access. The same applies to forms used for external purposes. Legal documents should also be included here, although access to them may be restricted by user security profiles and IDs, if necessary.
- *Security login and access*. Standardize security login procedures and access across the systems and the organization, respectively.
- *Employee titles*. This is sometimes controversial, but it assists with communicating with the right people at the right time.
- *Templates*. These are different from forms in that they involve correspondence both within and outside the company, such as letters, memos, e-mails, approvals, self-service printed brochures, and other marketing assets.

Consistency in Action

Consistency is to a business as training is to an army. Consistency is sometimes confused with standardizing; the fact is, consistency has more to do with alignment with a level of standards. Standards are a set of rules; consistency is behaving in accordance with those rules. When we speak of consistent customer service, the emphasis is not on the documentation or process, but rather on the way the interaction is performed that supports the values of the company. The documentation and process are the standards.

The distinction between the two is sometimes confused, and this can have a detrimental effect. Telling a customer that you cannot process an order because the form has not been filled in correctly is not being consistent. Helping the customer complete the task *is* being consistent. Consistency therefore needs to be seen as an attitude rather than a process.

In marketing, consistency means projecting an image that communicates the value of the company and and supports the brand. Brand is an emotional attachment, and the fact that there is a consistent look and feel at every touch point provides evidence that everything the company does is in accord with its value. In earlier chapters, we covered ways to increase recognition and add brand value in our communications and media by aligning with a core message and supporting that message with evidence from our customers and partners. Within the company, proof of consistent behavior comes from cognitive action.

Networking for the Good of the People

Part of developing a culture of small incremental improvement behavior is the requirement of networking with others, both within the company and outside of it. While that may seem like a strange statement to make, one of the growth impediments companies face is that employees do not want to have to deal with people outside of their immediate area of work. Modern business communications and technology allow a much more widespread capability for networking to take place efficiently.

Big companies have extensive networks that are far-reaching and varied. The reason is that everyone in the company has spread his or her areas of influence across a diverse range of organizations and people. In order to become a big company, then, you need to start acting like one, and that means starting with the people and the networks they extend and establish. I was speaking to an accountant friend who has been working for a large corporation for over five years, and when I indicated that he should develop networks the way the salespeople do, he looked at me with sheer surprise, indicating that his job did not require any outside networks; he just balanced the books and got the numbers out on time.

Every employee in every department has the opportunity to develop a network outside of the company that allows the employee to demonstrate the company's values and ethics. The most obvious way to do this is by attending nonprofit functions and community events. These are valuable opportunities to extend your network of contacts. Often this type of company exposure is left up to the marketing department. For growing businesses, all employees need to do their part and have management's endorsement. Small incremental improvements, therefore, may extend beyond the walls of the company. They may take the form of performing a duty or making a contribution outside of the company, participating in associations, and so on. Going back to my accountant friend, I know that there are several certified public accountants associations and societies that have gatherings during the year and that are always looking for speakers and other forms of value-added contributions.

Networking opportunities do not need to have a budget allocated. When I have encouraged networking as a key element of a team's role, the first question that comes up is, "What is the budget for networking?" The answer is almost nothing. It's *almost* nothing because some networking does require minimal travel costs, contributions, entry fees, and so forth; however, employees should look for networking opportunities that do not require large investments of money or time.

These small networking opportunities can have a big impact. I was asked to speak at a conference of the Association of Operations Management, formerly known as the American Production and Inventory Control Society (APICS), which gave me a good opportunity to network and expose my company. APICS is an organization that provides valuable training, resources, and advice to businesses all over the world. That small contribution of less than an hour spent with its members opened up many other opportunities that led to sponsorships, and eventually to a partnership between our two companies that created sales opportunities. Networking is fundamental to sales, and it should be encouraged for others as well. No matter where in the company the networking opportunity comes from, it may eventually lead to business.

The Knowledge-Passionate Company

In earlier chapters, we touched on the need to share knowledge across the company and how individuals' experiences are a precious source of information that cannot be gained anywhere else. Internal knowledge is specific to the environment and culture of the company. This is why internal sharing of experiences from projects and tasks has a far more immediate application than external education and training when it comes to efficiency. Data are not knowledge, and knowledge is not talent or IQ. Knowledge is information that is useful and that can be employed to make better decisions or actions.

Knowledge is also the foundation for creativity and ideas. Data alone are not enough of a stimulus to invoke any creative process. They are just data. When analysis or context is applied, then the result starts to become information. Information and experience create knowledge. For example, information about customers' satisfaction ratings analyzed by product, region, age group, segment, and other classifications is interesting; when experienced salespeople look at the data and explain them, that is knowledge. It is this type of knowledge that when made available and distributed across the organization becomes valuable for initiating small and incremental ideas for improvements in other areas.

We spoke briefly about the fact that small changes that improve one area of the company create a ripple effect that spreads across other areas of the business. Spreading knowledge has a similar effect, different only in that it is an idea generator for improvement.

At a large global technology corporation, a worldwide marketing program was underway; divisions in over 30 countries were basically asked to execute a similar marketing project to increase sales volumes for a specific market segment. The program involved a number of marketing activities, including a direct-mail campaign, followed by an e-mail blast, then a later follow-up with telemarketing. The results in most of the regions were not as good as had been expected. There was a lot of interest and response rates were high, but there was a poor ratio of leads generated to sales, with the exception of just one country that was doing extremely well. The results came in on a monthly basis, and this one country had consistently high lead ratios compared to the rest.

It was not until the end of the program, when a formal review of the campaigns was presented, that it was learned that the difference in what this one country was doing was so minor that it could easily have been adopted overnight by the other countries had it been shared with them months earlier. The difference was that the call guide or call script used during the telemarketing process had been slightly changed. The standard call script asked when the customer would be looking to buy. The scripted responses were one month, three months, six months, twelve months, or not interested. If the customer responded with either one month or three months, then these names would be sent to sales. However, there was a time lag between the call and the sales actually getting its hands on the names. The small change that was made in this one country was that instead of asking when the customer intended to buy, the caller asked for an appointment. Telemarketing did not pass a list of names to sales; it passed a list of appointments made for sales to keep.

This change was made by someone in the telemarketing department who had seen the lead rates data from a week before. This information and the person's experience created the new idea and small change. What did not happen was the transmission of that knowledge to the other countries that could have benefited immediately had they known about it.

Creating Value with Customers and Partners

It is called collaboration in some management texts and co-creation in others; basically, it is the way of the future and the most competitive position you can ever be in. This is when you are able to advance from satisfied customers to delighted customers, from business relationships to true business partners. The distinction being made here is that satisfied customers are not necessarily loyal ones. The modern definition of co-creation implies that there is a relationship with customers that involves them at a deeper level than being a user or a consumer. What does this really mean, and how does it fit into the context of making small incremental improvements?

To answer the former, you first need to look at how you relate to and transact with customers today. Basically, you have a product or service, and you propose a value attached to it that you believe the customer will be able to utilize. Customers become the recipient of a value set that you have built and about which you have made assumptions. The assets of your organization are largely based on delivery of your products and services, and you continue to make investments in those assets in order to remain competitive and financially stable.

To simplify, you will continue to invest in product development and the surrounding support operations, as this is the basis of your business; your core values come from this, and you depend for your growth on your ability to compete in your market. This is true on all counts, and here is where creating value with customers alters the arrangement of assets; some of those investments need to be focused on increasing the value of the customer's competencies and assets. To explain, let us continue along the product development line; you would invest not just in product-oriented people and technology to develop your products, but on competencies in your resources that would provide leadership and consultancy to the customer's products, resources, processes, and competencies.

To answer the second question, how small incremental improvements start us on this journey, you need to look at customer involvement at a simple level first and then move to more sophisticated areas as you advance this type of relationship. A good place to start, and the easiest area to administer, will be at the product level. In earlier chapters, we covered the idea that bringing in customers as advisors in the development of future plans can only benefit both parties; specifically, investments in functional enhancements will be better spent. This is the stepping-off point for engaging customers in the next-level discussion, which involves how they can best utilize your products and services for their business.

For this, you will need to make investments in people who have inherent business experience and knowledge of your customers' domain. We touched on this earlier when we looked at the importance of having industry-specific language in the materials you use to present yourself to target markets. Fundamentally, the point is this: when you sell a product or service to a customer, you are selling an assumed heightened value that the customer may be able to reach, but it is up to the customer to attain that value. You may provide support—true, it is called customer support, but in reality it is helping the customer use the product. If it were really customer support, your support center would have as many product experts as industry consultants.

Start with involving your customers in conversations regarding what their future will look like. Start with how your products and services need to be modeled and developed to help your customers with their upcoming challenges and opportunities, and then move from there to operational and tactical issues affecting their business. Finally, you should become a contributor to the development of their strategic intent and competencies. There is no better defense against competitors than to have customers with this level of loyalty.

Small Places to Find Profit Gains

Profit gains can be achieved almost everywhere in the company, and there are always opportunities to streamline, cut costs, and become more efficient. The problem is that most of us have little or no time to focus on this, as we are embroiled in the demands and pressures of our jobs. When there is a need for cost reduction, it usually takes the form of reducing expenses on travel, a head count freeze, rightsizing (which always seems to end up being downsizing), and generally putting a hold on spending on non-mission-critical items.

There is another approach that can be taken, and that is to pick focus areas within the company and concentrate on those for a period of time, then rotate to other areas. It is much like counting the inventory in a warehouse: you would count, say, the inventory in a third of the warehouse every quarter. By the fourth quarter, you will have counted all the stock, and then you will start again. Similarly, this idea can be applied in terms of giving deliberate attention to various departments and functional areas of the organization that have been given the task of finding ways to cut back on costs. This aligns with the philosophy of small incremental improvements.

An effective way to activate employees and managers to think about small improvements is to ask them to consider how they can operate their business units in a more effective way. The premise here is that a collection of small incremental savings aggregated across the company can have a significant impact on margins. The following are hand-picked areas where the focus should first be placed.

Operations

This is a logical place to start and the easiest to see improvements in, as this is where overhead builds up over the normal course of doing business. Employees can often find ways to make their unit of work, which may be embedded within processes and procedures, more efficient. The main problem when managers ask their staff members to cut costs is that they give them little guidance or objectives. How far should we go and where exactly should we look are questions that are typically left in employees' minds. To help give them some direction, the following are objectives that can focus their attention.

Minimize Costs

When business is experiencing a growth spurt, cost management takes a second place, but when slumps occur, as they invariably do, radical moves to slash costs rather than minimize them take place. A good example can be seen with telecommunications expenses. These often rank among the top expenses of most companies, especially when wireless and remote voice mail options are used by transient employees. According to leading industry analysts, research shows that 40 percent of CEOs do not know what their actual costs are. This research also estimates that as much as 10 percent of telecom budgets go to waste, largely because of lack of oversight by managers.

Using the small incremental improvement philosophy, it is in this type of expense area that costs can be *minimized* rather than slashed. In the case of telecom expenses, waste can be avoided just by looking more closely at the bills in each department. Typical findings are old rates or plans that have not been updated, duplicate billing, incorrect taxes, requests for disconnection that have not been complied with, and so on. If each department were to take the time to study its bills a little more carefully, operating costs would surely be less. Therefore, one of the objectives that can be given to initiate small improvements is to look at the basics and drill further to find exactly what is being charged.

Best in Class

"Best in class," "best practices," and "leading practices" are abstract terms primarily because it is difficult to establish a definitive definition of "best." In any case, there is value in this concept as an objective within the organization's operations. There are thousands of consulting services that have methodology and business process reengineering (BPR) strategies to assist a company in getting closer to this concept. However, as our focus is on dealing with the small things, we will isolate those areas where small ongoing efforts will help achieve a level of "best."

A lot of this starts with a reemphasis on standard roles and functions within the company. For example, a large retailer based in the United States decided to change the name of its call center from Telesales to Customer Awareness. This name change introduced a different set of priorities and began to build a different perspective and culture among the employees. Best in class with small changes is not about the kind of structural changes that a full-scale BPR project would require; it is about introducing a new way of looking at what each purpose and function is really all about. It is, in effect, a more sophisticated view of the department or business unit.

Another area is sales. Some companies are changing their salespeople's title from account manager to business services executive or customer services executive. Sales departments are touting the idea that customers are "our business partners," altering their view just enough to warrant handling and communicating with them with alternative approaches. This subtlety can make all the difference.

Initiate an internal campaign for selected department heads and business unit managers to come up with a proposal to rename their group based on a best-in-class terminology rather than a pragmatic functional term.

Talent Management

This is usually placed within the domain of the human resources department and given some other name, such as human capital management, employee relationship management, workforce management, or some other variation on the theme. Regardless of what it is called, this is not a new concept, and it is one that takes the spotlight every 8 to 10 years as expertise in specialized areas becomes scarce.

Manpower Inc., a global leader in employment services based in Milwaukee, Wisconsin, conducted a survey of nearly 37,000 employers across 27 countries to determine where talent shortages existed.[1] Not surprisingly, the top jobs that employers are looking for are in sales, skilled trades, technical skills including production and engineering, and accounting. However, what was staggering was that an average of 41 percent of employers indicated that they had difficulty filling these positions. One can appreciate why companies therefore must look inward to develop talent for their growth needs. Business technology vendors are responding with integrated applications that track, measure, and recommend staff for promotion and career planning.

A prerequisite for a company that intends to become bigger through organic growth is that it invests effort and management time in keeping and developing existing talent. As small incremental improvement behavior becomes the norm, employees will feel freer to demonstrate their abilities and expose their talents. When employees are encouraged to take the initiative and to bring out their ideas in an environment in which they know that even the smallest of improvements is a good one, those employees with latent talents and abilities will be the first to become apparent, and others will follow.

Technology and Information Systems

Technology is fundamental to accelerating growth. Nonetheless, technology alone does not create growth, and the improper use of technology can stifle progress. I have separated "information systems" because there are really two aspects of technology that need to be considered. The first is the underlying technology that you use to run the business; the other is getting the information to make decisions that the technology can provide. There are only a handful of IT vendors that have end-to-end business systems with built-in information systems. You will find that most of the business applications that your company has purchased have their own information and reporting functions, and that they are all different. This means that you need to collect the data from these various systems yourself to develop the reports you need.

At several conferences where I presented this topic, when I asked for a show of hands regarding the source of decision-making information, the unanimous answer was "from the C drive of my personal computer" and not from the systems that run the business. Some people indicated that they spent days after the end of each month preparing management reports for use in meetings.

With today's business pace, a management report created days after the end of a month provides nothing more than historical data. It is merely a snapshot of what happened. When exceptions are found from the data, the discussion is limited to repairing rather than rectifying the situation. The difference between repairing and rectifying in this context is, for example, if the monthly management report indicates that an expense item has gone over budget, then the only decisions available are attempts to repair the situation: find money elsewhere, stop purchases, or some such action. Rectifying is being able to take a proactive response and deciding to slow purchases when the indicators show that the item *is about to go over budget*.

The fundamental difference, therefore, is having information that will inform you of what is likely to happen rather than what has happened. In the same way that small improvement behavior is about making a change when something is not working or improving something when it is not working efficiently, information should provide you with indicators and alert you when something is not quite right or, equally important, when things are going well or better than planned.

Business Intelligence

It's a fact that information about the business is more important than efficient processes and integrated systems. Modern-day terminology for this type of on-demand business information is "business intelligence," "executive dashboards," "executive information systems," and other variants on these. There are several vendors in the market that are able to provide solutions that can bring a lot of the company information together to provide these types of informational portals.

In the context of what to do first, examine the systems that you have today with a view to making some fundamental decisions:

1. Do we need to introduce a separate business intelligence application that takes data from our existing business applications and provides us with the information consolidated as we need it to manage the business?
2. Should we systematically replace our current business applications and introduce a system that has a built-in business intelligence application?
3. Should we develop our existing information system further to allow it to provide more real-time processed information rather than going for a packaged solution?

Here are the advantages and disadvantages of each option in the context of small:

- *Option 1.* This is a valid strategy when you have made a heavy investment in the current business applications and where you have specific functionality and features that are unique and are giving you a competitive advantage. The advantage of taking this approach is that you are able to build up your data warehouse incrementally, making it more of a knowledge warehouse. We spoke of the importance of knowledge sharing in earlier chapters, and this will provide a good platform for launching it. The consideration to take into account that may be viewed as a disadvantage includes the need to introduce another application in addition to the ones you already have. This is, in effect, another system that you will need to maintain.

- *Option 2.* When there are legacy systems that (1) have a high
  maintenance cost for keeping the systems up and running and
  (2) do not provide the type of information needed to make
  decisions, then this is an option that should be considered,
  especially for the longer term. Selecting an application that
  has business intelligence built in with the business applications is the most ideal and cost-effective option. In considering the adoption of this option, careful analysis of the
  business system must be conducted to ensure integration both
  of the business processes across the modules and with the
  information system that it is updating. This option eliminates
  having another data warehouse, as the business application
  and the information system are one and the same.
- *Option 3.* This build option will produce a tailored information system that will be unique to your business, and that with
  continuous improvements will result in your having the exact
  information that you need. There are tools available on the
  market that allow information systems to be developed more
  efficiently than ever before. The cost associated with developing and maintaining such a system needs to be weighed
  against that of adopting a packaged solution. This option is
  mostly used where there is very sensitive information that
  needs to be handled under tight security; it is seen mostly in
  government and military applications.

Customers

Throughout the book, we have included customer satisfaction as a
guiding principle for where, what, and how to look for and make
small incremental improvements. A clear indicator can be found in
your customer base. How many of your customers would be willing
to be your reference or to recommend your products and services
to others if asked? Sometimes referred to as "customer advocacy,"
having a program in place that cultivates customers to become referrals requires a dedicated effort and a specific ongoing program. In
any industry, customer referrals are the most powerful endorsement.

This is therefore one of the areas you should focus on if your current programs are ad hoc or on a needs basis only, relying on relationships rather than having a broader customer community project in place. The challenge when it comes to customer advocacy is to attain a better than 90 percent reference rating for your *entire* customer base. There are ways to achieve this, and the best method is in fact by small incremental steps. Giving anyone in the company the task of making all customers references can be daunting, as customers will have various levels of happiness and cooperation. The program requires a number of steps, which, in most cases, cannot be rushed and need to be executed incrementally.

1. The first step is to isolate those customers that you know will be or are good references for you. Their treatment is one of maintenance. It takes a lot of time and effort to establish good relationships with customers; when they become references, the relationship moves to another level, and there is now a duty of care on both sides. Customers who accept reference calls and are used for promotional purposes view this as doing something extraordinary for your business and as investing their time to receive premier attention and treatment. These customers are in the "maintain" category, requiring regular, consistent, and personal proactive service. Having customers who are moving away from wanting to be references can be as damaging as not having enough references.

2. A deliberate recruiting program to move customers from their current state to a position where they feel comfortable providing public testimonial evidence of their level of happiness with you is essential. This means systematically contacting each customer, assessing that customer's satisfaction, and asking specific questions concerning the level of participation that the customer would be willing to commit to. Because there will be a diversity of responses, customers should be classified or coded to let you easily keep track of their cooperation.

There are in fact two dimensions of this categorization. The first is the customer's willingness to be a reference, and the other is to what extent. This means determining what exactly each customer is willing to provide. Prepare a list of activities and materials that you want your customers to contribute to. This will range from being available for sales reference calls from prospects, to having the story of their success with you formally documented and used for marketing purposes, to being quoted in the press. A log or inventory of what customers are providing needs to be kept. There are customer relationship management (CRM) applications that cater to this process of turning customers into references by tracking their status and approval of use. I have seen categorizing of customers based on levels of cooperation ranging from platinum customers (those that are willing to provide the full set of activities and materials) to gold, silver, and bronze levels (where customers will agree to only a subset or specific activities) used successfully.

3. Incentives need to be created and maintained on an ongoing basis. I have seen instances where customers are "under contractual obligation" to become references as part of the formal agreement or contract. In these situations, the incentive could take the form of increased discounts or preferential or premium services at the time of signing the deal. Consideration of adding an addendum clause to your standard contracts may be a good idea, but it needs to be followed up with the appropriate level of service.

Reliable Customer Information

When it comes to customer information, there are two areas where attention is required. One is the accuracy of your customer database and the information regarding customers' contact information, products being used, billing information, and so on, and the other is who are your most profitable customers and who are not. It is difficult to ascertain from all the surveys how accurate customer databases are, but the general average for in-house data is around 70 percent accuracy. When asked, senior managers from companies I have spoken to have indicated that their most reliable source of customer information comes from their billing systems, but they could not say with certainty that these systems were 100 percent accurate. Other industry metrics indicate that, depending on the industry, it can cost up to 6 to 10 times as much to acquire new customers as it does to keep existing ones.

Growing big will only make matters worse in terms of the quality of customer information and access. Depending on priorities, making a customer quality information project the initial project is a solid investment for the future.

Customers as Business Partners

In earlier chapters, we covered the need to find out more about your customers and their needs by establishing their pain points and directing your messages toward those pain points. Companies that are passionate about growing realize that the relationship they have with their customers represents access to their customers' success. Therefore, ways to strengthen relationships need to be cultivated. One of the ways to change the way customers are being viewed is to consider them as business partners. After all, they are the business.

Using regular communication media to keep your customers informed is necessary, but bringing them closer to your company has many benefits. A way to include customers is by selecting them based on common causes and needs and by creating both formal and informal forums where they can provide opinions and feedback on your performance as a company and on the products and services that you deliver. This is different from customer surveys and market research. The format is personal, and the discussion takes place in meetings attended by subsets of your customer base that are "special interest groups," or SIGs, as they are commonly called.

Order to Cash to Service Cycle

Taking an order, delivering the products and services, collecting the payment, and then continuing to service the customer so that the cycle starts again with another order is a fundamental business process. Repeat business is the best business you can have. It is in this core mission-critical process that arise most of the issues that affect your relationship with customers and that can make the difference between getting repeat business and not getting it.

In an accelerated growth environment, this process becomes the most stressed leading to dysfunctional operations, with staff members spending more time on resolving issues than on smoothing transactions. Another first step is to document this process. Chart the course that orders take in as much detail as possible, highlight the areas where the most issues or concerns arise, and use small incremental improvements to rectify these.

Marketing

Of the many areas that marketing needs to address, if there is a thing to do first, it concerns the company's message. In Chapter 4, the process of determining the core messages is outlined, and it is highlighted again here as one of the first projects to consider. Building an operationally excellent company has many benefits, but it is undervalued if no one knows who you are and what you stand for in a way that allows them, your prospective customers, to "get it."

Fortune 1000 companies realize that being big is not enough to ensure that their message reaches their customers. Smaller companies with the ability to develop precision messages for their niche markets have increased their market share relative to that of the larger corporations because they were able to develop a message that people related to.

To grow big, you need to be understood, and that means developing a simple, concise message that lets everyone speak with a single voice that has a pragmatic and emotional appeal to your customers and prospects. Irrespective of past attempts at messages, taglines, or corporate headlines, add developing your message to the list of first things to do as you embark on the growth curve, and constantly listen to feedback and refine your message along the way. Before outbound marketing takes place, communicate first internally, to ensure that everyone inside the company understands the message and company's positioning, and can express them during interactions with customers, suppliers, and channel partners.

Time to Market

Finding your new market segments and niches is a key to growth; however, once you have established what these segments or niches will be (Chapter 3), when is the right time to go to market? In other words, when do you know you are ready? The key to launching into new markets has as much to do with the preparation inside of the company as it does with knowing that there is a ready market to service. How often have you found marketing conducting campaigns and launching new initiatives when other people who should be involved are acutely unaware of them? If this sounds familiar, you are not alone.

It is possible for things to happen too fast. Whenever a revenue-generating event that has not had the involvement of other interrelated departments takes place in the company, the full value of the activity is rarely achieved. Therefore, any revenue-generating initiatives or major company events require internal preparedness. In some cases, it will be prudent to involve other associated departments and business units from the planning stages; in any case, at a minimum, senior management should mandate that there be comprehensive internal company communication of the impending events or initiatives.

Sales Morale

In the context of putting small things first, when it comes to sales, the main issue has to do with morale. Sales is one of the toughest jobs in the world, and there are many opportunities to feel frustrated, angry, depressed, tired, burned out, negative, isolated, use-less, insignificant, unappreciated, taken for granted, abused, dom-ineered—pick one. Positive and negative emotions show up in people's work, especially in sales work, as salespeople are inter-acting with other people most of the time. Whether negative or positive, emotions aggregate like deposits in a bank, and there comes a time when you are either so high because you have found your selling nirvana or so low that you want to change jobs as soon as the quarter is over and done with.

In a high-growth environment, sales managers' obsession with exceeding the numbers creates a tunnel vision toward the sales teams. The no-excuses tough sales manager is a holdover from the postwar era. But you say he or she brings in the numbers. The numbers may come in, but how many salespeople go out? Here are some of the common reasons that salespeople leave:

- Not enough training on products and company processes
- Not enough support from presales, marketing, and manage-ment
- No formal sales methodology supporting what is being sold
- Not enough or outdated tools and technology to support the sales process
- Unclear sales territory and compensation plan
- Hired for the wrong job in the first place or the position was oversold
- Relied on past experience that has nothing in common with current role
- Rarely got paid the right commission or bonus for the results achieved

Small is about finding that one thing that will make the biggest difference. In this case, it is about training that includes both information about the products and a sales methodology. If your company does not have a sales methodology, no matter how large or small your sales force may be, get one. If you have one and it is not optimizing the sales process, conduct a formal review to ensure that the methodology is aligned with the value and services you provide, and roll out any needed changes. (In most cases, it is simply a matter of fine-tuning existing sales methodologies and instilling them as disciplines.)

Competitive Pricing

Much of this was covered in Activity 3 in Chapter 8 as part of the pricing strategy module, where the process is to investigate and determine pricing alternatives so that the customer has more choices. One of the first steps before introducing additional purchasing methods is to make sure that there are rules in place for negotiating deals.

Every salesperson knows the importance of being able to close the deal at the moment when the customer is giving buying signals. In the past few years, because of compliance and other regulatory issues, the freedom to "cut the deal" with a handshake has been vanishing. What is now normal is that as soon as the customer says yes, the salesperson needs to go back to his or her manager, supervisor, legal officer, or someone else to gain approval. When you are in this precious area of the sales cycle, any sales manual will tell you that you are at your most vulnerable, as anything can and probably will happen. Leaving the deal closing site is like leaving a window wide open for the competition.

One of the big improvements that can be made by a small change is to provide salespeople with a full understanding of preauthorized, preapproved, and prepared negotiating tolerances for when they are out in the field. This is as important as the product demo. These tolerances should be part of the sales training, and they should be held in strict confidence. This does not eliminate the need for salespeople to consult with their managers when customers have exceptional requirements, but it can reduce the number of these consultations significantly enough to ensure that some deals are not lost as a result. The ideal metrics for negotiable tolerances are based on deal size, product mix, and geographic location. Accounting and finance will need to be involved in this discussion, as they can provide critical input regarding benchmarks and allowable thresholds.

Include Partners in the Sales Support Model

One of the most effective growth strategies is to involve partners. Winning with people, not from people, is a formula for success, and while this sounds like a cliché, it remains alarmingly true when it comes to partner relationship management. The power of channel marketing is often underestimated, largely because a lot of companies do not invest heavily enough in building support systems for their distributors, resellers, and value-added dealerships. While in previous chapters we covered a lot of ground regarding channel partners, if we were to pick one small thing to do first, before anything else, it would be to include them in the sales and marketing planning process as early as possible. This one change will provide a great deal of useful feedback that will also start the integration process with partners when you next go to market.

Small Things Scorecard

Now that you have some background concerning the issues, you can focus on the tactical areas by using a scorecard to help you determine where you should start your small incremental changes to provide the biggest impact. All of the areas that you covered in the SMALL Tactics workshop should be implemented; however, the scorecard in Figure 9-1 provides some indications of where to begin. Follow the instructions to derive your list of priorities:

1. There are four main growth areas or categories that are identified, along with some key questions. Look at the statements in the Area of Attention column, and use the Points

Category	Area of Attention	Points 0=Not Applicable 1=Highly Agree 2=Somewhat Agree 3=Disagree 4=Not Even Close	Totals
Operations	We are able to effectively and consistently reduce costs in key business areas		
	We have all the skills we need in order to effect growth in key areas of our business		
	Our business systems are vendor integrated and scalable to our business, with centralized data		
	We have quality business information and know what our trends are		
Customers	We are well aware of what our customers need and what they expect from us		
	More than 90% of our customers would be references for us		
	We know who and where our customers are and have a good contact database		
	We have regular formal and informal forums with our customers to determine their future needs		
Marketing	We have a clear, consistent message that we use to support our value and brand		
	Growth markets are known, and we have plans in place to develop new markets and niches		
	Sales and marketing work together to determine the best integrated activities to meet targets		
	Marketing communications are centralized, and they support our overall objectives		
Sales	We have a competitive pricing strategy and offer alternatives to customers that we know they like		
	Our channel partners are an extension of our sales force and are integrated in our planning		
	Competitive information and sales support materials are up to date and readily available		
	Our sales organization has less than 10% turnover in staff, including telesales		

Figure 9-1 First Small Things First Scorecard

column to enter the score that indicates your level of agreement with each.
2. Add the points for each of the categories, and enter that number in the Totals column.

This will give you an indication at a surface level of what areas of attention you need to focus on. Each of the statements in the Areas of Attention column has a relationship with the activities in Chapter 8. The next step is to apply a weighting factor that emphasizes areas related to growth. For example, sales has a weighting factor of 0.25 because sales is where revenue is the most directly affected. The weighting factor corresponds to the area's relationship to growth. Follow the next set of instructions to determine the priority order in which small incremental improvements should begin within your company. Using Figure 9-2,

1. Fill in the Scorecard Points column with the Totals from Figure 9-1.
2. Multiply the Scorecard Points by the weighting factor and write the answer in the Result column.
3. Rank the areas from 2 to 5 in the Priority column, where 2 is the result with the highest total and 5 is the result with the lowest. You will notice that the first priority has been identified for you as the prerequisite for this project. (Refer to Chapter 7.)

Category	Scorecard Points	Multiply by Weight Factor	Result	Priority
Prepare for Big				1
Operations		0.1		
Customers		0.15		
Marketing		0.2		
Sales		0.25		

Figure 9-2 First Small Things First Priority Analysis

Using this list of priorities, you are now able to look at the activities that were performed in the SMALL Tactics workshop and formulate a plan with ownership and milestone dates. A regular review of progress as part of any management and staff meeting is recommended.

CHAPTER 10

THE MEASURE MANAGE CYCLE

Measuring small incremental improvements is not as difficult as some people may imagine. The reason this is called the "measure manage cycle" is that when we are measuring the results of a continuous process, once a set of targets and goals has been achieved, the metrics are renewed and the process starts again.

There are definite ways to ensure that the improvements that are being made amount to something worthwhile and produce a result that is aligned with the company's objectives. One of the best ways of measuring and managing a set of activities is by using the Balanced Scorecard concepts. We will adopt the basic principles of the Balanced Scorecard and apply them across the organization, focusing on the improvements-based criteria. There are two applications for small incremental improvements, and they are for current business processes and for new projects and initiatives that are introduced to the organization. In previous chapters, we have introduced new ideas that may themselves be either assigned as new projects or incorporated as objectives into existing plans and integrated with current activities and processes. Measuring the effectiveness and outcome applies to either individual projects or a combination.

Manage What Can Be Measured

Essentially, improvement behavior is largely about attitude. What, then, are the metrics that need to be considered with small incremental improvements, and who should be responsible for them? Small incremental improvements may occur anywhere in the organization. What is important is that the changes are focused on achieving revenue growth and increased profits. The benefits of a deliberate emphasis on everyone in the company becoming involved with making improvements is that there is always going to be some benefit derived from the enhancements; however, this needs to be directed by all management levels.

If we look at the basic concepts of the Balanced Scorecard, there are two governing processes at work that operate in a circular motion. One is based on *output*, and the other is *feedback*. The output is the outcome or the result of an improvement that is being made, and the feedback is the status of that improvement. In other words, the output may be that a particular occurrence of a hiccup in a business process has been resolved by a small improvement, and the feedback may be that more changes may need to be made, as other exceptions may occur. The importance of documenting outcomes and improvements is that they will reveal *trends* over time. Trends are insights into the future. They show information, not just data, and *information* plus experience is the unique *knowledge* of your company.

The point here is that you may need to make some small incremental improvements in the way you measure if you are to fully understand and appreciate what is really going on. Are any of the improvements that everyone in the company is busily making each day amounting to something that aligns with the corporate objectives of becoming bigger, better, or both? The way to get the answer follows this path:

1. Small improvement actions that go from a current situation to a better one are taken in each of the departments or business units, and the outcome (*output*) is recorded.
2. Feedback or assessment of the outcome is used to make a judgment as to its usefulness and completeness overall.
3. A summary of the issues and the related changes shows trends, allowing tracking to the root of problems or enabling

better decisions as to how further improvements and fixes can be made.

4. The experience of staff and managers with the apparent trends allows them to deduce a broader picture of what is really happening so that other recommendations for small improvement actions can be taken—and we return to step 1.

In order for this continuous improvement loop to gain momentum, management needs to insist that the company be operated based on *facts*. Actions and decisions must be founded on information. Data must be gathered before you can get to information, and information alone does not provide the wisdom to make better decisions and take better actions; experience needs to be applied. The good news is that experience is built and learning is accelerated because there is better information available by this process.

As we indicated earlier, adopting the Balanced Scorecard supports the small incremental improvements practice, as it is a continuous cyclical process. The Balanced Scorecard has four main criteria that are constantly being measured and managed. Figure 10-1 provides an interpretation of the Balanced Scorecard with an emphasis on small incremental improvements as a vehicle for attaining them. In communicating corporate objectives regarding becoming biggger, better, or both, it is important to state the objectives in empirical terms.

Later in the chapter, there are recommendations regarding specific areas to measure that can be used to support the model's four major areas: financial, business work flow, knowledge sharing, and customers and channel partners. In each of these areas, there may be existing measurements and reporting functions; therefore, what is presented in the following sections is intended to complement any existing information systems you may have.

For clarity and simplicity, we will follow the major headings of the scorecard and add to those categories other criteria to which output, feedback, trends, and recommendations can be applied. Consider these suggestions as ways to turbocharge the existing

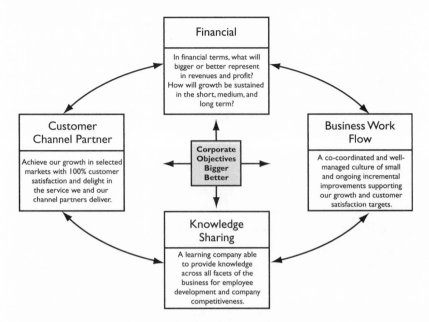

Figure 10-1 SMALL Balanced Scorecard

systems you have in place today. As with all Balanced Scorecards, their purpose is not only to provide a form of business intelligence to clarify your strategy and vision, but also to offer a management system with a signaling capability pointing to where improvement and actions need to take place.

Financial Measures

Most likely you have these in place, as most businesses start with their financial information first, especially with the increased regulatory and compliance requirements. Essentially, all activities percolate to here. This is the last measure of growth and profit. Financial information is historical in nature; it presents what has happened. In assessing whether small incremental improvements conducted across the company have any impact here, it is recommended that the accounting department make note of the periods in which some of the small initiatives were put in place and the time at which management introduced the strategy.

Apart from the obvious areas of increased revenues and profit, you should consider other "soft" areas of improvement as well, such as timeliness in closing the books and a decrease in erroneous data coming from the various business units or locations. In terms of budgeting, at the appropriate financial cycle, it is necessary to introduce to the rest of the company a clear definition of what success represents. Rarely is this communicated well enough for everyone to be aware of the actual numbers. If the objective of becoming big means a 20 percent increase in revenues this year and a 10 percent increase in profit margin, then *everyone* should be aware of this. Studies have indicated that when nonprofit organizations initiate fund-raising activities, those that informed their communities of the progress they were making toward achieving the target amounts, such as billboard-style thermometers showing the rising amounts, were more successful than those that did not. People want to involve themselves in progress. Add the following to the existing financial metrics you have today:

1. The increase in revenues from the time small improvements were implemented
2. The origin of cost savings and their impact on profit margins
3. The number of days taken to close books for the month
4. A decrease in errors as a percentage or unit measure
5. A process for communicating progress toward targets— monitor feedback

Business Work Flows

In order to manage process improvements, you need to establish a way to measure them. This means documenting processes to establish the root cause of improvements. Documenting the business process flow and the areas for attention will also highlight whether small changes are capable of achieving the desired result. It will also provide a useful reference regarding the department's processes. With the operational flow available in print, the staff will get a sense of the permissible scope, increasing the likelihood of finding new opportunities.

Documentation of a process can be made simpler to understand if the process is shown as a flow of activity. A diagram or schematic with notes indicating and identifying the basic units of work that make up that process is a good visual for describing what may be a complex set of activities. In each business unit, there will be different and related business processes. These have logical start and end points that should be easily traced. See Figure 10-2 for an outline of how a business process can be represented. In each of the steps, the more detail that can be included the better, in order to understand where improvements can be made. Avoid making too many side notes, and try to include as many of the details as possible within the boxes to ensure that you do not miss any of the exceptions and how to handle them.

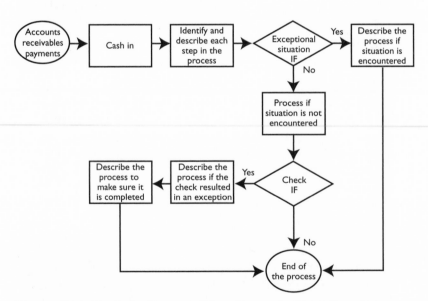

Figure 10-2 Business Process Flow Example: Cash Receipts Process

Figure 10-3 is an example showing the level of detail that can be included within the business process flowchart. After a business process has been described, an evaluation of where the small improvements can be made can take place. There are two important things that need to be done when preparing the chart. The first is to be as thorough as possible, and the second is to estimate where the inefficiencies are and where improvements will either increase the efficiency and productivity of the process or decrease the time and cost required to carry it out.

Once the process has been documented and the small areas for improvement have been identified, a log of the improvements can be kept and used to manage the progress and report on results. Figure 10-4 is a format that can be used to log and track process improvements. The Process Activity can be the unit of work that is being addressed. The Person Responsible will be required to report back and complete the change request when it is completed. The Communicate To column is filled in when the change

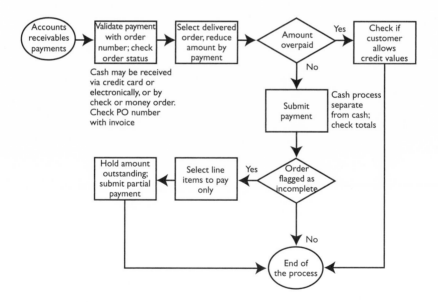

Figure 10-3 Detail of Business Process Flow Example: Cash Receipts Process

Process Name:

Process Activity/Recommended Change	Person Responsible	Start Date	End Date	Communicate To
Change Improvement Status				
Process Activity/Recommended Change				
Change Improvement Status				

Approving Manager:

Figure 10-4 SMALL Process Change Request

may affect other related departments or staff after it has been made. The Change Improvement Status box describes the difference the change made in terms of units or percent and what benefits can be derived. The approving manager should sign off on the changes prior to starting and ending.

This may at first seem to be an arduous task, but where the process has been successful, a template, such as the one in Figure 10-3, and guidelines are sent to each of the business units or departments so that they can develop their own versions. Storing the charts in a central repository for access and easy updating is not only efficient but also a way to share this knowledge with others, particularly if remote locations and branches could find it useful. The other value in doing this work is that it provides a starting point for user documentation that can be made available for new employees to supplement employee handbooks and departmental operating procedures.

The key is to select things in small increments. Do not attempt to make big changes at any one time, especially where others may be affected. To help kick off the thought process in selecting what to do within a process and how to measure the impact, here are some steps that will come naturally after some time:

1. The process being addressed is known and can be easily explained.
2. The item being improved occurs frequently or is intended to catch exceptions.
3. Improvement of this process is aligned with the overall goals of the company.
4. Others in the company will appreciate the benefits if this process is improved.
5. The change required is small and within our scope without further approval.
6. No one else in the company is addressing this item.
7. The change will improve a process without further outside assistance being required.
8. There is a high benefit-to-cost ratio with this improvement.

Where proposed changes may affect other departments or locations, consulting with those departments or locations as part of the change process has several benefits. First, it assembles a meeting with a well-defined agenda where decisions can be made on the spot, and, second, it promotes new ideas and knowledge sharing.

Measuring Productivity and Efficiency

Measuring efficiency and productivity can be done using highly sophisticated algorithms with historical performance and economic forecasts, or it can be simple, specific, and appropriate. I have seen companies invest a lot of resources and money in developing complex efficiency models to determine their economic competitiveness and benchmarking them against industry efficiency ratings. In most cases, the specialists built models that were either too difficult to understand or too theoretical. When business questions were posed to these models, they could not answer them, so many of these models ended up not being used.

Therefore, before continuing, productivity and efficiency must be defined in the context of small improvement behavior. The simplest definition is that productivity is output (or outcome) divided by input (or demand). Efficiency refers to the *time* it takes to produce the output. Working from that base, the fundamentals can include metrics that are *appropriate* to each individual unit. This will give managers an intuitive understanding of how well their unit is performing based on metrics in which they include their specific criteria and nuances. For example, output may have different measurement criteria in a marketing department, where creativity is fundamental, and in a manufacturing line producing widgets per hour.

In the context of measuring improvement, the focus is not on costs. Productivity formulas often include costs, and while that may be a valid approach, the concern here is ensuring that applying small incremental improvements to basic units of work is increasing the level of productivity toward common goals, not an overall companywide average. Cost of labor, materials, and so on will need to be taken into consideration, but they do not help in determining whether individual changes made by employees are taking the company in the right direction. Further, with the flurry of outsourcing both labor and component parts, a rigid assessment based on output from labor would show an improvement, but cost of goods would increase.

A multifaceted view of productivity and efficiency needs to be considered. Remember that you are measuring an improvement in behavior in order to influence and direct that behavior toward common aims. Therefore, there needs to be an assessment within each of the departments or operating units of what that entity's multifaceted measures will be. For example, in the accounting department, one measure may be the number of days required to produce statutory financial statements at the end of the month; in marketing, it may be the number of assets that can be produced in a given period of time. Both examples introduce a metric of "turnaround." In the manufacturing and supply chain management areas of the business, this is usually looked at in terms of units per hour, per machine, or per capital item or raw material. These are traditional metrics, however, and you need to come up with others that are based on empirical evidence but involve a number of related items. The example of the financial statements coming in earlier is measurable, but several people and processes may be involved.

Therefore, there are two elements that must be taken into account when it comes to behavioral productivity and efficiency, namely, time and the employee's unit of work or functional role. For example, during my tenure working for a large global beverage company several years ago, warehouse and distribution costs were closely monitored, as they represented one of the highest-cost elements in taking the product to market. Productivity was based on stock cycles, value of inventory remaining in the warehouse, and distribution costs related to the fleet of trucks. A traditional formula involving labor, capital, and materials (finished goods) was used. When a change in the truck-loading computer software program allowed the forklift operators to pick and assemble orders more efficiently, a daily dispatch metric was added that measured the number of orders per dispatch fulfilled and settled in any given shift. Before long, other warehouse operations using the same software were measured in the same way because this was necessary in order to compare the performance of each of them as apples to apples.

Managers should adopt metrics that are related to performance and aligned with the core objectives and how these objectives can be supported. Their view is different from that of the economist or accountant, as it includes ambiguities, such as effective working habits developed over time, which those professionals are unaccustomed to dealing with. One could argue that measures of profit are not perfect either, but despite their imperfections, they still produce valuable information regarding the state of the business. In developing metrics related to productivity, an importance factor associated with the metric should be included. For example, in the finance department, closing the books earlier in the month may not be as important as making sure that all journal entries are made accurately. A weighting factor indicating how each of the metrics represents the corresponding importance to the department's core values provides useful indicators for prioritizing when dealing with inefficiencies or problem solving.

The following is a set of suggested areas that have been adopted by companies that have implemented an improvement culture:

1. Identify the cost of administration and express it as an allocation per employee. The calculation is total cost of administration/number of employees (including contractors).
2. Estimate the cost of errors in administration, order management, and purchasing departments as a percentage.
3. Determine the time taken for processing transactions, categorized as incoming and outgoing. Incoming transactions are cash receipts and receipt of inventory items.

Outgoing include purchase orders, bill payments, contracts, and orders.

4. Identify a quality performance indicator (TQM, ISO 9000, or whatever is being used).

5. Calculate information technology utilization as a ratio of cost against actual use. (For example, if you are running a 24/7 system, what are the utilization rates during business hours, overtime, and overnight?)

Knowledge Sharing for Improvement Behavior

Volumes have been written on knowledge management and knowledge capital, where traditional measurement tools circle back to conventional systems, such as the costs of developing materials, of maintaining infrastructure, of providing knowledge training, and so on. Every size business is coming to recognize that knowledge, in the form either of intellectual capital as developed skill in employees or of assets (the documented versions), has a material impact on the value of the business. The fact is that knowledge can shape outcomes with regard to productivity and behavior.

What is knowledge? The definition varies widely between a learning institution and a corporation. Within a corporation, the definition changes depending on who is asking. In the accounting department, for example, knowledge has a collateral value associated with costs (and savings). In the human resources department, it represents a core value. There it is the raw materials used to train, develop, promote, and motivate employees. In other areas it may represent a resource used for support and assistance. Whatever the definition you may have, and irrespective of the way it is being accounted for, knowledge in the context of small incremental behavior is about sharing objectively the documentation of and access to a practice and/or the outcome of an improvement at any level of operation. This type of knowledge stems directly from activities coming out of projects, best practices, business flow enhancements, templates for efficiencies, and so on. Those small but significant ideas and changes constitute knowledge.

Companies of all sizes have come to realize the enormous benefits of recording even the smallest of improvements or findings and making them available to others. This improves performance, and measurable results are becoming evident. Take, for example, the following companies:

- *3M (St. Paul, Minnesota).* This company has introduced over 60,000 products through its own innovation processes and has encouraged a culture of creativity and risk taking. It has also implemented a "knowledge for business" culture in which managers are required to use continuous learning as part of generating revenue.
- *Analog Devices (Cambridge, Massachusetts).* Directed by the CEO, this company implemented a collaborative knowledge-sharing culture in order to break down the corrosiveness of the internal competitiveness and functional barriers within the company. Senior managers are required to create and participate in "communities of inquirers."
- *Ford Motor Co. (Michigan, United States).* This company is transforming itself and adopting state-of-the-art new technologies as they become available by extending its knowledge platform, creating a virtual network of vendors that includes back-office operations such as procurement intelligence.
- *British Petroleum (London, United Kingdom).* This company implemented a system that brings together talent from all over the organization, with an emphasis on tacit knowledge rather than on accumulating data. A communication system has been installed, allowing networks of people to use multimedia, including electronic white boards and videoconferencing, to bring them together.
- *Buckman Laboratories (Memphis, Tennessee).* This company, which makes chemicals for water purification and other products, has created a knowledge-sharing department. Employees at Buckman who are recognized for their exceptional

investment in the knowledge system gain both financial rewards and promotions to management.

- *Chevron (San Ramon, California).* Chevron has formalized a database of best practices that captures the experience of drilling conditions and the innovative solutions that employees come up with to solve problems on site, and shares them on a worldwide basis.
- *Hewlett-Packard (Palo Alto, California).* This company implemented a culture of collaboration and virtual innovation teams in which the sharing of knowledge using technology is essential, encouraging risk taking at all levels of the company with access to support for those who implement ideas that are not working.
- *Skandia (Stockholm, Sweden).* The creation of a formal process and procedure to capture customer experiences while starting new financial services products has increased this company's return on investment on new products.
- *Xerox (Stamford, Connecticut).* This company has designed specific areas within its offices, routinely called the "distributed coffeepot," where people can get together to exchange ideas.

While the companies in this list have been able to make large investments in their knowledge-sharing systems and processes, the examples of what they have done can be scaled to allow any size company with any amount of investment to start introducing such a system and gaining the advantages. As we covered in earlier chapters, there is a lot of untapped knowledge and expertise that is specific to your company, your customers, and your industries that your employees have gained through their jobs but that are not utilized to the fullest potential.

If you take out the economic aspects of knowledge, looking at it not as capital, assets, economic value-added (EVA),[1] or property, but rather measuring the process of developing knowledge-sharing systems and applications as a companywide initiative, then you can focus on those specific conditions that indicate that (1) knowledge is being created by individuals and teams, (2) the use of and access to this knowledge is increasing, and (3) output is increasing. What are the metrics for knowledge sharing?

It is recommended that you set up a "knowledge program office" that has the primary role of managing content and making it available. This function can be a shared role, but allocating it to an individual owner has the benefit of providing accountability. This does not mean that one person is responsible for building the content; this is the responsibility of everyone in the company. Instead, the owner has a coordinator function. Providing guidelines and managing access and distribution will become a key role as the knowledge system is built over time. The following are metrics that can be used to measure the knowledge system and the sharing capability of the organization:

1. The participation in and adoption of the knowledge management system or application, expressed as a percentage of overall employees
2. The number of managers and the corresponding business units or departments that have implemented knowledge objectives within their teams and have tied them to rewards, compensation, performance objectives, or promotion criteria for their staffs
3. The percentage of companywide initiatives that management has approved in which the knowledge system was a central or key source of information access, update, and distribution
4. The percentage of existing fragmented and decentralized information and content that has been categorized and catalogued in a central knowledge system or application
5. Investments being made in technology to support knowledge systems and access, such as multimedia and communication media, by business units or locations
6. The number of key business processes that are supported by technology, including business applications such as ERP,

CRM, and financial, human resources, and payroll systems that have been integrated into the knowledge-sharing process

Customers and Channel Partners

For specific reasons, partners are included in the same category as customers when it comes to measuring success. Channel partners have multifaceted relationships with you. While they are your business partners, there are similarities to customers in the way you deal with them. Building and developing a channel requires a recruitment effort that involves attracting channel partners and "selling" them on the value of your company and its products and services. Once they are signed up, you establish an ongoing relationship with them that requires supporting them and servicing their needs. The value proposition is different, but the process is essentially the same. Today we have systems and methodologies that help us support and manage our partners, with partner relationship management applications holding different types of data but acting for the same reasons as customer relationship management systems do.

Therefore, in keeping with measuring progress through small improvements, there are fundamental areas that can be quantified that increase the attractiveness and loyalty of customers and partners alike because their reasons for continuing to do business with you are basically the same. The lists of metrics that follow can be used to ensure that small incremental changes are being managed toward the goals you have set.

Metrics Specific to Small Incremental Improvements

1. Number of business units that have implemented small incremental improvements aligned with corporate goals as part of their performance objectives

2. Number of managers that have a reward system that recognizes achievements for initiatives taken by small improvements
3. Percentage of departments that have tracking and change management procedures in place and that report on a regular basis

Metrics Specific to Customers

1. Number of customers (if possible, sort these according to tenure with the company)
2. Average tenure per customer in years
3. Customer churn rates as a percentage (arrange by location, product group, or both)
4. Reasons for customers leaving codified and the number of reasons tracked (by code)
5. Percentage of overall customer revenues from top 10 customers
6. Customer satisfaction rating (based on an independent study; if possible, arrange the questions in such a way as to relate to departments in the company, e.g., satisfied with timely delivery, satisfied with accuracy of payments, satisfied with service and support)
7. Average revenue spent per customer as a percentage

Metrics Specific to Sales to Customers

1. Win/loss ratios (number of deals won against number of deals lost during a given period of time)
2. Number of prospects being handled at any one time per salesperson
3. Percentage change in revenues per salesperson
4. Number of salesperson days spent visiting customers

Metrics Specific to Marketing to Customers

1. Percentage of attendance at marketing events (include online and offline events)
2. Percentage of customers attending events that become opportunities and leads
3. Number of neutral to positive press and analyst reviews and reports
4. Number of sales support materials generated by campaign
5. Number of sales support materials generated per period
6. Number of positive customer responses to marketing activities (based on feedback forms and surveys)
7. Number of customer forums formed based on interest groups
8. Percentage of customers attending or participating in customer forums
9. Percentage response to direct mail sent to customers
10. Percentage accuracy of any mail sent to customers (based on customer database accuracy rating)
11. Percentage of revenues generated per campaign (if possible, isolate by location and campaign type or product category)
12. Number of new niche markets/segments added over period
13. Number of new customers coming from new niches/segments over period
14. Percentage of revenues from new customers
15. Number of new product enhancements applied based on customer feedback
16. Number of customer conversions from competitors
17. Average number of years of marketing staff tenure
18. Number of local integrated marketing campaigns
19. Number of national/international integrated marketing campaigns
20. Number of customer references added to customer advocacy list

Metrics Specific to Channel Partners with Customers

1. Number of partners added over period
2. Percentage of revenues from partners (all indirect channels)
3. Percentage of total products partners are selling
4. Number of market segments covered by partners
5. Number of sales support staff by partners (average)
6. Percentage of marketing budget allocated for partners
7. Number of deals closed by partners
8. Win/loss ratio for partners (in specific product categories)
9. Number of partner relationship staff allocated for period
10. Total cost for partner enablement (including setup costs)
11. Percentage of partners signed compared with competitors
12. Average percentage of investments made by partners for marketing
13. Average tenure of partners with company
14. Percentage of revenues from top 10 partners

The metrics listed may already be in use within the company at some level; they are intended as suggestions and potential additions to any existing metrics that you may be using and managing today. These metrics have been selected, first, because they have a correlation with growth factors and a direct connection with revenue, and, second, because they have been addressed in the other sections of the book where small incremental enhancements have been introduced.

The activities, ideas, and disciplines that have been discussed in previous chapters will directly affect and improve each of the line items listed here. The challenge for most companies is being able to develop a data capture system to enable the monitoring and management of the information. It is recommended that while initially the systems will not be precise, the important thing is to *start*. Just as the small incremental improvement behavior acts upon a problem or an issue, similarly it will apply when developing a measuring capability, and tracking will become easier as the systems become more sophisticated.

Start Smart with People

When considering the rollout of small improvements behavior and gradually instilling it as a culture, it is prudent to look at the organization, taking into account the resources that are available. Small thinking and small incremental changes even at the lowest levels of the company mean that everyone can become involved from day one. Line managers and senior managers need to be well versed and prepared with a plan so that everyone is clear about the nature of the changes that are expected and the scope of the changes (see Chapter 8).

A reality check or assessment of current projects and initiatives and the resources they are consuming needs to be taken into account as part of the introduction of small thinking. Invoking the philosophy of small incremental change behavior in current projects while they are in progress is smart for a number of reasons:

- The effects can be seen and managed immediately.
- It adds a boost to projects that have stalled, enabling teams to feel empowered.
- It opens opportunities for collaboration across divisional lines.

The people factor has been touched on throughout, and while the focus has been on operational and tactical issues that relate to growth, small incremental improvement behavior has a human element that should not be overlooked. The nature of small incremental improvements implies that employees have the underlying approval and freedom to take a different level of ownership of their jobs and responsibilities. If this is done properly, there will be a change in attitude toward the company and their jobs. The human aspect is included in this discussion of measure and manage because there are intangible assets regarding the development of employee skills. These will become evident in economic and empirical terms over time.

In cases where I have seen a culture of constant improvement, and where the basic philosophy is that good enough is not good enough, employees and their managers develop a competitive energy to be the *best*. This sometimes leads to competitiveness across business unit and departmental lines. Senior management needs to be vigilant to prevent this from evolving into a corrosive or protective attitude on the part of individuals or teams seeking to guard their success from others.

There are telltale signs that this type of mindset is taking root. One is that some teams are far exceeding others, but doing so in isolation. Another sign is that individuals who are making small incremental improvements in private show their results only after they have made huge improvements and can demonstrate to their managers their ability to outperform. This is why it is important to develop knowledge systems that encourage the sharing of experiences and content. Adopting some of the suggestions from the companies listed earlier may be beneficial if these trends become evident.

Management at all levels needs to agree on how to handle this type of behavior and these situations. It is recommended that while improvements be acknowledged and rewarded, individuals or teams need to be counseled to maintain equilibrium, a spirit of collaboration, and tolerance of others who make smaller advances than they do. Without this realignment of what small is about, over time, if laggards are perceived as not making as big a contribution as others, they will become discouraged and withdraw from attempting to implement changes. The balancing act that management needs to maintain is to continue to encourage both those who are not as creative with their opportunities and those who are able to make the most of them.

A way to do this is to instruct line managers to focus on their teams' strengths and build on those, not on their weaknesses. The tendency will be for managers to surrender to the idea that some of their staff members are not able to make the kind of significant changes that others can make because of their skill levels. This is often a misconception, and it is fueled by the fact that most of the attention is given to addressing the weaknesses rather than the strengths. Where weaknesses are affecting progress, they need to be addressed; however, in the context of allowing employees to use their creative and intuitive abilities to improve their business unit, working on developing strengths produces a much more meaningful outcome with faster results than resorting to the inevitable "not good enough" mentality.

Big companies stay big and get bigger because they focus on their strengths and manage their weaknesses. Improvement theory suggests that by making small incremental and consistent improvements, weaknesses are challenged at the personal level. In earlier chapters, we touched on the fact that overcoming personal barriers and achieving personal goals are done faster and with much longer-lasting effects when attempted in small increments. The same applies with teams in a company setting. Fear of failure is somehow sabotaged by the notion that things will be done a little at a time.

Another phenomenon involved in thinking and doing in small steps is that people feel smarter, and their confidence in their ability to do more increases. Irrespective of the task performed, a sense of accomplishment reminds the brain of the intellectual resources used. (In much the same way that a small personal failure can create anguish out of proportion with the failed task, the same effect can apply with successful outcomes.) Consider what happens when you fix something small around the house. That sense of accomplishment registers in the subconscious in the same way that a much bigger achievement would. The only difference between the two is the emotional reaction caused by the benefit received. The emotional consequence is based on the size of the result; the subconscious response *is the same*. Apply this to individuals and teams and you can see the point of concentrating your time on strengths in order to bring about more positive outcomes.

Getting Bigger the Small Way

The saying that the next big thing is an improvement of the last big thing is true. The process of small thinking and small incremental improvement, and the attitude and behavior that it invokes, follows a natural path, which leads to becoming even bigger. Big becomes hindsight when *bigger* becomes relative. Everyone forgets big when you become bigger. Therefore, this is a frame of reference. No one says that you were big five years ago if you are much bigger today.

When I was speaking to the CEO of a large software company a few years ago, he told me that when approaching each level of his company's growth, everyone knew that the secret was doing more of the same, but better than before. Every time the company improved on important areas of its business, it showed a result. Mergers and acquisitions aside, getting bigger was not a function of doing something big, but of adding on from where the company was.

The extent of growth is not in question here, and growing bigger the small way is not an endorsement of growing a little at a time. In fact, our objective throughout the book is to demonstrate how making small incremental changes and additions in very specific and select areas can unleash unprecedented growth for any size company. What is relevant is that you grow to your maximum capacity and build from there. The displacement of resources, technology, and investments is almost always a result of not achieving maximum growth with what you have today. Mediocre performance fueled by huge investments in employees, assets, and technology rarely produces the outcomes or returns expected. This is because what was unknown is what was keeping the company from growing; therefore, it was not clear where the investments needed to be made.

The pyramids were built over many years using more than 20,000 men, and this is symbolic of small ways of becoming big. However, in our society and our economic world, we want pyramids to be built in months, even weeks. Luckily for us, we have modern technology and advances in engineering techniques at our disposal. Still, the principles remain the same. Leaving the physical attributes to one side, the key to constructing the pyramids was the workers' commitment to the task, a commitment based on a religious belief and an unwavering dedication that spanned generations. In order to get bigger, management needs to commit to the implementation and maintenance of a culture of improvement. Once employees realize that success is achieved through their contributions, which come from their own ideas and actions, they will feel more ownership of that success, and it will seem more meaningful. That alone will suffice to start improvement on its path along a continuum.

Big, therefore, is only a stepping-stone to even bigger the small way.

ENDNOTES

Chapter 1

1. Reprinted from Environmental Nutrition Inc., *Small Weight Changes Have Big Impact* (Norwalk, CT: Belvoir Media Group, LLC, 2000), www.environmentalnutrition.com.
2. Corinne T. Netzer, *The Complete Book of Food Counts* (New York: Dell Publishing Group, 2006).
3. Geoff Williams, *Innovative Business Practices* (Farmington Hills, MI: Entrepreneur Media, Inc., 2005), gwilliams1@cinci.rr.com.
4. Malcolm Gladwell, *The Tipping Point* (New York: Little, Brown, 2000).
5. Chan Kim and Renee Mauborgne, *Blue Ocean Strategy* (Boston: Harvard Business School Publication Corporation, 2005).
6. Piers Steel, *The Nature of Procrastination* (Calgary, Alberta: Haskayne School of Business, University of Calgary, 2007).
7. Federal Consortium Benchmarking Study Report, February, Washington, DC: U.S. Government Printing Office, 1995.
8. Ajit Kambil and Cabrini Pak, "Marketing Information Technologies to Small and Medium-Sized Enterprises,"

Deloitte Research, Copyright Deloitte Development LLC, 2004, ISBN 1-892383-05-5, p. 3.

9. Donald N. Sull, "Why Good Companies Go Bad," *Harvard Business Review*, reprint 99410, 1999.

10. Lowell Bryan and John Kay, "Can a Company Ever Be Too Big?" *McKinsey Quarterly*, no. 4, 1999, p. 106.

11. Robert M Tomasko, *Bigger Isn't Always Better* (New York: AMACOM, 2006), p. 214.

12. Robert Slater, *Jack Welch and the GE Way* (New York: McGraw-Hill, 1999).

Chapter 2

1. Gartner Research, *SMB IT Spending Will Rise, but Vendor Commitment Will Fail*, December 4, 2002, COM-18-8242, p. 3.

2. SAP official corporate Web site.

3. Jim Collins, *Good to Great* (New York: HarperCollins, 2001).

4. Collins, *Good to Great*.

Chapter 3

1. U.S. Census Bureau, www.census.gov/epcd/www/naicstab .htm.

2. Trademark registered by United Brands Company Inc., Los Angeles, California.

3. Trademark registered by Vitabiotics Limited, London, UK.

4. Trademark registered by National Beverages Corporation, Fort Lauderdale, Florida.

5. Trademark registered by Distribuidores De La Energia Inc., Burlingame, California.

6. Trademark registered by Uno Mas Inc., Long Beach, New York.

7. Trademark registered by Tampico Beverages, Chicago, Illinois.

8. Figure does not include local, state, or federal government agencies.

Chapter 4

1. Seth Godin, *Purple Cow: Transform Your Business by Being Remarkable* (New York: Penguin Group, 2003).
2. NLP is a registered trademark of the model's founders and creators, Richard Bandler and John Grinder.
3. Interbrand, *2007 Brand Marketers Report*, January 2007, p. 16.

Chapter 6

1. Edward de Bono, *Sur/Petition* (London: HarperCollins, 1992), p. vii.
2. Sun Tzu, *The Art of War*, trans. Thomas Cleary (Boston: Shambhala Publications, Inc., 1988), p. 67.
3. Microsoft Word is a registered trademark of Microsoft Corporation Inc.

Chapter 7

1. Peter M. Senge, *The Fifth Discipline* (New York: Random House, 1990).

Chapter 8

1. "Our Rising Ad Dosage: It's Not as Oppressive as Some Think," *Media Matters*, February 15, 2007.

Chapter 9

1. Talent Shortage Survey, 2007 Global Results, Manpower Inc., 2007.

Chapter 10

1. This is a measure of a company's financial performance based on the residual wealth calculated by deducting its cost of capital from its operating profit, e.g., net operating profit after taxes − (capital × cost of capital).

INDEX

ABOUT THE AUTHOR

Frank Prestipino is a former vice president of Global Enterprise Applications Strategy for Oracle Corporation. He has been profiled in the media and is a highly sought after speaker. Prestipino was also the president of UnicornHRO and is currently the general manager of the International College of Management, Sydney.